GASLIGHT AND SHADOW
The World of Napoleon III

1851–1870

THE MACMILLAN COMPANY
NEW YORK · CHICAGO
DALLAS · ATLANTA · SAN FRANCISCO
LONDON · MANILA

BRETT-MACMILLAN LTD.
TORONTO

GASLIGHT

AND

SHADOW

The World of Napoleon III

1851–1870

by

ROGER L. WILLIAMS

ANTIOCH COLLEGE

THE MACMILLAN COMPANY · NEW YORK

1957

Permission to quote from copyright works is acknowledged to the following publishers:

Alfred A. Knopf, Inc., for permission to quote from Gerstle Mack, *Gustave Courbet*, New York, 1951. Copyright 1951 by Gerstle Mack.

Hamish Hamilton, Ltd., for permission to quote from Francis Steegmuller, *The Selected Letters of Gustave Flaubert*, London, 1954. Copyright 1953 by Francis Steegmuller.

Harper & Brothers, for permission to quote from Robert C. Binkley, *Realism and Nationalism*, New York, 1935; copyright 1935 by Harper & Brothers; and André Maurois, *The Life of George Sand*, New York, 1953; copyright 1953 by André Maurois.

Librairie Félix Alcan, for permission to quote from Jean Maurain, *La Politique ecclésiastique du Second Empire de 1852-1869*, Paris, 1930.

Librairie Hachette, for permission to quote from Marcel Boulenger, *Le Duc de Morny, Prince français*, Paris, 1925; and Victor Duruy, *Notes et souvenirs*, 2 vols., Paris, 1901.

Librairie Plon, for permission to quote from Pierre Saint Marc, *Emile Ollivier*, Paris, 1950.

Longmans, Green & Co., for permission to quote from F. A. Simpson, *The Rise of Louis Napoleon*, London, 1909. Copyright 1909 by F. A. Simpson.

Pantheon Books, Inc., for permission to quote from Goldwater and Treves, *Artists on Art*, New York, 1945. Copyright 1945 by Pantheon Books, Inc.

Library of Congress catalog card number: 57-6555

A André Lobanov-Rostovsky:
hommage de profond respect

PREFACE

Clio, Muse of History, plays deceptive tricks; she often hides her most confounding problems under a façade of flippancy. The masquerade ball is a sign of a society which has become infinitely complex, a society which confuses the *haut monde* with the demi-monde, and at the very moment when we most need our analytical faculties our attention is captured by décolleté.

There was much more than *gaieté parisienne* in the France of 1851–1870. The political creed of Bonapartism, born of myth and misunderstanding, was practiced for nearly twenty years by a doctrinaire—if un-Napoleonic—Bonaparte. The régime stands nearly unique in its evolution from dictatorship to limited monarchy. What is even more remarkable is that this orientation from Order to Liberty was Bonapartism's *raison d'être*. We are treated to an instance when a party platform was honored.

France has never ceased pulsing from her great Revolution, though, admittedly, subsequent developments like industrialization retarded the recovery from revolutionary wounds. Every postrevolutionary government has been confronted by this phenomenon, and those who are fond of casting stones at Napoleon III would do well to reflect upon the success and stability of all French régimes after 1815.

The words *liberty* and *equality* were used in the eighteenth century to suggest the ideal toward which mankind must strive, and the major economic transformation then beginning virtually guaranteed that *equality* would be a word which would raise blood pressures as the nineteenth century unfolded. Napoleon III was in the vanguard of those who recognized the new economic facts and the political doctrines which they engendered, though he was perhaps unaware that the new economic conditions could well affect the vitality and creativity of French culture. Great wealth can patronize creativity, or it can stimulate a greed for more wealth and power.

The schisms in the fabric of modern French life—for which the Revolution was a catalyst—are illustrated by a factor characteristic of the Second Empire: every major faction within the nation, as well as the Emperor himself, seems eternally on the horns of a dilemma. Nothing is ever resolved to the satisfaction of all. Napoleon III wishes to be liberal and modern, yet finds he must protect the Papacy which condemns liberalism and modernity. The Republicans approve His Majesty's liberalism, but cannot forgive him his support of the Papacy and clerical interests. The Church wishes to support the Emperor's authoritarian régime, but cannot tolerate his liberalism. The Army is delighted to have a Bonaparte as Emperor, but ignores his suggestions for reform which might have markedly improved the Army.

The crux of the difficulty was the creed of Bonapartism itself: the attempt to heal the wounds of the eighteenth century and the Revolution by pleasing everybody. But how does one reconcile the eighteenth century faith in the natural goodness of man and in Reason with the older faith in the necessity of Divine Revelation and in the notion of original sin? And in nineteenth century France, one's political, economic, social, educational, and clerical views were usually contingent upon one's faith. Napoleon III's answer was to offer a program which seemingly offered some satisfaction to every party, and to offer himself as a national symbol—above the factionalism. Even under the Liberal Empire, he retained considerable authority to provide a counterweight against the likelihood of a badly divided Parliament.

Not intending this book to be a text, I have abandoned the more orthodox chronological approach in favor of a mosaic; here are ten vignettes chosen to portray the many facets of the Second Empire: The Duc de Persigny, the professional Bonapartist, was useful as a political hack, but a troublesome ignoramus as an ambassador or statesman. Napoleon III's half-brother, the Duc de Morny, was the most glittering ornament on the Empire's façade.

Beginning as chief architect of the *coup d'état* of 1851, he was successively Minister of the Interior, President of the Corps législatif, and for a few months Ambassador to Russia. A practical man (he called his own kind the "considerable people"), Morny profited handsomely in his country's service.

The Empire suffered opposition, not merely in the form of republican platitudes shouted from the security of exile, but from the braver and wiser who remained at home. The Comte de Montalembert, theologian and statesman, was the leading Liberal Catholic of the Second Empire. His liberalism made him few friends in a period when the Church was well disposed to His Majesty's dictatorship. Emile Ollivier was the most critical of Napoleon's enemies, since he modified his republicanism to fit the promised constitutionalism. Early in 1870, Ollivier emerged as leader of the Empire's first responsible cabinet.

Cologne-born Jacques Offenbach was a cellist who chose to live in France. His music was not particularly celebrated for its intellectual content, which accounts for his popularity during the Empire. He caught the spirit of bourgeois taste as a student during the July Monarchy, but his triumphant cancans were saved to shake the stages of a less respectable era. Gustave Courbet was a realist too, but of another sort. No intellectual, he selected mundane subjects which the bourgeois preferred to ignore and enraged the academicians with his disdain for tradition.

The poet Charles-Augustin Sainte-Beuve is better known as a literary critic. His influence was enormous, but his sympathy for the Empire put him at odds with many writers of the day, a time when few writers were found ignoring politics. The gap between society and politics is bridged with the Countess of Castiglione. Many men were ready to attest that she was the most beautiful woman of the century, but we shall not be concerned with any absolute standards of feminine charm in discussing the "Divine Countess." It is more to the point that her supremely adequate physical endowments were employed in France on behalf of Italian ambition. It might be added that the Countess was temperamentally well suited to perform her patriotic role.

It is not difficult to choose the most able of Napoleon's ministers from the mediocre selection which served the Second Empire. The historian Victor Duruy rose to imperial favor when His Majesty required professional assistance in compiling his *History of Julius Caesar*. Ultimately, Duruy became Minister of Public Instruction. His zeal to revitalize public education reopened an ancient quarrel with the Church, and when he sought to extend education to young girls the sultans of morality quivered in anticipation of the end of the world.

The tenth person to be included, Louis Pasteur, needs the least introduction, as his name has become a household word. Chemist and humanitarian, he represents the finest tradition of experimental science.

The Emperor does not appear as a chapter heading, but in every chapter. More often than not, he has been reviled by historians: his long career of throne seeking made him appear a fool; the Roman expedition and the *coup d'état* of 1851 revealed him a tyrant and a slayer of democratic republics; military failure in 1870 was unpardonable in the eyes of a world which believes in its heart that might is right.

We may view the Second Empire as a laboratory period. The men of that time were challenged to redefine liberty in an age which had been sorely upset by a great political revolution; they were obliged to face the social and economic implications of this revolution. To complicate the picture further, industrialization did much more than increase the supply of economic goods available for consumption. It meant the political ascendancy of the "useful people," to recall the Comte de Saint-Simon's parable, and the grave possibility that virtue would become a utilitarian commodity. Traditional values might either be cast aside as outmoded or practiced without understanding. But even as this process was in action, there remained the uncorrupted who either practiced or preached integrity. In sum, the Second Empire, confronted with the moral crisis of modernity, should loudly speak of questions still pertinent to our age.

More important, it was a dazzling, wicked, wonderful, and gaslit world. France has not been the same since.

In the bibliography, I have indicated my obligation to many

excellent works from which I have gleaned information necessary for the synthesis I present. And while I shall add here the names of kind colleagues who have encouraged me in this project and criticized its various chapters, I cannot begin to thank all those whose minds I have probed in the process of the book's creation.

Specific thanks, however, to Professors Elting E. Morison, John M. Blum, and George R. Healy of the Massachusetts Institute of Technology; to Dean Jacques Barzun of Columbia University and Professor William B. Willcox of the University of Michigan; to Professors Stanley J. Idzerda, Ralph Lewis, John A. Garraty, Marjorie E. Gesner, and Professor and Mrs. Charles C. Cumberland, all of Michigan State University; to Mr. Charles D. Lieber of Random House; and finally to two members of my family, Margaret B. Williams and Richmond B. Williams.

ROGER L. WILLIAMS

Yellow Springs, Ohio
December 2, 1956

CONTENTS

I

The Duc de Persigny

AND THE RENASCENCE OF BONAPARTISM

The absence of a sense of humor is a double disaster: those deprived are unconscious of the ridiculous and are left unarmed against the perversity of their neighbors.

—ROGER DE MORAINE

The man who called himself the Vicomte de Persigny, having just been dismissed from the French Army in 1831, went to Germany on family business. Driving through Augsburg one day, his coachman suddenly pulled up short, waved his hat, and shouted, *"Vive Napoléon,"* at a passing carriage. Persigny had only a glimpse of a young man in the carriage, but his coachman explained that this was Louis-Napoleon, son of Louis and Hortense of Holland, nephew of the only Emperor of the French. In this casual fashion, Persigny met his career.

It is fitting that a parvenu dynasty should have found its most vociferous support in a parvenu. For whatever the eulogistic biographies of Persigny report of his "ancient and noble family," he was born Jean-Gilbert-Victor Fialin, son of a tax collector. The Fialin family, according to the official legend, came from Dauphiné to Lyonnais early in the seventeenth century, moving a second time later in the century to Saint-Germain L'Espinasse in Forez. By the time of Victor Fialin's birth, January 11, 1808, the Revolution had erased the old provincial names, and Saint-Germain L'Espinasse was in the Department of Loire.

The tax collector sent his son to the Collège de Limoges, which served as Victor's preparation for the Cavalry School at Saumur. After two years at Saumur (1826–1828), where he was an able student, Fialin joined the Fourth Regiment of Hussars as sergeant major. In these last years of the Bourbon Monarchy, he came under the influence of a Captain Kersausie, who preached republicanism, and Fialin became a convinced and outspoken republican. The Revolution of 1830 overthrew the Bourbons but not the crown, and the new government of King Louis-Philippe dismissed Fialin from the Army.

If we can believe Persigny's own words, this chance meeting

in Augsburg was a religious experience for him. His republicanism was suddenly converted to Bonapartism, even though he had
not spoken one word to the Prince; and, when he returned to
France, he began an intensive study of First Empire history. "I
want to be the Empire's Loyola," he wrote, and in the sole issue
of the *Revue de l'Occident français* he published his faith in
Bonapartism.

Persigny's view of the French Revolution and Empire does
not suggest that his study of history was as intensive as he claimed.
From his point of view, the French Revolution was bad because
it had created class struggle; the Empire was good because
Napoleon had reunited the classes into a single people; after
Waterloo social war had begun again, and presumably would
continue until a second coming of the Bonapartes. This conversion of history into simple arithmetic was accomplished by adding
up the superficialities and ignoring the complexities of the Revolutionary Era.

Seen in a more kindly light, Persigny was a nationalist, a patriot
who believed that France as a whole could be served by Empire
and the Bonapartes alone. He regarded political parties as serving
some class or factional interest and not the interest of France.
Since there was no Bonapartist party in the 1830's, he could see
no reason why all parties should not support Bonapartism (which
for him was the nation) while still maintaining their respectability
and identity. It was again just a matter of arithmetic.

The publicity Persigny gave these ideas won the attention of
several Bonapartes. Jerome, former king of Westphalia, then
living near London, granted Persigny a letter of introduction
to Louis-Napoleon, who was regarded as the one member of the
dynasty not to have abandoned the idea of restoration.

The Bonaparte family was, of course, exiled from France. King
Louis had moved to Italy, but Queen Hortense, having always
found him dull, settled at Arenenberg Castle in Switzerland. She
was solicitous for her son's education, instructing him herself
when it came to memories of the Empire, and sending him off to
Augsburg for more orthodox schooling. In this way she was
responsible for inculcating in Louis-Napoleon a sense of his

French destiny and for the development of his German accent, neither of which he ever lost.

Returning to Arenenberg from school, Louis-Napoleon received Persigny in 1835. It was the beginning of a collaboration that would last nearly thirty years. It is evident, however, that the Prince had not awaited his "Loyola" before planning the return to Empire. The previous year he had published his *Manuel d'Artillerie*, and he took pains to have it distributed to ranking army officers. Historical rather than technical, it was considered to have merit; even more, it was a reminder that a Bonaparte prepared his way with artillery.

Furthermore, Louis-Napoleon had begun to frequent Baden-Baden. He could do this unobtrusively, as Baden-Baden was an international resort, but it gave him opportunity to meet officers from the French garrison of nearby Strasbourg. He had first recruited a Lieutenant Laity of the Engineers; then a more important conquest, Colonel Vaudrey, commanding the Third and Fourth Artillery regiments. Attempts to win the garrison's governor, General Voirol, failed; the general naturally reported the plot to Paris, where Louis-Philippe's government found the matter too absurd to notice it.

Having done this groundwork himself, Louis-Napoleon sent Persigny into Strasbourg in October of 1836 to make the final preparations. It was Persigny who set the date for the uprising on October 30th. In addition to the two artillery regiments, the garrison included three regiments of infantry and a battalion of engineers. Persigny's idea was for Louis-Napoleon to present himself to the Third Artillery and rally its support. He reasoned that the Fourth Artillery would join immediately, as it was Napoleon I's old outfit, and Bonapartist out of sentiment. With all the guns and the arsenal, Persigny expected to force the adherence of the remaining troops and the town.

Louis-Napoleon entered Strasbourg two days in advance of the scheduled rising and immediately vetoed Persigny's plan. Presumably he did not wish to identify himself too closely with only one branch of the Army; more important, he insisted on avoiding bloodshed and the appearance of military terror. He thought it better, therefore, to present himself to the Fourth Artillery, which was certain to acclaim him, and then to try winning the Forty-sixth Infantry. In any event the new career was not to begin with a whiff of grape, whatever the Napoleonic tradition; but such scruples gave birth to suggestions of coward-ice.

Early in the morning on the thirtieth of October, Colonel Vaudrey introduced Louis-Napoleon to the Fourth Artillery, and he was cheered as anticipated. Then, with the Prince at its head, the regiment marched out to test the sentiments of the Forty-sixth Infantry. Meanwhile, the governor was arrested, but managed to escape; it was a bad omen. The townspeople, on the other hand, seemed friendly enough, and offered no sign of a zealous loyalty to the government.

When Louis-Napoleon arrived at the Forty-sixth Infantry barracks, he found the courtyard too small to bring in his regiment. There was only room to draw up the infantry in order to introduce himself. Thus, he came into the courtyard with only a small escort. Infantry officers loyal to the King rallied the troops, and it was quickly evident that a fight between the two regiments was essential if the *coup* were to succeed. As Louis-Napoleon refused to give the order, Persigny alone tried to get the artillery to fire on the infantry, but his was not the magic name. The momentum was lost, and with it the cause. The artillery vanished, and Persigny made his escape.

After a brief skirmish inside the courtyard, the Prince and his suite were arrested, and the affair was finished less than three hours after it had begun. The government chose to be lenient, and pardoned Louis-Napoleon unconditionally, though he was put on a ship bound for America. In so doing, the government minimized the rising to a point of ridicule and successfully obscured the fact that Louis-Napoleon had received considerable popular response in Strasbourg. In fact, a more decisive man would have won the day, and the near success was a guarantee that a second attempt would be made.

The Prince spent the spring of 1837 in the United States, and then rushed back to Arenenberg to be with his dying mother. A small group of loyal adherents, including Persigny, rallied to his side, and their presence in Switzerland soon brought protests from the French government. The Swiss were disinclined to be bullied by Paris, and made no move to expel Louis-Napoleon and his friends; but, as French pressure increased, the Prince saw the opportunity for a politic gesture. He moved his suite to London to save the Swiss further embarrassment, simultaneously making himself extremely popular in Switzerland and making the government of Louis-Philippe appear ignoble.

Much to Persigny's disgust, Louis-Napoleon seemed in no hurry to gain the French throne once they had arrived in London. He readily fell into the social life of the British aristocracy, and the agents of the French government may well be pardoned for taking his plotting lightly. His existence appeared to be a series of frivolous entertainments. In 1839, for example, Louis-Napoleon and Persigny went to Lord Eglinton's castle in Ayrshire for a fantastic costume ball. The guests were to participate in a medieval tournament and were, therefore, invited for a good many days of preliminary practice before the actual event.

The best description of this organized folly appears in Disraeli's novel *Endymion,* where Louis-Napoleon is referred to as Florestan. If Disraeli is correct, Florestan, garbed in blue damascened armor inlaid with silver roses and calling himself the Knight of the White Rose, commanded more admiration than any other knight in the procession. Though a major part of the tournament was rained out, it was clear that he was also one of the best horsemen. Persigny was cast in a fitting role: squire to Florestan.

Some of their moments in England, however, were given over to literary projects. Louis-Napoleon worked on a pamphlet entitled *Idées napoléoniennes,* in which he presented the Empire as the ideal government for France and explained how Empire in France meant peace and stability for all Europe. For his part, Persigny composed his *Lettres de Londres* (1840), in which he introduced Louis-Napoleon as the man necessary for the restoration of Empire. His enthusiasm for Louis-Napoleon led him into the following description:

One is not long in perceiving that the Napoleonic type is reproduced with an astonishing fidelity. . . . There are . . . the same lines and the same inclination of the head, so marked with the Napoleonic character that when the Prince turns, it is enough to startle a soldier of the Old Guard; . . . and it is impossible not to be struck . . . by the imposing pride of the Roman profile, the pure and severe—I will even say solemn—lines of which are like the soul of a great destiny.

In the summer of 1840, having been in Britain over a year and a half, the two men finally completed plans for a second attempt on the French government. The channel port of Boulogne was the target this time, and Persigny had recruited an expedition of fifty-six men. The landing was to take place just north of the port, and the men were to be dressed in uniforms of the Fortieth Infantry, one of the local regiments. Not all the party knew the object of the expedition, but an ample store of liquor on board was designed to guarantee general enthusiasm and courage. Someone who was devoted to symbolism had tied a live eagle to the mainmast; but, having been waved about on a rough sea, the wretched creature was anything but imperial. The presence of the bird gave rise to a legend that Louis-Napoleon had worn bacon in his hat to keep the eagle happy on his shoulder.

The debarkation took place early in the morning of August 6, 1840. Despite the local uniforms, some customs officers thought the operation odd, and investigated. They were seized; but, because Louis-Napoleon had forbidden bloodshed, and because the party had no personnel to spare as guards, they were ultimately released. The alarm was soon given. Meanwhile, the expedition marched to the barracks of the Forty-second Infantry to rally its support. They were interrupted there by an energetic and loyal officer, Captain Col-Puygélier, whom Persigny tried to kill. The Prince interfered to prevent violence, and his party retreated from the barracks. As they were not pursued, they might have escaped to the boats; instead, Louis-Napoleon led them into the town in hope of winning popular support. At the approach of troops, however, his men scattered, and Persigny and he rushed for a boat with several loyal followers.

Though they reached a small boat, it was in vain. They were

fired on from shore, Napoleon was slightly wounded, and the boat capsized. Made prisoners, they were removed to the fortress of Ham on the Somme River to await trial. The government could no longer afford to be lenient, and in September Louis-Napoleon was brought before the Chamber of Peers. His defense was undeniably clever. It was an attempt to win sympathy rather than deny the government's case:

I stand before you representing a principle, a cause, a defeat. The principle is the sovereignty of the people; the cause is that of the Empire; the defeat, Waterloo. That principle *you* have recognized, that cause *you* have served, that defeat *you* would avenge. No, there is no difference between you and me.

He moved the court, but that could not remove the guilt. The Peers ordered his return to Ham for the remainder of his life, while the other prisoners were given terms ranging from two years to transportation for life.

Persigny was to be interned at Doullens for twenty years; but, once there, he became ill and was transferred to a military hospital at Versailles, where he had relative freedom. When word came that the Master at Ham was devoting his leisure to study and writing, Persigny could do no less. He had been interested in the Egyptian pyramids, and had a notion that they were not the funeral monuments which scholars supposed. His thesis was implicit in the pamphlet's title: *On the Object and the Permanent Use of the Pyramids of Egypt and Nubia Against the Sandy Inroads of the Desert.*

Persigny's official biographer, Delaroa, ever courageous in the line of his duties, tells us that Persigny consulted history, geography, archaeology, geometry, mechanics, aerostatics, and meteorology; he consulted documents from Herodotus to Champollion-Figeac, weighing all assertions and facts; he even devoted himself to "lofty considerations" drawn from politics and religion. And finally we are informed that, having mustered every discipline (there is no mention of common sense), Persigny concluded with the "moral and mathematical proofs" for his problem. This contribution to learning was published in Paris in 1845.

The following year, Louis-Napoleon made his escape from Ham and scurried back to Britain, where Persigny, who had had virtual freedom since his illness, hastened to rejoin him. The story of Louis-Napoleon's escape—how he shaved his beard, donned the clothes of a workman named Badinguet, and walked unnoticed from the fortress with a board on his shoulder—endeared him to the French public at a time when the government of King Louis-Philippe was regarded with increasing distaste. It was obvious that trouble was brewing in France, and trouble could be Louis-Napoleon's and Persigny's opportunity.

II

Louis-Philippe's government, often called the July Monarchy, dated from the July Revolution of 1830. His régime suffered a fatal weakness from the start: it could not appeal to any traditional principle of French political experience. As a constitutional monarchy resting on the suffrage of the well-to-do, the principle of legitimate monarchy had been rejected without embracing the political democracy of the French Revolution. Compromise is, of course, a well understood political mechanism; but, to be practical, a compromise must itself rest on a moral basis. Otherwise it has the appearance of selfish interest.

The July Monarchy, unable to accept either legitimacy or democracy, took liberalism as its official philosophy, and liberalism in the 1830's was defined, in brief, as *laissez faire.* This gave the government a moral basis but, unfortunately, not a basis entirely free from the taint of selfish interest. France was then beginning the economic transformation brought by industrialization, a transformation which held the promise of realizing equality for *all*. Such a period of dislocation and aspiration would have been trying for any government; but a government whose official philosophy seemed designed to confer benefits upon only a few—in the face of more general expectations—was numbering its days.

To the troubles of early industrialism—the migration from farm to town and the frequent depressions—was added the hu-

miliation of a foreign policy which gave the appearance of spine-
lessness. The program offered by Louis-Napoleon and seconded
by Persigny made more sense than *laissez faire*. It seemed to offer
peace with glory, liberty with order, and profits with honor.

Meanwhile, the government met growing criticism intransi-
gently. Elections were manipulated and patronage was carefully
managed so that political power became the property of an even
smaller oligarchy. Criticism grew into demands for electoral
reform and came from conservatives and radicals alike. A bad
depression, which began in 1846 and lasted into 1847, further
embarrassed the government, and when the régime tried to solve
all problems by simply crushing the reform movement it found
a revolution on its hands.

This was the February Revolution of 1848. Sensing the magni-
tude of the opposition, King Louis-Philippe was not long in
packing himself off to Britain. Persigny, always impetuous, urged
Louis-Napoleon to go at once to Paris, but the Prince knew he
lacked sufficient support in France and preferred to bide his time.
The Provisional Government, in the meantime, dissolved the July
Monarchy and thus accomplished the only act on which the
factions comprising the new government could agree.

The Radical Republicans, representing the workers of Paris,
were much influenced by the various socialist doctrines of the
nineteenth century. They understood liberty and equality to
be social and economic as well as political. The Moderate Republicans, while they favored universal suffrage, held liberal
social and economic views. It was to their advantage to preserve
the provisional nature of the government in the hope that the
combined weight of the bourgeois and conservative rural votes
would eventually swamp the Radicals. Accordingly, the Radicals
favored the immediate formation of a socialist republic while
the Parisian mob was still the predominant political force. Such
a threat was a ghastly nightmare for the propertied classes, and
accounts for their increasing demand for a government dedicated
to *Order*, by which they meant the protection of private property.

The Moderates were able to postpone national elections from

February of 1848 until late April by conceding an important point to Louis Blanc, one of the Radical leaders. Blanc believed that any government worthy of the name must guarantee every man the right to work. Thus, to appease the Radicals, the Provisional Government established National Workshops in Paris and guaranteed work for the unemployed. The Workshops were an expedient for all except Blanc: the propertied classes hated the principle which underlay their establishment, and too many workers regarded them as a republican road to subsidized idleness. Blanc's humanitarian principle was lost in the struggle of selfish interests.

Elections for a National Assembly were scheduled for April 23rd, and Louis-Napoleon sent Persigny to France in March to discuss with several Bonapartists the advisability of standing for election. They decided against his candidacy for the moment. As the Moderates had predicted, the country as a whole was alarmed at Parisian radicalism and returned an overwhelmingly moderate Assembly. As a result, Louis Blanc was dropped from the government.

Supplementary elections were held for the National Assembly on June 4th, and this time Louis-Napoleon decided to risk his name. He was elected by four departments, a clear indication that instability had created an interest in Bonapartism. The Republicans were nervous, and when Persigny was seen entering France from Britain on June 12th the government issued orders for his arrest—and Louis-Napoleon's, too, should he set foot in France. This decree had to be set aside the following day as too illogical. Having failed to deny Louis-Napoleon the right of candidacy, the government could not deny him the rights of an elected member of the Assembly.

Louis-Napoleon well understood that his name meant security and order to many of the French. He would now demonstrate that their faith was not misplaced. "Since involuntarily I am the excuse for disorder," he wrote the government, "it is with deep regret that I place my resignation in your hands." It was his good fortune to have made this gesture immediately before the bloody insurrection known as the June Days.

Ever since the inauguration of the National Workshops, laborers had been streaming into Paris, and the government found itself paying an ever increasing horde for whom it could not supply productive work. Aside from insulting bourgeois virtue, this practice was spawning a dangerously large army of potential enemies inside Paris. In June the government screwed up its courage and made an honest attempt to limit state employment to cases of legitimate need. The Workshops were greatly reduced, to the dismay of many workers. The Radical leaders were quick to make political capital of the situation, and the workingmen were urged to risk their lives for principles they did not fully understand.

The Army, under General Cavaignac, fought the mob for four frightful days, and at the end a grateful National Assembly made Cavaignac the Provisional President of the Republic. Meanwhile, the Assembly continued work on a republican constitution, which was ready in October of 1848. It provided for the election of a president by universal suffrage; he would appoint his ministers, but as a check on executive power—ever a French concern—the ministers were to be responsible to the Assembly.

The presidential election of December 10, 1848, was a contest between four men: General Cavaignac, the darling of the Moderate Republicans; Ledru-Rollin, representing the Radical Republicans; Raspail, a Socialist; and Louis-Napoleon, who had no party but an unbeatable name. He swept the field. His election, and that of the regularly constituted Assembly, revealed a strange illogicality: the French elected a Bonaparte as President and returned a majority of monarchists to a republican Assembly. In this way the Second Republic was dealt a mortal blow at birth, although it lingered for three more years. The new Assembly, comprising 300 Orleanists, 200 Legitimists, and only 250 Republicans, was bent on reaction. When the Deputies disenfranchised 30 per cent of the electorate, they made the President the only hope of Democracy as well as Order.

Oddly enough, the new President did not name Persigny as one of his ministers; instead, in the late summer of 1849, Persigny was sent on a six-week good-will tour of the German states, including Austria. In the wake of the February Revolution in Paris, the German world had been shaken by revolutions, but by the time of Persigny's trip the old régimes were once again in the saddle. Upon his return, Persigny made a report to De Tocqueville, the Minister of Foreign Affairs, but some of his observations were reserved for the President alone.

According to the dictates of the Napoleonic Legend, Persigny was prepared to be more friendly with the Prussians than with the Austrians. The Treaties of 1814–1815, which proscribed the Bonapartes, were regarded by them as essentially Austrian in spirit: legitimist, antinationalist, and illiberal. Thus, when in Austria, Persigny was not surprised to be rather coldly received at first by Prime Minister Schwarzenberg. Later, they had two private dinners together, probably because Schwarzenberg quickly sensed Persigny's shortcomings as a diplomat and hoped to glean information about Louis-Napoleon's future intentions.

Persigny made it his duty to warn Schwarzenberg that Louis-Napoleon would never tolerate snubs like those given to Louis-Philippe; he warned against underestimating the vigor of a united people standing behind one man, and in particular against underestimating the strength of France. In short, he blustered and threatened when there was as yet no occasion. The judgment of a French contemporary is fair: that Persigny, although intelligent, was "an old tomtit who knew nothing of statesmanship."

Persigny's attitude changed once he arrived in Prussia. According to Bonapartist definitions, Prussia was a relatively good power because she looked favorably on a unification of the German peoples, just as Austria was bad in her obstruction of this ambition. Persigny's report to De Tocqueville must have caused some annoyance at the French Foreign Office. He pictured King Frederick William IV as illiberal, but as willing to accept liberalism as an aid to unifying Germany under Prussian rule. This, according to Persigny, was the reason the King had willingly granted a liberal constitution in Prussia. He seemed unaware of the actual reason for the constitution—that Frederick William had granted it during the Revolution of 1848 to save his throne.

During the revolutionary upheavals in 1848, German liberals,

eager for unification, had gathered at Frankfort and offered
Frederick William the crown of a united Germany. Persigny
explained the rejection of this offer as the King's unwillingness
to have anything to do with the trappings of liberal, constitutional
government, which "inevitably led to republicanism." That the
King's opinion was in direct contradiction to his earlier judgment
on the Prussian constitution never seems to have occurred to
Persigny.

Not mentioned in Persigny's official report was a private conversation he had with the King, who was curious to know
whether Louis-Napoleon's following had diminished since his
assumption of the presidency. Assured of the President's continuing popularity, Frederick William said that he failed to understand why Louis-Napoleon had been willing to be circumscribed
by a constitutional republic. Persigny regarded the King's question as legitimate, and replied that he had advised Louis-Napoleon
against becoming a constitutional president.

Nor had he any hesitation in suggesting that the form of the
French government was temporary, "a matter of opportunity."
Persigny tells us in his *Mémoirs* that the French Foreign Service
was full of officers hostile to the Bonapartes. Hence it was his
obligation, when abroad, to reveal the true situation in France
and to herald the coming of Empire. The Prussians and Austrians
alike were astonished at his words, which he attributed to the
enlightenment he was bringing them. Shortly after his return
from the German tour, Persigny was appointed Minister Plenipo-
tentiary to Berlin, where he served without particular distinction.

Persigny's sympathy for Prussia reflected the Napoleonic
scheme to create a Rhenish buffer state between France and an
enlarged Prussia. This plan, which would have permitted a degree
of German unification without—according to Louis-Napoleon—
jeopardizing French security, was pondered well into the 1860's.
There was always the precedent of Napoleon I's Confederation
of the Rhine, and such precedents, supported by Louis-Napoleon's own written version of the Napoleonic Legend, comprised
the sacred doctrine for convinced Bonapartists.

By 1851, the year Louis-Napoleon forced a revision of the

constitution in his own favor, Persigny's self-esteem had raised him from *vicomte* to *comte*. Despite this improvement, Louis-Napoleon did not see fit to entrust one of the key roles in the coup to Persigny, though as an old friend and intriguer he was included in the plot and given lesser tasks to perform.

Once the *coup d'état* had secured the President a ten-year term at the Elysée Palace, he turned his attention to properties owned by the Orléans family. It was an ancient principle that French kings joined their properties with those of the crown, but in 1830 Louis-Philippe, then Duc d'Orléans, transferred the bulk of his property to his sons a few days before ascending the throne. His lawyers argued that the old custom of devolution was no longer binding in view of the end of legitimate monarchy, but the Duke's haste in transferring the property suggests that he was not completely confident of their opinion.

Thus the matter rested until January of 1852, when Persigny urged Louis-Napoleon to rectify this wrong. The Decrees of January 22nd spoke of Louis-Philippe's "fraudulent donation," and characterized the seizure of the Orléans properties as "restitution," not confiscation. Whatever the legality of the matter, the propertied classes in France were aghast. They had voted for a Bonaparte as a guarantee of order, and this seizure smacked of socialism as they defined it. A serious political mistake, the confiscation provoked the resignation of several ministers; and Persigny, whose advice had for once been taken, emerged as Minister of the Interior.

Persigny's honest devotion to Bonapartism, when combined with an absence of humor which bordered on the sullen, produced a minister whose intense seriousness of purpose was in marked contrast with the mood at court. Moreover, this lack of a sense of humor warped his sense of proportion and made him blind to the ridiculous. We see him, for example, several months after his assumption of office, talking to Count Nieuwerkerke, the Superintendent of Museums. He announced his intention to take over the Louvre for ministerial uses, to centralize the various governmental departments in a great barracks, where the government could sit with all its power. Poor Nieuwerkerke, who thought that for once Persigny must be joking, forced a smile. Advised of this mistake, Nieuwerkerke suggested that it might then be necessary to sell the masterpieces in the Louvre, to which Persigny replied: "Why not? The arts amount to little in the face of serious political requirements." Small wonder that Viel-Castel, Nieuwerkerke's assistant, classified Persigny as "a vulgar intriguer, lacking in courage and honesty," and as "pompous and spiteful. . . . To my mind he is as much like a gentleman as chicory is like coffee."

During 1852 Persigny was haunted by the fear that the Second Republic would never evolve into Empire. If he spoke to the President in private, he was always put off in a manner which suggested that Louis-Napoleon regarded presidential rank as sufficient. If, as Minister of the Interior, he raised in cabinet meetings the problem of what the official attitude should be if cries of *Vive l'Empéreur* were heard during the President's projected tour of France, he got nothing but angry argument. Unable to conceive of anyone less Bonapartist than himself, forgetting that the ministers of a republic might regard a discussion of the possibility of Empire as lacking in taste or even seditious, Persigny concluded that the ministers were too preoccupied with self-interest to take advantage of "this unique opportunity to set France in her rightful track." How had such selfish men come to be ministers? By default, he tells us; more eminent men had been thrown into hostile parties by the turn of events, giving these "upstarts" opportunity to achieve fortune.

Five days before Louis-Napoleon began his tour of the nation (September of 1852), Persigny decided to see to it that the "desired political orientation" would take place. His technique was simple; he informed the prefects of the first departments to be visited that Bonapartist demonstrations would be favorably regarded by the President, knowing that the remaining prefects would emulate these performances in the competition to please Paris. Skipping the prefect of Loiret, who was a friend of one of the ministers, he summoned the prefects of Cher, Nièvre, and Allier to Paris for secret instructions, which specified, incidentally, that Bonapartist cheers be for Napoleon III, not II.

Persigny suggests that all went as planned, but that the President guessed his initiative in the demonstrations and was furious. Since the general outburst of Bonapartist enthusiasm which Louis-Napoleon met on his trip ended in the transformation of the Second Republic into the Second Empire, it is clear that Persigny hoped to imply that the Empire was his own work. Yet it is difficult to believe that Louis-Napoleon, after his history of plotting in the name of the imperial tradition, went off on a national tour in the innocence which Persigny claimed. In fact, he openly spoke of his trip as an "interrogation," and the question was as obvious as the desired response.

The Second Empire was not an empire by inadvertence. A study of Louis-Napoleon reveals certain consistencies, and one of them was his refusal to go in directions he had not anticipated. Those around him were free to advise, urge, and push, but not until painful illness broke his resistance did he succumb to the will of others. His guide was a legend and he, alone, the legend's heir. Traditional histories have pictured Louis-Napoleon as an opportunist whose policies were strangely unrealistic. To regard him, however, as a sincere believer in the principles of the Napoleonic Legend, who designed his actions to fit the Legend, gives a more faithful portrait of the man. The legend was crystalline on one point above all: to be Napoleonic, one must first become an emperor.

Why, then, did Persigny seek to enlarge upon his own part in the establishment of Empire? No doubt he had been galled by the secondary role he had played in the *coup d'état* of 1851. As the longest and most faithful supporter of Louis-Napoleon, his ambition was to be the primary inspirer of policy. It must be said that money and honors were not his goal, and he had strong sentiments about the morals and characters of more selfish men in politics. He had no love for non-Bonapartist ministers like Thiers and Falloux, and when men like Morny, Bonapartist only after 1848, took precedence in the *coup d'état*, he was plainly jealous.

Even so, 1852 was Persigny's year. He became Minister of the Interior in January, saw the birth of the Second Empire on

December 2nd, and was named to the Senate on the last day of
the year. Furthermore, on May 27th, he married Albine-Marie-
Napoléone-Eglé Ney de la Moskowa, granddaughter of Marshal
Ney. No one could ever claim that the Comte de Persigny was
not devoted to dynastic principles. But, if he brought a splendidly
Napoleonic name under his roof, he did not marry a reputation
as lofty as the name. Happily for him, he was too blinded by his
wife's name to know the extent of her later infidelities, though
they were common knowledge and offered much amusement to
the court society. Mme. de Persigny was also known for her love
of English ways, and behind her back was called Lady Persington.
She was the mistress of the Duc de Gramont-Caderousse, a roué
much frowned upon by his prominent family; and her taste for
embassy clerks, when her husband served as Ambassador to Britain, gave rise to the following anecdote: "Mme. de Persigny is
lost; it is impossible to find her." "Well, have you looked carefully under all the furniture? The tables, buffets, and secretaries?"

III

Persigny and his new Emperor received a rude shock early
in the régime. Europe, understandably, was not pleased to have
another Bonaparte as Emperor of France, but since his elevation
to the throne was sanctioned by an overwhelming vote by the
French no power deemed it prudent to intervene. Some of the
conservative monarchs even welcomed Napoleon's accession, as
it marked the end of a Republic, but when he assumed the numeral III they disapproved. Taking the numeral III instead of II
was a pretension of legitimacy and recognized the existence of
the King of Rome, son of Napoleon I, who had never reigned.
It suggested the illegitimacy of all governments since 1815 and
was a slap at the powers who had proscribed the Bonapartes in
1815.

Nicholas I of Russia, urged on by the courts of Prussia and
Austria, greeted Napoleon III as *"Monsieur et bon ami,"* the
proper salutation for a President. It was a deliberate snub, and
no one felt it more keenly than Persigny, who was ready for war

in case a *Sire et bon frère* was not forthcoming from St. Petersburg. When Napoleon and the other ministers overruled
Persigny's belligerence, he regarded the affair as further evidence
that he alone was devoted to Bonapartism and to France.

In a similar vein, Persigny regarded Napoleon III's tastes as
too simple, and insisted on a court with "conditions of magnificence." He did not mean a return to the etiquette of Louis XV,
but a studied effort to avoid the stingy atmosphere of Louis-
Philippe. As Louis XVI had had a civil list of nearly twenty-five
million francs in 1789, Persigny felt that double that figure would
be satisfactory for Napoleon III. The Council of Ministers, however, was so parsimonious as to propose twelve million francs,
forcing Persigny to alter their proposal to twenty-five million,
the sum voted by the Senate.

On June 21, 1854, Persigny temporarily left the imperial service
and received the following note from His Majesty:

I regret very much that your health forces you to give me your
resignation, and I regret no less that you feel unable to accept the
post of Minister without Portfolio, as this last arrangement would
not deprive me of the insights and friendly advice of a man who, for
twenty years, has given me so many demonstrations of his devotion.

As a token of my personal satisfaction, I name you Grand Officer
of the Legion of Honor, and I hope that your health will permit you
to render me new services later.

On this, I pray God to keep you in His holy care.

NAPOLEON

Shortly afterward, on May 28, 1855, Persigny returned to the
Empire's service, this time as Ambassador to Britain. He replaced
Walewski, who became Foreign Minister. Napoleon III was determined to make friendship with Britain the keystone of his
foreign policy, since, as a good student of the Napoleonic Legend,
he was convinced—and with some reason—that Britain had been
the power most responsible for the defeat of Napoleon I. The
British were naturally hostile to the rise of a new Napoleon, and
Palmerston had been dismissed as Foreign Minister for approving
the *coup d'état* of 1851 without cabinet approval.

Ironically enough, Palmerston's successor, Lord Malmesbury, was one of the few aristocrats sympathetic to Napoleon III. He was the youngest member of the cabinet and had not lived during the First Empire; but he had known Louis-Napoleon in Britain, first meeting him at Eglinton Castle. Friendship with Britain was not a hopeless matter, and Walewski had been instructed to impress upon the British the fact that Napoleon III had nothing but pacific intentions. Persigny was wont to claim that it was he, not Walewski, who discovered a basis for good Anglo-French relations, but actually neither of them could prove such a claim.

Persigny supposed that the First Reform Bill in Britain in 1832 had given commercial interests predominance in the formation of foreign policy. His formula was thus quite simple: Develop Anglo-French trade as the basis for political alliance. His notion that the British statesmen of the eighteenth century had slighted commercial interests while devoting themselves to the colonial rivalry with France must have caused some astonishment in Britain, but before his embassy was completed the British were to experience a number of surprises from the same source.

When Persigny went to London in 1855, Britain and France were allied and fighting the Russians in the Crimea. It was an alliance of convenience; both powers worried that Russia was about to break into the eastern Mediterranean and upset the balance of power. But the Russian defeat, accomplished by an army three-quarters French, served to enhance Napoleon III's prestige and, thus, to increase British uneasiness. Even during the war, at a time when neither side could achieve a decisive action, the British were suspicious of Napoleon. He had wanted to go to the front to assume personal command in the hope of hastening the war's end, but the British were dead set against his going. It was not that they feared his untried generalship, but that they feared his victories. The problem was to win the war without simultaneously whetting Napoleon III's ambitions. Persigny was duly informed by the British that Napoleon's departure for the East would strain the alliance, and this was probably the primary consideration which kept His Majesty in Paris.

In short, despite the Crimean alliance, Anglo-French relations were never as harmonious as Napoleon III would have liked, and Persigny's faith in trade was not the key to good relations. Ironically, trade increased between the two nations as their political estrangement grew. Unfortunately for France, Bonapartism and victory combined to give the appearance of great power and ambition, an appearance that was greater than reality. When Napoleon III said, "The Empire means peace," few believed him. Only after 1870, when an isolated France had been quickly beaten, was Europe convinced that the balance of power had actually shifted.

In his double desire to maintain the British alliance and to keep Persigny employed, we have Napoleon III reading his new Ambassador a lesson in elementary diplomacy:

My dear Persigny, When one occupies a position like yours, one must become imbued with the fact that one is not free to develop personal ideas, however good and useful they may be. A minister or ambassador can give authority to his words only if it is well understood that they faithfully echo those of his government. And if, by accident, this conviction should become weakened, the words lose all influence and political importance. It is thus necessary, when you communicate an idea to the British government, that they be convinced that you are the official and faithful organ of my views and intentions. Now in your last communication to the British government, which contained, I admit, some good things which will perhaps come to pass sooner or later, you proceeded without really knowing whether such is the present determination of my government. . . . Receive, my dear Persigny, the assurances of my sincere friendship.

Persigny and his cohorts regarded this letter as a perfect example of Napoleon's coldness, but a better description of it would suggest His Majesty's kindness to old friends.

By his refusal to cast out faithful adherents of his younger days, Napoleon III made himself vulnerable to the charge that he lacked political acumen—that he could not select talented lieutenants. A good many able supporters of earlier régimes, of course, refused to serve Napoleon III, but his appointment of some extremely capable officials is often overlooked. Historians, like the public, often measure a man by his errors rather than by his virtues.

Meanwhile, Persigny's responsibility was to keep the Crimean alliance from going to pieces. At the Congress of Paris (1856), following the war, Napoleon III had shown himself too lenient toward the Russians for British taste, and he was suspected of playing a double game. Some of the postwar problems were not settled at the Congress, and remained to trouble the international scene (see the chapter on the Duc de Morny). An example was the Romanian question, the solution of which nearly broke the Anglo-French alliance.

The Treaty of Paris had removed the Russian right to protect the Christians in the Danubian Principalities, and placed this portion of the Turkish Empire under the joint protection of the signatory powers. This removal of Russian monopoly which the Romanians had enjoyed for thirty years was regarded as a check upon ambitions which the Russians might have in the direction of Constantinople. The Treaty left the Sultan of Turkey the sovereign of the Principalities but granted each one of the Principalities—Moldavia and Walachia—autonomy in domestic matters. It was an arrangement satisfactory to none of the parties.

A majority of the Romanians favored unification of the Principalities and complete independence from Turkey, and their claims soon had the backing of Napoleon III, ever the champion of nation-states. The remaining great powers chose sides according to self-interest: Turkey, of course, opposed unification as a direct territorial loss to her Empire; Britain, anxious to preserve Turkish integrity, backed the Turks; so did Austria, always concerned to defeat the principle of nation-states. Napoleon gained the support of Russia, who smiled on weakening Turkey, and Sardinia and Prussia threw in their support, happy to be opposed to Austria and themselves having a stake in the nationality issue.

In compliance with the Treaty of Paris, the Turks held elections in the Principalities to choose representatives for the divans (legislatures) in Bucharest and Yassy, the two provincial capitals, but—knowing that there was a small group of Moldavians

who feared the preponderance of Bucharest in a unified state—
the Turks rigged the Moldavian election so as to elect opponents
of unification to the Yassy divan. This was July of 1857. The
Turkish trick was so obvious that France, Russia, Prussia, and
Sardinia demanded the annulment of the elections. Backed by
Britain and Austria, the Turks said No.

The British could not see the logic of fighting a war to preserve the Ottoman Empire, and then turning around the following year and carving an independent state out of that Empire.
Napoleon III answered that peace and order in Europe depended
on satisfying national rights of self-determination. Thus he was
ready to break relations with Turkey, and the Russians, hoping
such an act would smash the Crimean alliance and pave the way
for the removal of the 1856 Treaty, agreed to break with Turkey
also.

Napoleon III, however, valued his British alliance, and he instructed Persigny to tell Lord Clarendon, then Foreign Minister,
that he would like to visit Queen Victoria. The Queen responded
by inviting the imperial couple to visit her at Osborne, and it
was understood that the Walewskis—he was still French Foreign
Minister—would be included. At the last moment, the Empress
Eugénie announced that she would not have Mme. Walewski in
her suite, forcing Clarendon to obtain a special royal invitation
for her. Eugénie had been rightly informed that Mme. Walewski
was a current favorite of the Emperor, and was disinclined to
suffer the humiliation of seeming to sponsor his infidelity.

This crisis solved, it was possible for Napoleon III to arrive
at Osborne on the very day that the Russians and he broke relations with Turkey (August 6, 1857). Franco-British discussions
immediately got under way, and a compromise was achieved.
Napoleon promised not to insist on a complete fusion of the
Principalities, while the British agreed that the elections should
be annulled. This compromise was actually a French victory,
since honest elections in the Principalities would mean the ultimate victory of the Romanian unionists. The British softness
may be explained by the Sepoy Mutiny, which was causing
anxiety in London. It was hardly the time to push France into

Russia's camp. Thus, the Crimean alliance endured the storm, but it was shaky and vulnerable to further blows.

The French were, in particular, sensitive to criticism which could be freely published in British newspapers. Perhaps it was natural that a government which had the power to silence journalists at home should expect to hear nothing but kindness from the ally's press, whereas in reality a free press, like that in Britain, would be by definition hostile to Napoleon's government. Persigny, who regarded himself as something of a liberal and a student of British historical experience, was, among the French hierarchy, the least inclined to tolerate the idea of a free press.

Late in 1857, Persigny informed his government that he had discovered the secret of the *Time*'s hostility to Napoleon III: it had been bought by the Orléans family. Walewski found the report amusing and laughingly showed it to Lord Cowley, who duly reported the incident to his government. Lord Clarendon replied: "Persigny's cock and bull story about the *Times* having been purchased by the Orléans family, ought to be the measure of faith to be put in his reports."

The right of asylum which the British granted to political refugees was another mysterious and unfriendly practice from the French point of view. Napoleon III, who had profited from this generosity and who was not despotic in temperament, understood the British tradition; but the majority in his government failed to see why the ally across the Channel allowed enemies of His Imperial Majesty to live in peace.

This irritation almost ruptured the alliance in 1858, when Orsini, an Italian patriot, made an unsuccessful attempt upon the Emperor's life outside the Opera. Many Italians were anxious about the unification of their country, having expected speedy action after Sardinia's participation in the Crimean War. The Sardinian Prime Minister was convinced that Napoleon III's cooperation was essential for success and was busy securing it (see the chapter on the Countess of Castiglione), but Orsini preferred to follow the dictum of Schwarzenberg: "When France catches cold, Europe sneezes." He would start a revolution in France by assassinating the Emperor in the hope that chaos would develop elsewhere as it had in 1848.

After the attempt on Napoleon's life, the police discovered that the plotters had come into France from Britain, and that their bombs had been manufactured in Birmingham. An immediate and unthinking outcry was raised against the British government, and though Napoleon allowed some intemperate security measures at home, he alone was calm when it came to attacking the British. When the news of the attempt reached London, Persigny donned court dress and rushed to the Foreign Office. Half-drawing his little ceremonial sword, he shouted, *"C'est la guerre!"* Even if it meant depriving the British of a source of amusement, it was now necessary to withdraw Persigny from London, and as a gesture of friendship Napoleon replaced Persigny with Pélissier, the Duc de Malakoff, a man whose title symbolized the recent Anglo-French victory.

It is remarkable that Persigny, having been Minister to Prussia, Minister of the Interior, Grand Officer of the Legion of Honor, Senator, and Ambassador to Britain, could feel that he was insufficiently regarded. Humility, indeed, is the possession of those who see themselves in a true light. Yet, honors still came to him. Lord Cowley, British Ambassador to Paris, tells us of the charming way Napoleon chose to confer the Grand Cross of the Legion of Honor upon Persigny. It was June, 1857, and time for the Prince Imperial's baptism, an auspicious occasion for those enthusiastic for the dynasty's continuance. The Persignys were at Saint-Cloud in the morning and were urged to remain for dinner. Since they did not have the proper dinner clothes, the Empress offered Mme. de Persigny a gown, and the Emperor promised the Count a coat. The coat arrived with a star on it, and when Persigny began to unpin it, as he was only a Grand Officer, the Emperor prevented him from doing so.

Persigny's first term in London lasted from May 28, 1855, to March 23, 1858. He was reappointed Ambassador on May 9, 1859, when Pélissier was needed for military command, and served until November 24, 1860. During this second term in London,

Persigny took great interest in Anglo-French negotiations for a commercial treaty. Much of the spadework for the treaty was done by Richard Cobden and Michel Chevalier, who tactfully kept Persigny informed because of his supposed credit with Napoleon III. Chevalier, the French economist, recognized that Persigny was for free trade and in favor of a commercial treaty as a support for the sagging Anglo-French alliance.

As early as 1852, Persigny spoke out for free trade in principle, but at that time he felt that French industry was not yet strong enough to compete with British industry. Even so, he regarded competition as the right way to build a healthy economy, and rejected the protectionist argument which equated economic self-sufficiency to national security. By 1859 Persigny gave vigorous support to Cobden and Chevalier. Napoleon III also wanted to reform the tariff system in the hope of lowering the prices of consumer goods while increasing their supply, as he was solicitous for the welfare of the people.

But the Emperor also knew that French business and industry were profoundly protectionist, and he dreaded the outraged clamor certain to develop in the Corps législatif should he employ his treaty powers. Thus, he hesitated. Persigny reminded him how much this treaty would please the British, and in the end the Emperor decided to fly in the face of the very interests which supposedly were the régime's chief support. The Cobden-Chevalier Treaty, which provided for a reduction of duties, was signed on January 23, 1860.

Despite the treaty, Anglo-French relations continued to deteriorate. It was the old problem that always had plagued the alliance: the British feared Napoleon's ambition. In this instance, it was Napoleon's aid to Sardinia in 1859–1860 in the interest of Italian unification which upset them. They favored unification in itself, as a check upon France, but disliked French assistance.

Napoleon III proceeded in the full knowledge of British displeasure. His armies defeated Austria in 1859 and provided the Sardinians with the province of Lombardy. The following year, he sanctioned plebiscites in Parma, Modena, Tuscany, and Romagna; all voted to join Sardinia. Meanwhile, Garibaldi overran

Sicily, crossed the straits and took Naples in September. His Neapolitan Majesty fled to Rome to find a refuge with Pius IX and the protection of French troops, who had been in Rome since 1849. Napoleon III's dilemma was now sharply outlined: he had to maintain the Pope in Rome out of consideration for the French Catholics; he had to favor Italian nationalism as a Bonapartist principle; and the one possible compromise—getting the Pope to be president of a federation of Italian states—was vetoed by Pius IX, who, with logic on his side, refused to become a national leader.

Russia and Austria, with many national minorities within their empires, were certainly not friendly to Napoleon's championing of nationalism, and Persigny was making trouble in London. Instead of attempting to reassure the British that France had no ulterior motives in assisting the Italians, he adopted a menacing attitude. Lord Clarendon wrote to Lord Cowley in Paris, "People are very much disgusted as well as tired of him," and Napoleon took the hint and extracted Persigny from London a second time. In November of 1860, Persigny moved to Paris and assumed the Ministry of the Interior. It was to be his last post.

The government of Sardinia, meanwhile, had the good sense to recognize a dangerous situation, and moved to halt the machinery of unification short of Rome. The Sardinians did move into Umbria and the Marches, defeating the Papal forces at Castelfidardo, and then joined Garibaldi's army; but while despoiling the Pope of territory the Sardinians were able to prevent Garibaldi from attacking Rome, and avoided what would have been a most embarrassing clash with French arms. Sicily, Naples, Umbria, and the Marches all voted to join Sardinia, and thus by November of 1860, when Persigny came into the cabinet again, only Rome and Austrian Venetia remained in hostile hands.

The Roman Question had developed into such a boiling issue by late 1860 that every ministerial change was watched for a sign of the Emperor's intentions. Persigny's appointment to Interior was regarded as significant, since he was known to be anticlerical and to favor Napoleon's Italian policy. On the other hand, Walewski, who had lost the Foreign Ministry in 1859

owing to his hostility to the Italian policy, came back into government as President of the Council of State. He was a leading
champion of a Franco-Papal accord. Even so, many of the French
clergy thought that Napoleon III might be preparing a religious
schism in the fashion of Henry VIII and were uneasy about the
presence of the Bourbon King of Naples at the Papal Court. If
the Pope made too open an alliance with a legitimate monarch, a
Bonaparte emperor might well be goaded to break with Rome.

Actually, there is no reason to believe that Napoleon III ever
pondered a schism. He was not an ardent Catholic, but his Spanish Empress was sincerely devout, and, while he was never the
slave of her opinion as is sometimes suggested, it is unlikely that
he would have risked the household explosion that a schism would
have produced. But schism was a phantom in the closet, whose
possibilities, though unmentioned, haunted the imagination. The
Vicomte de la Guéronnière, head of the press and library of the
Ministry of the Interior, wrote pamphlets suggesting that the Roman Question was being exploited by political enemies of the
Empire. He implied that there could be no simultaneous loyalty to
Paris and Rome.

These government pamphlets stimulated some equally immod-
erate editorials from clergymen. Bishop Pie of Poitiers, for example, likened Napoleon III to Pontius Pilate:

> In the summary of Christ's doctrine, "which all Christian lips re-
> cite every day, the abominable name of the man who sent Him to
> death figures. This man marked with the deicide brand, this man
> thus nailed to the pillory of our creed, is neither Herod nor Caiaphas
> nor Judas. . . . This man is Pontius Pilate and this is justice. . . .
> Pilate could have saved Christ, and without Pilate they could not
> have put Christ to death."

As Bishop Pie sent his message to all French bishops, Persigny
presented the situation to the Council of State and claimed it was
a misuse of power, an attack upon the head of the state under the
mask of religion. Then on March 1, 1861, Prince Jerome-Napoleon, the Emperor's cousin and a well known liberal, rose in the
Senate to call Rome an anachronism and to announce that France

did not represent reaction but did stand for modernity. Persigny telegraphed all the prefects that the Prince's address had been "magnificent," suggesting that the opinions were actually those of the Emperor.

Among the ministers, however, Persigny was practically alone in approving Italian unification, and it was highly unpopular in the Corps législatif. When Jules Favre, a Republican, proposed the French evacuation of Rome, his measure was defeated 246 to 5, and the vote was not merely the work of a captive assembly. Nor were the Deputies overwhelmingly clerical. They rather cynically regarded the Church as a preserver of social order and disapproved of any measures which would enhance the possibility of chaos.

By 1861 the government had in fact assumed a neutral attitude toward Italy and Rome, neutral at least in the eyes of most politically conscious Frenchmen, who were favorable to either one of the two extreme positions. Napoleon was still sympathetic to Italian nationalism, but he did not propose to despoil the Papacy any further. Persigny did circularize the prefects on March 4th, inviting them to publicize Article 21 of the Code Napoléon, under which no Frenchman could, except by imperial permission, take service abroad without losing his citizenship. The law was to be strictly applied to those enlisting in the Papal Army. Otherwise, Persigny became more lukewarm for Italy and tried to avoid any action which would give the appearance of persecuting the Church. Napoleon did maintain his pro-Italian Foreign Minister, Thouvenel, until October 15, 1862, but in reality the neutral policy was by then well over a year old.

Most historians have assumed that Napoleon did not push Italian claims to Rome out of consideration for the upcoming elections of 1863. This thesis has some merit, though it is weakened by the general assumption that Thouvenel's dismissal marked the change in policy. His dismissal was, incidentally, welcomed in France where there was little sympathy for Italy, but the new Foreign Minister, the pro-Papal Drouyn de Lhuys, was unable to get Napoleon III to drop Persigny from the cabinet. It is odd— if the Emperor was concerned that the Roman Question might seriously affect the elections of 1863—that he should have retained the anti-Papal Persigny as chief of the ministry which prepared the elections. No other minister was as heartily disliked by the Catholic party as Persigny, for it was recognized that he had opposed Napoleon's decision to adopt a neutral attitude in 1861.

It is not usually noted that Napoleon's activities in Italy were conditioned by his relations with Russia. He had begun to court Russia in 1856 and had not felt free to proceed with war in 1859 until he had a secret Russian commitment to smile upon the campaign. And when, during that campaign, the Russians did nothing to retard Prussia's sudden mobilization, Napoleon had hastened into armistice. By 1861 Russia was using the Italian situation as an excuse for reopening the Eastern Question, blaming the success of liberal ideas in Italy for unrest in the Balkans and for encouraging the Poles. In short, to avoid reopening the Paris settlement of 1856 for modification, Napoleon III had to put the brakes to Italian nationalism in 1861.

Persigny's unpopularity with the Catholics was only magnified by his attitude toward the Society of Saint Vincent de Paul, a charitable and religious organization founded in 1833. Its original function had been to visit the poor, and though in time the Society grew into a large-scale charity organization its impetus was always religious zeal. The Society originated in Paris, but chapters were later developed in the provinces. Under the Second Empire these chapters were vulnerable to the laws which prohibited combination (associations); recognizing their peril, they were careful to do nothing in secret. When Persigny first came to Interior in 1852, he remarked that these chapters were hostile to the Empire but took no action. Only later, when the Roman Question became acute and Persigny began to regard every Catholic as a subversive, did he determine to strike at them.

The Society had, by 1861, nearly 100,000 members, and it is true that it enjoyed rapid expansion under the Second Empire. The number of chapters increased from 500 in 1852, to 1,000 in 1859, to 1,549 in 1861. As its period of greatest growth coincided with the sharpening of the Roman Question, it was only natural that the government should have been curious. Investigations revealed that many of the Society's recent recruits had entered for reasons other than the love of charity. In the West, Legitimists dominated the chapters, and though the rules forbidding political action were honored the government suspected that the chapters concealed a conspiracy.

Tackling the Society of Saint Vincent de Paul involved two hazards: the Society enjoyed a popular reputation for integrity, and the Empress considered herself the guardian angel of charitable and religious affairs. Thus, Persigny began by commending the Catholics for their "remarkable zeal in the pursuit of a goal that could not be too much applauded." But—and this was in his circular dated October 18, 1861—he noted the hierarchy of the Society's organization. "Such an organization cannot justify its claim to be interested solely in charity. . . . Christian charity does not need to be organized in the form of secret societies." Alone, it would seem, the chapters were fine; in total they merited police attention. This information, which went out to all prefects, was followed by an order dissolving the Society. In the future, charity would be dispensed under the auspices of the sovereign. Her Majesty, in short, would play an increased role. It should not be assumed that Eugénie had encouraged Persigny in this action, for in fact the two detested each other to a point precluding collaboration. She organized the Society of the Prince Imperial to replace that of Saint Vincent de Paul.

Having provided for charity, the government turned its attention to the coming elections of 1863, which would renew the Corps législatif. Morny, perennial President of the lower chamber, was a liberal and had been urging the Emperor to modify the constitution in the direction of true parliamentary monarchy. Changes in this direction had in fact been made (and are considered more fully in the chapters on Morny and Ollivier), but Persigny was actually authoritarian despite his pretensions of liberalism, and bitterly opposed any leftward swing. Furthermore, Persigny and Morny despised each other. Morny, who was suavity personified, profited well while giving the Empire good service. To line one's pockets was, for him, the morality of office, and he was revolted by the self-righteous Persigny strutting his disinterestedness about court. Poor Persigny, who had little wit, was the target of many jibes, and Morny was forever proposing him for a post in Kamchatka or some other distant spot.

In closing the last session of the Corps législatif (May 7th) before elections, Morny asked the Deputies to remember that a government can become blind if there is no contradiction or criticism. "Our discussions have strengthened security more than a misleading silence would have done. Despite some most lively debates, the most extreme opinions have been moderated and a bit reconciled." The mission of the Empire, as Morny saw it, was to marry the more traditional forms of monarchy to the more recent spirit of liberalism. Only then could the government expect the enthusiastic adherence of those who, in 1863, still styled themselves as Orleanists or Republicans.

But Persigny, whose task it was to prepare for the elections, ignored Morny's appeal for the development of an enlightened opposition. He regarded French parties as factions, because they were not devoted to the fundamental institutions of the government. Therefore, debate on the conduct of affairs was insincere and only masked a more basic hostility to the Empire. His argument may have mirrored the situation of the moment, but his weakness lay in his inability to envision any means of reconciling these factions to Empire.

Autocracy for an indefinite period was the logical conclusion for Persigny. He admitted to the prefects that the constitution provided for free and universal suffrage, but reminded them of their duty to make known which candidates were most worthy of government favor. It was the prefect's obligation to see that the citizens of his department were not led astray by clever politicians. "The government in fact," wrote Persigny, "can only support those men who are devoted without any reservation or second thought to the imperial dynasty and our institutions." Politics, according to Persigny's definition, was the blindly devoted leading the blindly devoted.

If the press was unfree under the Second Empire, the controls were surprisingly less arbitrary than we—who are accustomed to the greater efficiency of twentieth century autocracies—would expect. Especially in Paris, newspapers openly supported candidates unfriendly to the régime, and there was considerable actual freedom of the press. There was less freedom in the provincial regions, because in many departments the only local paper was the prefecture's. Journals were often warned and occasionally suspended, sometimes for petty grievances; but an editor who could modify his insults and oppose through innuendo might publish in confidence and know that his readers understood his point of view. Persigny tried to rig the elections, however, less through control of the press than through using techniques well known to students of dirty politics. He had recourse to official candidates, the purchase of votes, and gerrymandering the city districts so as to attach fragments of their radical vote to the suburbs.

The balloting took place on May 30–31. The earliest returns came in from Paris and suggested an astonishing Republican victory, but when the provincial totals came in it was clear that the Republicans had been swamped outside Paris. They did, however, win seventeen seats, a dozen more than in 1857, and it was generally admitted that Persigny's electioneering had really excited a protest vote in Paris. It was significant, too, that many leading Orleanists and Legitimists were beaten. Only one Legitimist, Berryer, gained a seat. The nonradical protest vote went to men who ran as Independents. They represented in particular the clerical faction, whose vote normally went to the monarchist or Bonapartist parties. The Independents won fourteen seats, making the total opposition thirty-two.

On June 21st Persigny put out another circular in which he congratulated the prefects on the victory; but though the government was safe enough with 250 seats, Persigny was whistling in the dark. The Emperor was convinced that his Minister's inept management of the elections had not only swollen the Opposition's gains, but—more important—had cost the government in prestige and dignity. No one could deny that the proceedings had been shabby and unworthy of the government's obvious strength, and two days after Persigny's victory bulletin he was removed from the Ministry of the Interior, though retained in the Privy Council.

Even in this moment of annoyance, Napoleon III did not forsake his loyal friend. By letters patent, he raised Persigny to be a *duc,* an especially gracious gesture, as it put an end to several legal inquiries into Persigny's title of *comte.* A second decree on June 23rd, however, betrayed the significance of Persigny's retirement. The Emperor created a new post in his ministry, though it was not immediately fulfilled: Minister of State, actually a minister without portfolio who would henceforth serve as a liaison between the executive and legislative powers.

It would be inaccurate to conclude that Persigny owed his fall solely to his bungling of the elections of 1863. His service was more notable for length than quality; his fixation that he alone gave disinterested and devoted service made him quarrelsome and given to intemperate words and acts; and Napoleon III may well have been weary of his rude friend before 1863. Furthermore, the trend toward a more parliamentary régime had already begun, and Persigny was out of step; he refused to believe that the French were capable of parliamentary government. Yet, the new Ministry of State was a sign of the Chamber's rising importance, and in October of 1863 Napoleon nominated Eugène Rouher to the post.

Finally, Persigny had a dangerous enemy, the Empress Eugénie. He had opposed her marriage, for which he could not be forgiven, and he continued to oppose her influence and even her presence at meetings of the Privy Council. The many indiscretions of Mme. de Persigny only increased Eugénie's hostility. Like many others, Persigny was wont to see the Empress's hand in every policy and, in particular, every policy which went sour; his bitterness against her flourished out of power. In 1867 he wrote the Emperor a memorandum on the Empress's position, which quite inadvertently fell under her eyes. He began by admitting the greatness of her soul, her courage, and her private virtues, but thinly disguised his own views by claiming that the public generally regarded her influence in the Council of Ministers as baneful. He accused her of being more Legitimist than Bonapartist (which was true only in the sense of making the Bonapartes a new legitimate dynasty), and he claimed that her clerical interests had produced the difficulties between Church and State. In 1869 he wrote an essay in which he attributed all the foreign and domestic troubles of the 1860's to her influence. In reading Persigny, one sometimes gets the impression that Eugénie was the only force at work in nineteenth century Europe.

Meanwhile, Persigny had returned to his native department, Loire, where Napoleon named him prefect. Here he began his *Mémoirs* and began to think about the administrative reform of the Empire. This project, which he outlined and read to the Emperor in 1866, antedated his memorandum on Eugénie about a year. In this document he suggested that the dynasty had suffered from setbacks in foreign affairs, which the public was tempted to attribute to the Emperor's loss of vigor or to his mental enfeeblement. Therefore, it was essential to expose the true causes of the Empire's difficulties and to provide reforms.

He did not mention the Empress in this memorandum. Instead, he found the Empire seriously undermined by corruption and threatened by parliamentarianism. Responsible government meant corruption, in that a loyal majority in the Chambers could be secured only through effective use of patronage. An authoritarian régime, which he advocated in place of parliamentary monarchy, would give the appearance of honesty and efficiency, and would not suffer from "the disorder of ideas."

Persigny's various memoranda came to nothing, as his authoritarian views were no longer tolerable at the Tuileries. Then, with war in 1870, he wrote to the Emperor:

I appeal to your heart. I ask to be employed in Paris where my devotion can be useful to Your Majesty, or to be permitted to go with you to fight in the ranks of your most courageous servants.

Receiving no answer, he then begged Napoleon not to leave Paris and its "demagogic army," and he urged emergency laws to end the freedom of the press and of association. But to no avail.

With the war lost and the Empire in ruins, Persigny went to Britain to avoid possible trouble. Those who were wise after the disaster were reviewing Franco-Prussian relations for the purpose of identifying scapegoats. Persigny was cited as blind to Prussian power and intentions, largely on the strength of his advice to Bismarck in 1864 to keep the Prussian Army in fighting trim. Admittedly it was an unfortunate remark, but it is true that Persigny's view of Prussia was in keeping with opinion of his time, which regarded Austria as the stronger power. Furthermore, Persigny was Minister in Berlin in 1850, when Prussia suffered a galling diplomatic defeat at Olmütz through Austrian intervention.

His distress at the turn of events allowed him to believe that his personal intervention would have saved Alsace and Lorraine and that it was Eugénie who had prevented his action. In a similar vein, he was apt to recall that it was her failure to assist him properly which cost him the Parisian vote in 1863. In the meantime he received a delegation from Loire, but rejected their request that he stand for the new Assembly of the Government of National Defense on the grounds that British parliamentarianism "was incompatible with the excitable character" of the country.

Toward the end of July, 1871, Persigny returned to his retreat at Chamarande in Seine-et-Oise. Six months later he suffered a cerebral congestion and was sent to Nice to recover. Mme. de Persigny had already gone off on a lengthy pleasure trip and was finally located in Egypt. Napoleon, then living in Chislehurst, was also notified; but, being ill himself, he did not promptly respond. Persigny's valet and secretary were understandably furious when the Duchess postponed her return with flimsy excuses and when the letter from Chislehurst, which would have given such pleasure, failed to appear. They did not realize, of course, the seriousness of Napoleon's illness.

On January 12, 1872, however he managed to post a letter:

My dear Persigny, I learn with pain the state of your health. I hope that you will be able to triumph over this illness; but while awaiting your recovery, I must tell you that I forget what it was which divided us in order to remember only the demonstrations of devotion that you gave me for many years. Believe in my sincere friendship.

NAPOLEON

By cruel coincidence, Persigny died the day Napoleon's letter was written; he did not learn that he was gratefully remembered.

II

The Duc de Morny

AND THE GENESIS OF PARLIAMENTARIANISM

*May the reader not be scandalized that
the frivolous is taken seriously.*

—BAUDELAIRE

His life lacked austerity.

—EMILE OLLIVIER

The constitutional system of the Second Empire did not provide for a vice emperor, though several notable personages of the period were so classified in usage, if not in fact. One of these was Auguste de Morny, whose presence was both a bulwark and an embarrassment to the régime, for he was not only capable but illegitimate. As the Grand Duchess Marie of Russia once observed, Morny was "*heureux comme un bâtard.*" But if connected to the Bonapartes by questionable lines, Morny could point with some pride to the "dynasty" from which he descended.

His paternal grandmother was Adélaïde Filleul, born in 1761 to Louis XV and Adèle Filleul, a peasant girl from Normandy. Adélaïde was deposited in a convent, educated, and then married off at eighteen to the fifty-seven-year-old Count Alexandre de Flahaut. He had been a colonel in the King's Army, then graduated to be Superintendent General of the King's Gardens. This gave Adélaïde access to the society of court and salon, where she met a refined and handsome young cleric, the Abbé Maurice de Talleyrand-Périgord. He disguised his clubfoot with high-heeled shoes, padded and adorned with large buckles, and managed to carry on with the ladies in a manner which suggests that neither infirmity nor ecclesiastical position weighed heavily upon him. In 1785 Mme. de Flahaut, with Talleyrand's cooperation, presented old Count Flahaut with an heir: Auguste-Charles-Joseph de Flahaut.

The French Revolution caught up with Count de Flahaut in 1793 and chopped off his head for failure to fill it with the newest virtues. The Countess tarried nine years before marrying the Marquis José Maria de Souza, who had for a time been Portuguese Ambassador to France. Meanwhile, she reared her son into an elegant, graceful, handsome man, whose superb voice and smile became fabled. The young Count entered the army when fifteen, two years later became an aide to Murat, and in the best Napoleonic tradition was made colonel at twenty-four and brigadier at twenty-eight.

Historically speaking, General Count de Flahaut's most significant tour of duty was at the court of Holland, where he served as aide to King Louis Bonaparte. Here he met the Queen, Hortense Beauharnais, who, forced into a dynastic marriage against her will, posed as a virtuous and unhappy woman. In truth she was merely unhappy; as her uncle-in-law, Joseph Cardinal Fesch, once said, Hortense always became confused when referring to the paternity of her children. No doubt she had Flahaut in mind when she wrote the hymn *Partant pour la Syrie*, which, as the national anthem during the Second Empire, caused her legitimate son, the Emperor, many painful thoughts.

Partant pour la Syrie,	Departing for Syria,
Le jeune et beau Dunois	The young and handsome Dunois
Venait prier Marie	Went to pray Mary
De bénir ses exploits;	To bless his feats;
"Faites, reine immortelle,"	"Ordain, immortal Queen,"
Lui dit-il en partant,	He said to Her in leaving,
"Faites, qu'aimé de la plus belle,	"That, loved by the most beautiful,
Je sois le plus vaillant."	I shall be the most valiant."

The "most beautiful" and the "most valiant" had a child on October 21, 1811, Hortense having gone on an extensive trip to prepare for the event. The baby was named Auguste-Charles-Joseph Demorny; the given names were Flahaut's, while Demorny was borrowed from a Prussian officer who was living in retirement in Versailles. Little Auguste was taken to his grandmother, Mme. Flahaut-Souza, while Hortense did her share by providing a modest life annuity. She sent additional sums in 1818 and 1820, signing herself the Countess Henry de Morny of Philadelphia.

Mme. Souza felt honor-bound to protect Hortense, and never revealed to Demorny the identity of either his father or mother, but Flahaut called often on his own mother and was thus able to

watch his son develop. He took Demorny abroad in 1829, the
pretext being a course in German at Aix-la-Chapelle. Hortense
just happened to be there too, which suggests that Demorny was
by that time acquainted with his antecedents. Meanwhile Mme.
Souza was trying to envision a suitable career for Demorny. She
thought first of agriculture, but this was quickly overborne by
her own preference for literary gentlemen. She encouraged
Morny to write letters, madrigals, and epigrams. General Flahaut
had more practical ideas; he thought his son should be a mathema-
tician.

The Revolution of 1830 returned the tricolor and Talleyrand to
France. General Flahaut was invited to take a seat in the house
of Peers and to become a Lieutenant General in Louis-Philippe's
Army. The following year he was named Ambassador to Berlin.
Suddenly we find that Demorny had become De Morny, in fact
Count de Morny. He entered the General Staff School and
graduated as a Second Lieutenant in 1832, to join the fashionable
First Regiment of Lancers.

Raised to a lieutenancy in 1834, Morny was dispatched for
service in Africa. If we can believe his friend, the Duc d'Orléans,
he left many anguished women behind in Paris. General Oudinot
appointed Morny his orderly officer for the Mascara campaign, a
risky position in a day when a commander's orders had to be delivered in person. He won a commendation from Lieutenant
General Duc de Montemart, but his bravery was no defense
against gastritis and dysentery, which annoyed him constantly.
He got a brief respite at Nevers, but was back in Algeria in 1835,
and two more campaigns were the limit of his endurance. On the
campaign to capture the town of Constantine, he was orderly
officer for General Trézel, whose life Morny had the good luck
to save. The reward was the medal of the Legion of Honor. After
the subsequent Kabylie campaign (1836), dysentery won the
day, and Morny resigned his commission.

Despite General de Flahaut's displeasure over Morny's resignation, he tried to arrange a brilliant welcome for his son. The story
of their relationship was generally known, if not openly discussed,
but owing to General and Mme. de Flahaut's unpopularity at

court it was up to Morny to make his own mark. Fortunately, he had winning qualities: elegant manners, wit, good looks, a talent for composing and singing ballads. He was a dandy and a participant in *le sport*. Fortunately, too, social climbing was encouraged by the defection of the greatest aristocrats from the July Monarchy's official society; they sulked in their exclusive salons, feeding their expectations a rarefied diet of epigrams, little suspecting that Legitimacy had no future.

Morny quickly became an arbiter of fashion: black waistcoats edged with gold thread were his innovation, and the hat pulled down over the eyes was *à la Morny*. Horses assumed a greater role in the social world. Morny, the former cavalryman, was attracted to *le steeple-chase*, recently imported from Britain, and soon found himself elected to the *Jockey-Club, cercle et société d'encouragement pour l'amélioration des races de chevaux en France*. As its members had to pass a rigid social inspection, Morny's election brought him into a group which included the Duc d'Orléans, the Duc de Nemours, the Prince de la Moskova, and Lord Henry Seymour.

The role of *jeunesse dorée* requires an income in any age; Morny's came from a variety of sources. Hortense had provided an annuity much earlier, and no doubt he received something upon her death in 1837. General de Flahaut contributed, and he received a small sum under Mme. de Flahaut-Souza's will. Finally, Morny had the foresight to select a wealthy mistress—Mme. Charles Le Hon. He had many other affairs, but he was remarkably faithful to this one liaison.

Countess Le Hon, née Mosselmann, was the daughter of a ranking Belgian banker and the wife of His Belgian Majesty's first Ambassador to France. She kept up a discreet correspondence with Hortense until the latter's death, became a lioness in French society, and made important cash advances to her lover. Presumably it was her money which enabled Morny to play the stock market and to invest in a newspaper. The latter venture was not exactly a success. He was induced by one of his Jockey-Club friends, the Viscount Alton-Shée, to join the staff of the *Messager*, a paper owned by Count Alexandre Walewski, a natural son of the first Napoleon. Morny's social obligations, however, were too pressing to allow a flow of words. He eventually managed to write one article, a defense of the beet-sugar industry in its struggle against West Indian cane.

Countess Le Hon then encouraged Morny to participate directly in the sugar business. She owned land around Clermont-Ferrand, and in 1837 Morny purchased a sugar refinery in the neighboring town of Bourdon. His success was immediate; not only did he prosper, but he won the favor of his fellow entrepreneurs—men to whom he was inclined to refer as the "considerable people." They responded by electing him president of the beet-sugar manufacturers' association. This advancement probably encouraged him to run for Parliament in 1842, and no doubt contributed to his victory. He showed political skill, too, during his campaign, though he was not a great speechmaker. "The peasants will be for you?" jibed an opponent; "what have you been able to offer them?" "An eclipse on July 10," replied Morny, alluding to astronomy; "even two, if I count yours!" This was an early example of his trademark: the retort facetious.

His parliamentary demeanor lacked brilliance. He never spoke impromptu but occasionally read from a prepared text, and his messages were laden with orthodox Orleanist notions of Law and Order. The "considerable people" of Clermont-Ferrand returned him again in 1846, but he was beginning to sense the approaching collapse of the July Monarchy and had begun to consider the possibility of adjusting his principles. Flahaut, then Ambassador to Vienna, had been advising the abandonment of the Orleanist régime, and Morny considered throwing his weight for Henry V and the Legitimists. Ultimately he concealed his hand (the Talleyrand blood ran true!), and only after the Revolution of 1848 did he make an effort to meet his half-brother, Louis-Napoleon.

Before 1848 Morny had had no more than a glimpse of his relative, and that was years earlier in London, a chance meeting on the street. The half-brothers had never spoken, and apparently Morny had remained unmoved by Louis-Napoleon's spectacularly abortive attempts to seize power at Strasbourg in 1836 and

Boulogne in 1840. He was very much moved, however, by the latter's sudden elevation to the presidency of the Second Republic in 1848.

An interview was arranged by Morny's friend Count Félix Bacciochi, Louis-Napoleon's cousin, and took place at the Castellane Mansion. This edifice served as the Bonapartist headquarters, though there was virtually no Bonapartist party in France, despite the fact that a Bonaparte had been elected President. In the oddest election of the nineteenth century, the Radicals had supported Louis-Napoleon, thinking him a Socialist: the Moderate Republicans, thinking him a Jacobin; the Orleanists, supposing him a Liberal; the Catholics, confident he would defend the Faith against radical onslaught. Louis-Napoleon seemed bent on pleasing everybody and on reversing Aesop's law that he who pleases everyone pleases no one. And now, in 1849, his half-brother came forward, newly elected to the National Assembly, to encourage the restoration of Empire. The initial meeting was friendly but reserved; that is, there was no mention of their mother Hortense. But Morny's advice was repeatedly sought in the subsequent months.

Had Louis-Napoleon merely wanted power and position, he would have been satisfied with presidential rank, but as he was possessed—body and soul—by the Napoleonic Legend, the imperial title was clearly prescribed. The constitution of the Second Republic, in limiting the President to one four-year term, served to hasten the transformation. When Louis-Napoleon could not get sufficient votes in the Assembly to pass an amendment allowing a second term, the nation should have been forewarned of what would follow. Perhaps his demeanor was disarming; he was a dreamer, and dreamers are reckoned by the "considerable people" as inept and harmless.

The *coup d'état* of 1851, which lengthened the presidential term to ten years and was merely the prelude to Empire, was the joint effort of Hortense's sons. The dreamer was supplemented by the man of action. Morny was wont to take full credit to himself:

I believe I can affirm that there would have been no *coup d'état* without me. I should even dare say that without my participation it would not have succeeded as it did.

But Louis-Napoleon never allowed himself to be pushed in directions he did not already anticipate, though indeed he often needed prodding to execute his own intentions. This was Morny's role.

Four other men were included in the plot: General Jacques de Saint-Arnaud, who owed his rise to Algerian service and who was made Minister of War shortly before the coup; Jean-Constant Mocquard, the President's secretary; Victor Fialin, Count de Persigny, a faithful Bonapartist and rival of Morny; and Charlemagne-Emile de Maupas, an ambitious young bureaucrat whom Morny detested. We are told that the conspirators set and canceled at least three dates for the coup before settling on the night of December 1–2, 1851. This is remarkable, as December 2nd was an auspicious Bonaparte date (Napoleon I consecrated by Pius VII in 1804; Austerlitz in 1805). Was it chance or design?

December 1, 1851, was a Monday. It was the President's custom to hold a reception every Monday evening at the Elysée Palace, and he proceeded as usual, appearing friendly and undisturbed. Morny went to the Opéra-Comique for a performance of Limnander's *Bluebeard's Castle* and made himself much in evidence. During the evening he slipped away to the President's private chamber, where the other five had discreetly gathered. Louis-Napoleon produced a roll of instructions and decrees, neatly packaged and inscribed *Rubicon*. He read his proclamation for their edification and distributed instructions to each. Morny was to be Minister of the Interior, Maupas Prefect of Police, Saint-Arnaud to remain Minister of War, and Mocquard to become *Chef de cabinet*. The meeting broke up before eleven o'clock. Louis-Napoleon returned to his drawing-room duties, while Morny repaired to the Jockey-Club for a rubber of whist.

In the execution of the *coup d'état*, Morny's direction and efficiency certainly contributed to success. By dawn the city had been placarded with the presidential proclamation, which announced the dissolution of the National Assembly, the restoration of universal suffrage, and promised constitutional changes that would, among other things, extend the presidential term to ten years. Morny arrived at the Interior about seven-fifteen to rout the incumbent Minister, Thorigny, out of bed. "Monsieur, you have been dismissed. Do pardon me for informing you of it so suddenly. It is I who have the honor to succeed you. Please do me the favor of removing yourself without losing a minute."

Meanwhile, Morny selected a group of leading politicians and military chiefs for temporary incarceration. The list included Adolphe Thiers and Generals Cavaignac and Lamoricière. Their roundup was accomplished with dispatch and delicacy; there was no violence, and the rank of the prisoners was carefully observed by saluting, bowing officers. During the day of December 2nd, about three hundred Deputies, who were unable to take the hint, made an attempt to assemble in the Tenth Arrondissement. They too were forcibly detained.

There was still the possibility that the Parisians would rise in defense of the Assembly despite their relative lack of leadership. The experience of previous revolutions suggested that the presence of troops did not necessarily intimidate the mob. Worse, troops kept on duty for use against their fellow countrymen tended to sympathize with the mob. Morny's strategy was simple: keep the soldiers away from the infecting influences of the radical leaders; allow them to rest while the opposition coalesced; then strike to break the resistance in one blow. Presumably, hunger and boredom would already have broken the resistance of many by the time the troops charged the barricades. Certainly Morny's strategy was designed to be both efficient and humane.

According to plan, the troops went into action on December 4th. There were casualties, more than there should have been, considering the rather apathetic response the Parisians made to parliamentary appeals, but it is hard to limit slaughter when street action begins. The records of such events are untrustworthy, and casualty figures are really partisan estimates. The Army probably lost less than thirty killed; the insurgents lost between two and three hundred killed. No one regretted these losses more genuinely than Louis-Napoleon.

The fighting was over by the evening of the 4th, and everyone knew—in Paris at least—that the President had triumphed. Discreet inquiries continued to come in from the provinces from those whose futures required an enthusiastic adherence to the winning side. "They say in my Department," telegraphed an anxious prefect, "that the Assembly is triumphant all along the line. Is it true?" Morny wired back: "On the contrary, the Line is triumphant all along the Assembly."

The new Minister of the Interior's immediate tasks were the preparation of new elections and the repression of hostile parties. He was temperamentally qualified for the former but too lenient to relish the latter. His work was hampered by rancor within the Cabinet; Persigny, Maupas, and Achille Fould, the Finance Minister, were jealous of Morny, and sought to turn Louis-Napoleon against him. Of the three, Morny found Persigny especially trying, and considered him crude and stupid. It was a durable enmity; somewhat later Morny was to remark of Persigny: "He has above all else the gift of hindsight; the first view always defeats him." However efficient Morny may have been, and quite apart from petty jealousies which sought to ruin him, his station commanded delicacy. Louis-Napoleon was entirely devoted to the memory of Queen Hortense and did not take kindly to evidence of her shortcomings. In this regard Morny served as a red rag to a bull, and he would have been well advised to be a paragon of discretion. Instead, his official dignity moved him to adopt arms which were as subtle as a bugle blast: a blooming hortensia (hydrangea) with the words *Tace sed memento:* Be silent, but remember. The Parisian wits were not silent, but remembered; "Count Hortensia" was the boulevard jest. There were spoken indiscretions by Morny as well.

To the departmental prefects fell the task of selecting parliamentary candidates worthy of official support, support which in 1852 virtually guaranteed election. Morny dispatched hints to the prefects to guide them in their choices: "When a man has made his fortune by work, through industry or agriculture, has improved the lot of his workers, has made good use of his wealth, he is preferable to what is generally called a politician. He will bring a practical sense to the formulation of laws and will second the government in its work of pacification and reconstruction." As despotism this had a benevolent ring, and Morny's successors at Interior would have done well to imitate him. Various indiscretions, however, made his tenure at Interior short, and he found it necessary to resign from the Ministry on January 22, 1852. The resignation coincided with the imperial decrees confiscating Orléans property, and the official pretext for his resignation was his protest against this seizure of property belonging to old friends.

Morny settled back in his parliamentary seat and renewed his business and speculative activities. The Emperor was zealous for railroad building and industrialization, and the early years of the Second Empire in particular were characterized by rapid economic expansion. Speculation became a national game, played by rich and poor alike. Since the greatest profits were to be earned by companies which received concessions and subsidies from the government, it was only natural that speculators sought advance information about the government's intentions. As usually happens under such circumstances, government officials either sold information or made a traffic of their influences. Furthermore, they were themselves in a fortunate position to invest. Anyone with court connections, including the imperial half-brother, was watched or bribed. *"Morny est dans l'affaire"* was the investor's clearest guarantee of handsome earnings.

The imperial marriage in 1853 was deplored by the Bonapartes —indeed by most of the court—and Morny alone encouraged his half-brother in the unpopular alliance with the Spanish noblewoman Eugénie de Montijo. The issues were legitimacy and jealousy. In the first place, the Bonapartes were not counted among the legitimate royal families of Europe. The previous year, Napoleon III had not been recognized as an equal by several European monarchs upon the inauguration of the Second Empire. Russia's Nicholas I, for instance, welcomed Napoleon as "friend" instead of "brother," and Napoleon's conciliatory response about not being able to choose one's relatives—merely one's friends—did not conceal the snub he had received.

In this light, a royal alliance for Napoleon was clearly prescribed. His Majesty found, however, that there was a shortage of royal daughters that year, a shortage enforced, no doubt, out of consideration of Marie Louise's fate. His answer to Europe's matrimonial blockade, and it was fair revenge, was to marry a beautiful woman. It was also in this light that the promotion of the illegitimate relatives seemed even more odious to antique King Jerome Bonaparte and his children, who now resided in Paris. Morny was not the only illegitimate relative in the competition; Count Alexandre Walewski, natural son of Napoleon I, was an important link in the dynastic hierarchy. Walewski was jealous of Morny and insisted on being recognized as the precedent bastard. He kept himself clean-shaven (like Napoleon I) as a measure of his dynastic rank, while Morny wore an "imperial" as a symbol of his relationship.

By 1854 Napoleon again required skillful assistance. The Crimean War had begun, and Georges Haussmann had started the modernization of Paris. Both were expensive and unpopular projects. From among the clan, the Emperor knew Morny's hand to be the steadiest; furthermore, Morny's attitude toward the imperial marriage had acted to repair the breach of the previous year. The other Bonapartes were bent on preventing his return to high office, and his appointment to the presidency of the Corps législatif enraged Jerome's branch. To forestall it, King Jerome had threatened to resign the presidency of the Senate, and Prince Jerome-Napoleon instituted inquiries into Napoleon III's own legitimacy, but the blackmail failed.

Punch greeted Morny's nomination with a cartoon. He was pictured in the presidential chair, saying: "My mother is Queen Hortense; my father is Count de Flahaut; Emperor Napoleon III is my brother; Princess Louise Poniatowski is my daughter; all that is natural." These lines were repeated, modified, and distorted to suit the teller and the occasion. Morny's own version was: "I call my father 'Count,' I call my daughter 'Princess,' and

I say to my brother 'Majesty'; I bear the title of Count, and all this is most natural."

The Princess Louise Poniatowski was generally believed to be the daughter of Mme. Le Hon and Morny. There was some astonishment in royal circles when Joseph Poniatowski took the illegitimate Louise as his wife. Sophia of Holland inquired of Jerome-Napoleon whether this marriage was really a fact. *"Oui, c'est la petite Pologne qui a épousé la grande Bohême!"* The wits on both sides of the Channel never wearied of these Bonaparte entanglements. After Morny's death, Walewski was nominated to the presidency to succeed him, and a new basic epigram was coined: *"Chassez le naturel, il revient au galop"* (What is bred in the bone comes out in the flesh).

Morny was the perfect presiding head for a captive legislature. He had had a dozen years of parliamentary experience, and was closely allied to the executive authority. He was a kind of imperial go-between and owed his success to a double illusion; each power believed itself the better served. His competence was obvious: he knew agriculture, industry, and finance, and was only lacking in extemporaneous oratory. Morny turned this disability to his own benefit (and the Emperor's) by frowning on highflown speechifying. His own speech was widely copied by aspirant politicians: informal, hesitating, chatty, long pauses punctuated by a peculiar hissing sound like escaping steam. When a forgetful Deputy launched into a cascade of words, Morny would retire into the shell of his presidential chair, and his glacial indifference usually frightened the offending Deputy into ending quickly.

Morny held this post for the remainder of his life, though he was briefly absent after the Crimean War in order to serve as Ambassador Extraordinary to Russia. Napoleon III was anxious to forge a strong bond with Alexander II, because one of his Napoleonic ideas was to base the peace and order of Europe on an Anglo-Franco-Russian entente. Morny was exceedingly pro-Russian, and regarded a Franco-Russian alliance as a bulwark against the British and Germanic states, which he distrusted. The British in particular recognized Morny's hostility, which

they returned in kind. They attributed his Russomania to the
vast opportunities for the investment of foreign capital in Russia,
and in this regard the British were partly correct. Yet it would
be unfair to disregard his patriotic dislike of the British and his
fear of the Germans. In fact, his Anglophobia made him an un-
faithful exponent of Napoleonic designs, which did not include
a rupture with Britain.

The Morny embassy to Russia was monumentally sumptuous.
More like a court than a suite, the embassy required several pal-
aces, and its carriages and horses became celebrated for elegance.
The Morny arms, in hibernation since 1852, were emblazoned
on the Ambassador's own carriage. The crest not only included
a blooming hortensia, but a bunch of lilies and a bend sinister.
This pompous display and flaunting of bastardy regaled the
Russians, though it might well have had the opposite result. No
one had been more pointed in refusing to recognize the Bonapartes as equals than the Romanovs, and now, the Russians having suffered a humiliating military defeat, the principle of successful illegitimacy was advertised all over St. Petersburg. But,
as the Russians were not offended, Morny succeeded in over-
coming much of the late war's ill-will. A Franco-Russian rap-
prochement was achieved, though Morny's hopes for an alliance
were not realized, chiefly because Napoleon III was unwilling to
scrap his alliance with Britain.

Morny's second achievement in Russia was the discovery of a
wife. He fell in love with the blond and young—she was not
half his age—Sophie Troubetzkoi. Sophie had been brought up
at court, as her father, Serge Troubetzkoi, had been stripped of
princely title and banished to Siberia by the Czar for abducting
a beautiful woman from her husband's arm. Alexander II consented to Sophie's marriage, which took place on January 7, 1857.

For more than twenty years, Mme. Le Hon had been Morny's
faithful mistress, and the note he sent her from Russia to announce the affair's end, "France disapproves our liaison," was
not calculated to appease her jealous anger. She showed the note
around Paris to everyone's entertainment, actually went into
mourning, and received calls of condolence.

But her grief was apparently limited, for she was soon seeking an indemnity, a campaign which smelled faintly of blackmail. The actual circumstances are not clear and perhaps never will be. It is probable that Morny still owed Mme. Le Hon money lent him when he invested in the sugar industry: it is also probable that she knew many of his business secrets and was in a position to demand liberal settlement. She took her grievance to Eugène Rouher, a political protégé of Morny's from Puy-de-Dôme, who held the portfolio of Public Works, Agriculture, and Commerce. Rouher gave a decision rather favorable to Mme. Le Hon, for which he was never forgiven by Morny. The latter regarded himself as betrayed, while Rouher believed himself unjustly maligned. In either case, the affair bred a lasting enmity. Probably there was wrong on both sides: surely Morny wished to escape his obligations to Mme. Le Hon; surely the stolid Rouher was scandalized (made jealous?) by Morny's success in the *demi-monde*, and "hell hath no fury. . . ." It should be added that Napoleon III paid the bill (nearly three million francs) which silenced Mme. Le Hon.

Morny returned to his presidency of the Corps législatif in July, 1857, after an eleven-month absence. An unwelcome situation faced the Empire that year. The parliamentary elections produced a bloc of five Republicans, not dangerously numerous to be sure, but an ominous sign in the light of heavily supervised electioneering and official candidates. It was soon known that Morny was in favor of "liberalizing" the Empire. He believed in disarming opponents by granting concessions and favors, but since the Republicans assumed the high moral attitudes typical of an Opposition it was evident they would accept nothing short of constitutional reform.

Both Morny and the Emperor were liberals. Morny, the Orleanist, the man of the "considerable people," thought of liberalism as embodied in limited monarchy, and presumably would have made Napoleon III into a latter-day bourgeois king. His Majesty often wrote and continually spoke of liberty, but he was not the defining sort. Did he mean Democracy? Did he mean Order? Did he mean economic prosperity? Or in espousing

the eighteenth century notion that Liberty derived from Order
(this was explicit in the Napoleonic Legend), did he simply
mouth his inherited doctrine uncomprehendingly?

Probably Napoleon III, with his double faith in the Legend and
his Star, believed himself Liberty incarnate. His assumption of
total power was the guarantee of liberty, and when it became
clear that the nation did not share the Emperor's definition he
had no constitutional program to replace his beneficent humanitarianism. He really meant to establish liberty, but it was up to
Morny to lead him toward true parliamentarianism as the logical
means to inaugurate it. Liberty was a vague principle for Napoleon III; it was Morny who was the concession maker. Hence
the famous Decree of November 24, 1860, which permitted parliamentary response to the speech from the throne.

The reform was at best a mere token, but Morny pursued the
leftward course. The Italian War of 1859, which Morny opposed,
had alienated the clerical faction; the obvious strategy was to
rally liberal opinion to the Empire. Once a protectionist, Morny
supported freer trade in backing the Cobden-Chevalier treaty
of 1860. He became more avowedly anticlerical, and courted the
friendship of Emile Ollivier, a leading Republican Deputy, who
was attracted by hints of further parliamentary freedoms. The
liberalizing of labor legislation was another bait to lure Republicans.

Actually, the government was too committed to Order simply
to emerge as a flaming incarnation of the Goddess of Liberty.
Napoleon might pardon some typographical workers who had
struck illegally, but the effect was dimmed by the suspension of
Ernest Renan's controversial courses at the Collège de France the
same year (1862) after the publication of his *Life of Jesus*. Morny
may have desired to attract the intelligentsia, the artists, the
writers, and the students, but a government which slapped immorality charges on Flaubert and Baudelaire did not find itself
suffocated by adulation from this quarter.

The dilemma was apparent during the Polish Revolt of 1863.
As the Polish cause was one of the few issues which could arouse
French Catholics and Liberals alike, it was the government's

opportunity to unite the nation in common effort and, incidentally, in the cause of Liberty. Moreover, Napoleon would have been serving his principle of nation states. The price was the loss of Russian friendship, which neither Napoleon nor Morny wanted to pay. In particular, Morny regarded the Franco-Russian entente as his responsibility. The only course was to aid the Poles by urging the Russians to be reasonable. This produced nothing for the Poles, but it did wreck the Franco-Russian understanding. Morny's biographers have usually deplored the loss of Russia's friendship in 1863, suggesting that Morny's foreign policy would have saved the Empire in 1870. Their thesis, however, does not take into account the community of Russo-Prussian interests in the decade 1860–1870.

The Polish fiasco was all the more damaging to French prestige because it came at a moment when Napoleon III was deeply involved in the Mexican campaign, a project so fantastic that one is tempted to suppose it was conceived by an assemblage of mental pygmies. Actually, no such synod was convened; the Mexican venture was born of skulduggery and disorder, of misinformation and bizarre calculation. The name of Morny has always been linked with the Mexican affair, though there is disagreement as to his exact role.

The story began in 1859, when a Swiss banker, J. B. Jecker, lent about 750,000 pesos to the Conservative Mexican government of Miguel Miramón. In exchange, Miramón gave Jecker bonds valued at about 75,000,000 francs. The nature of the loan suggests the instability of the Mexican political situation, where the struggle between the clerical Conservatives and anticlerical Liberals kept the country in turmoil. The issues provoked international interest in Mexican affairs, and for a number of years, on both sides of the Atlantic, there was talk of foreign intervention. The Mexican parties sought foreign support; the religious quarrel in particular won partisans abroad; and Europeans were nervous that chaos in Mexico invited intervention by the United States, where an occasional voice suggested a southward expansion to turn the entire Western Hemisphere into one mighty (and Protestant) state.

Jecker found himself bankrupt less than a year after he made the loan to Miramón (1860). Moreover, the political tide had shifted in Mexico, where the Liberals were in the ascendant, and in 1861 Benito Juárez suspended payments on the Miramón debts to foreign creditors. Britain, France, and Spain were quick to organize joint action against the Mexican government; in the meantime Jecker sought Morny's aid, urging him to press for intervention and to arrange the inclusion of Jecker's claims among those of French citizens. If we can believe Jecker, Morny consented to use his influence in exchange for 30 per cent of whatever Jecker managed to recover. In March, 1862, Jecker was naturalized as a French citizen, and his claims soon formed more than half of the sum which the French government required from Mexico.

Morny did not have to do much pushing to force the intervention issue. Napoleon III had long had utopian visions about developing the economy of Nicaragua, and no doubt Mexico would have served him just as well. The Empress was an ardent pleader for the clerical cause, though it is doubtful that her influence was very strong in foreign affairs. She did welcome the Mexican clerical leaders to court, where they represented the Mexican people as thirsting for Catholic monarchy. These vows were substantiated by the French ministers to Mexico, De Gabriac and his successor, the Marquis Dubois de Saligny, who served clerical interests before those of France. In this way the Mexican trap was baited with a delicacy to which the imperial appetite would surely succumb: the issue of self-determination. The British and Spanish soon sensed His Majesty's game and withdrew from further participation. They, like Morny, were solely interested in the financial problem, but not in "reorganizing Mexico" nor in creating a new Constantinople in Central America, with or without the consent of the Mexicans.

Napoleon's dream of a Central American canal, of a vast commercial center, of natural resources rich enough to benefit the entire world, received a rude shock before Puebla on May 5, 1862. Juárez's army, setting its face against this invasion of sweetness and light, repulsed the French. The "honor of the flag," that sacred cow of modern nationalism, was thus introduced, and a Bonaparte in particular was expected to retaliate with the appropriate vigor. Retreat became inadmissible at the very moment when it became advisable. "We have no partisans here," General Lorencez wrote to the Minister of War. "The moderate party does not exist; the reactionary party, reduced to nothing, is odious. I have not met a single proponent of monarchy."

And here is the Commandant Mangin writing to General de Castellane, July 1, 1862:

The Emperor has been shamefully misled by his Minister, M. de Saligny, or by others, on the situation in this country. We are supporting a cause which neither has, nor can have, any partisans. We have in our train men like Almonte and Miranda, who are objects of horror in this country.

And so, on and on toward the conquest of Mexico and the rigged plebiscite, which brought the Archduke Maximilian of Austria to Mexico City as Emperor in 1864. By this date Napoleon III had awakened to the true state of Mexican sentiments, but the inevitable evacuation of the French troops was not ordered until Prussian victories in Central Europe required it.

At a moment when the imperial market was bearish, Morny's stock was bullish. Shortly after Puebla, Their Majesties went to Auvergne, the region most clearly identified with Morny's economic and political career. There, the Emperor raised his half-brother to a dukedom and presented him with new arms in silver and sable: three blackbirds (from Flahaut's arms) framed with a border of imperial eagles and Auvergne dolphins. It was another anecdotal blazon, but it pointed a finger at Flahaut, not Hortense.

The year 1863 meant parliamentary elections. A much greater Opposition was returned than in 1857. Instead of Les Cinq, there were now thirty-two Opposition deputies, of whom seventeen were Republicans. They owed their election in part to Persigny's ineffectual and clumsy electioneering on behalf of the government, but Morny was not sorry to see Thiers and other Independents in the Chamber. He opened the new session on November 6,

1863: "The people's votes have placed some venerable parliamentarians among us; for my own record, I must say that I rejoice." Presumably the Emperor did not rejoice.

But what of Morny the man? The nineteenth century historian, Jules Michelet, believed that a knowledge of man's bodily habits revealed much about his soul. Accordingly, he divided the reign of Louis XIV into two periods: *Avant la fistule* and *après la fistule*. We cannot find such a convenient watershed in Morny's life, though it is true that his marriage in 1857 changed his mode of living. He loved Sophie dearly, and willingly put up with her idiosyncrasies.

She was a social liability for a man in his station, but he was uncomplaining. They resided at the Petit-Bourbon, which had to be overheated, owing to *Mme. la Russe*. She did not like Paris nor things French; she thought French women felt and loved "smally"; she remarked about the vulgarity of the French court, compared it unfavorably to the legitimate court in St. Petersburg, and wore a fleur-de-lis emblem to emphasize her sentiments. They had a good table, fine wines, were very hospitable, and were popular with servants, owing to Morny's attention. Sophie would not be bothered being mistress of a great house. She spent many hours secluded with a few friends, mostly Russian, and since it was known that they had recourse to cigarettes it was rumored that they indulged in a multitude of other exotic vices.

Because Sophie was fond of rare birds, the house was equipped with an aviary. Morny preferred animals; Siamese cats and Pekingese pups were eternally underfoot, and for a time two bear cubs terrorized Morny's guests. He had a particular passion for apes and monkeys, and kept them caged in the antechamber where business and political associates waited on him. The monkeys greeted the visitors with piercing screams and a frightful odor. Morny called them all by the same name, Glais-Bizoin, who was a member of the Opposition.

Visitors called early in the morning, and Morny received them either in sky-blue pajamas or in a fur dressing gown, depending on the season. The doctors took precedence over all other callers, for he had great faith in doctors and medicines, as well as considerable need of them. His social, commercial, political, and official activities were carried on without respite, and he expected the physicians to remedy his unending overindulgence. He consulted quacks as well as reputable physicians, and in this way fell victim to Dr. Oliffe, one of the more celebrated rejuvenation artists of the nineteenth century. Dr. Oliffe dispensed pills he called pearls—he is the Dr. Jenkins in Daudet's *Le Nabab*—which probably contained arsenic, though not advertised as such. These pills gave quick stimulation and a sense of strength; but they were drops of death which hastened the end of life while creating the illusion of eternal youth.

Morny was not the sole partaker of Dr. Oliffe's "pearls." They were devoured by that small group which equated social entertainments with civic obligation. To fall dead on a ballroom floor was to die in line of duty; as lavish functions provided employment for many people, it was a patriotic obligation to attend them. This justification of good works accounts in part for the constant frivolous activities which characterized the court life of the Second Empire and the ready market for "pearls" among the wealthy.

Morny also saw his children in the morning. He had four, two boys and two girls, and was extraordinarily fond of them. Marie was born in 1858, Auguste (the second *duc*) in 1859, Simon-Serge in 1861, and Sophie-Denise (Missie) in 1862.

Morny's marriage was unquestionably happy, but it came too late in his life to alter a lifelong addiction to many women. One night, for instance, when the court and the artists' world had been invited to the Petit-Bourbon for a ball, the Polish wife of a young novelist returned to the ballroom with Morny's Grand Cross of the Legion of Honor clinging to her bodice. Morny could not have planned a more amusing incident for his guests.

His interest in sexual matters sometimes led him beyond the barrier of propriety in conversation. It is reported that at a dinner at Giradin's in 1863, he dominated the talk. His thesis: that women have no taste and do not know what is good; they are neither gourmets nor libertines, but respond to caprice and whims. Remarking that a little debauchery "softened the mores" of societies, he suggested that tribadism ought to be practiced by women because it "refined" them, "perfected" them, and made them "accomplished."

Most portraits of Morny are deceiving, because they picture him in court dress or formal attire, posing in the sober role of statesmanly selflessness. Behind the dignity of the presidential façade lay the racy, horsy dandy; there was more Brummell than Richelieu in him, as he preferred salon and boudoir to official chambers. He was an excellent horseman and delighted in steeplechases. Long a member of the Jockey-Club, Morny had been associated with French racing practically from its start.

The first French Derby was run in 1836 at Chantilly, about twenty-two miles north of Paris. Until there was direct communication by rail (1859), the racing enthusiasts made a short season of Chantilly, but swifter transportation made the track accessible on a daily basis. Other tracks were built in Paris on the Champs de Mars, but they were very inferior to Chantilly. When, in 1852, Napoleon III began to improve the Bois de Boulogne, Morny urged the construction of a hippodrome in the Longchamp district. In those days Longchamp was divided between swamp and farm, but its location—between the Bois and the Seine—seemed ideal to Morny. He eventually won over the Jockey-Club, and in 1856 the government granted a fifty-year lease. The tracks were completed the following year and were considered excellent. It may be added that Morny's horses were not celebrated for their ability to win on these courses!

If, upon Morny's death, his heart had been opened, they would have found there inscribed *Deauville*. It was "his town." Trouville was an earlier seaside resort, which had become increasingly popular. By the 1850's, as the Parisians discovered the salubrious sea air, Paris suddenly became quite insupportable in July and August. Morny found Trouville too crowded, too commercial, and he took an interest in developing a more exclusive resort. Collaborating with a banker named Donon, they began in 1860 the construction of villas, streets, hotels, a harbor, a church, gardens, and a railroad. The tracks were completed in 1864, but

Morny did not live long enough to see "his town" become a Mecca for Europe's "considerable people."

He had a lifelong liking for painting, though probably he had no profound notions about the philosophy of art. When only a second lieutenant, he had begun to buy canvases, and he occasionally bought and sold as his interests changed. He took a considerable collection along on his embassy to Russia, and other diplomats, probably unfairly, suggested he meant to sell them advantageously to the Russians. His taste ran to the seventeenth and eighteenth century Dutch masters; he liked Delacroix; and though he ordinarily did not care for the Barbizon school, he did own a Rousseau and a Diaz. He worried about the genuineness of a Metsu, "The Visit to the Accouchement," because of an identical canvas in the Hermitage in St. Petersburg, but during his embassy he became convinced that his own was the original.

Mme. de Souza, in encouraging Morny to be literary, had bent the twig farther than she knew and in a direction which might not have entranced her. He had a passion for featherweight musical comedy and wrote under the name M. de Saint-Rémy. Such was the man generally regarded, particularly abroad, as *Homo economicus*. But great financiers might sit indefinitely in Morny's antechamber, suffering the slings and arrows of those outrageous monkeys, while Morny received physicians, played with his children, or hummed tunes with his collaborators. The latter were men of ability. Ludovic Halévy, who had been an official in the Ministry for Algeria, was given the task of editing the records of parliamentary sessions for publications in the *Moniteur*. He collaborated with Morny in this delicate job—and helped with librettos on the side. Alphonse Daudet was employed by Morny as an *attaché de cabinet* for presumably the same reason.

Most of Morny's artistic efforts received their first performances at his own home or at Princess Mathilde's: *Sur la grande route* (May 31, 1861); *Les Bons Conseils* (April 1, 1862); *La Manie des proverbes* (same date); *Pas de fumée sans un peu de feu* (April 10, 1864); *Les Finesses du mari* (May 14, 1864); *La Succession Bonnet* (June 4, 1864). These works were published by

Michel Lévy in 1865 under the title, borrowed from Musset, *Comédies et proverbes*. From them it can be clearly seen that M. de Saint-Rémy was of the "*crayon est sur la table*" school.

One work, *M. Choufleuri restera chez lui*, deserves special mention as it achieved some success and much notoriety. In fact, it has been produced as recently as 1951 in Paris. The premiere was September 14, 1861, at the Bouffes Parisiens. St.-Rémy wrote the original manuscript, with additions and subtractions by Halévy, and Jacques Offenbach set it to music. A few samples of this verse should suffice: here are the words of the opening aria sung by Ernestine:

> J'étais vraiment très ignorante
> Quand j'ai quitté ma pension
> Mais depuis j'ai su, je m'en vante,
> Finir mon éducation.
>
> Je sais que toute fille honnete
> Doit avoir au moins un amant
> Et vite j'ai fait la conquête
> D'un un jeune homme aimable et charmant.
>
> C'est mon voison Babylas
> Cher Babylas, Hélas
> Pourquoi donc ne m'entends-tu pas
> Cher Babylas, Ah! cher Babylas.

Then we have the second number, a bolero sung by Ernestine and Babylas:

> *Babylas:*   Pédro possède une guitare
>   Une guitare bizarre.
> *Bab-Ern:*   (Four measures of Bing, bing, bing, etc.)
>
> *Ernestine:* Qui jusques au fond des familles
>   S'en va troubler les jeunes filles.
> *Bab-Ern:*   (Four measures of Bing, bing.)
>
> *Babylas:*   Lorsque sur sa mule
>   A travers Madrid circule
>   Notre beau Pédro

Ernestine: Chantant sa musique
Sur sa guitare magique
L'effet est complet Ah!

Bab-Ern: Pédro possède une guitare
Une guitare bien bizarre
Une guitare bien bizarre
(Seven measures of la, la, la, etc.)

If one remembers the press censorship of the Second Empire, it will explain the enthusiasm of some of the critics. Here is Albéric Second in the *Comédie parisienne:*

How fortunate it is for us poor writers that the author of this delightful play should be absorbed in higher politics! What would become of us if he could devote his leisure to theatrical matters?

But this tribute was followed by a blunt review next day in *Figaro,* written by Henri Rochefort (Comte de Rochefort de Luçay):

How fortunate is this author whose participation in a fruitful *coup d'état* has saved him from the necessity of living by the pen! If one of us dared bring such an inept production to a theatrical director, he would forthwith have been seized and thrown into the den of the theater's old hag ushers, whose instructions would have been to beat him to death with footstools.

Cartier de Villemessant, the publisher of *Figaro,* was summoned at once by Morny. The two had long been friends, and Morny wanted an explanation for the attack. Villemessant pleaded that he had been absent and had not seen the proofs, but he was unwilling to discharge Rochefort. Morny then tried to get acquainted with Rochefort, but the critic proved elusive. Perhaps he disliked Morny too much, or perhaps he feared that he would be attracted and compromised by Morny's fabled charm.

Morny became ill in the first week of March, 1865. There had been little forewarning, and since he had been quite active the Duchess disputed the doctors when they found his situation grave. She went right on with her own plans. Alphonse Daudet has described in *Le Nabab* the gathering of the anxious business associates and various clients, wringing their hands over the dying Duke, though actually grieving for themselves. He was suffering from pancreatitis, which the physicians of the day could not treat; he also had liver trouble, and influenza further weakened him.

It fell to his old friend Fernand de Montguyon to reveal the truth: "My poor Auguste, you are done for." Morny then gave his friend instructions for the destruction of personal papers. Bundles of letters were consigned to the fireplace, and when the flames did not consume them swiftly enough Montguyon speeded the operation by flushing documents down the bathroom drain. It was a conspicuous waste of precious records and an example of a too frequent practice in French officialdom.

The imperial couple called on March 7th. At first, Morny did not recognize them. The Emperor held his hand and was very much affected; the Empress was on her knees in prayer. After some minutes Morny appeared to realize their presence, and bade them farewell. Both of Their Majesties sensed the greatness of their impending loss. Morny had not only been an able servant and a strong support for the dynasty, but he had been almost alone in approving their marriage.

The end came quickly. Last rites were performed by the Archbishop of Paris, and the Duke expired early next morning—March 8, 1865. In the chilly stillness, the wail of a beggar's clarinet was heard, coming from the Concorde bridge. Morny had hated its sound in life; now the tones could mock, but not disturb.

III

Montalembert

AND LIBERAL CATHOLICISM

It means little for a Christian to be right;
a philosopher often has that advantage. But
to be right and to suffer the appearance of
being wrong while allowing him who has
all the wrong on his side to triumph—that
is indeed good vanquishing evil.

—FÉNELON

The tiny village of Montalembert in the department of Deux-Sèvres hardly suggests the ancient glory and the fighting qualities of the Counts of Montalembert. From the Middle Ages to the nineteenth century, the men of this family were born to the military profession; but the French Revolution divided the family and broke the traditional devotion to arms. One brother, Marc-René de Montalembert, remained in France and was the senior member of the Académie des sciences and the dean of French generals at the time of his death in 1802. The other brother, Jean, emigrated to England in 1792, taking his fifteen-year-old son, another Marc-René. Six years later, the latter married Eliza Forbes, a descendant of the Scottish Earls of Granard, who had been settled in Ireland by Charles II. To this Franco-Scottish union Charles-Forbes-René de Montalembert was born on April 15, 1810, in London.

His early education was directed by his grandfather, James Forbes, as the Comte de Montalembert returned to France in 1814 to serve his friend Louis XVIII. Charles remained in England until 1819, where he became intensely pious in the company of his grandfather. Forbes, though ardently Protestant, was content that the child should remain Roman Catholic, and worked to strengthen the alien faith in the boy. Meanwhile, the Comte de Montalembert, who had been made Minister to Württemberg, was anxious for his son to be trained in France, and in 1819 he ordered Charles to Paris and entered him at the Lycée Bourbon. The following year, Charles visited his family in Stuttgart and began to study German, but upon the end of the vacation he was forced to return to his academic "prison."

Shortly afterward, the Montalemberts returned from Württemberg and liberated their restive son. He lived at home, read a great deal, and attended lectures which were open to the public, essentially directing his own education from his tenth to his sixteenth year. His Scottish mother was indifferent to intellectual matters and failed to understand his devotion to books, but after her conversion to Catholicism in 1822 she was at least sympathetic to his piety. The *Comte* devoted himself to the Chamber of Peers until 1827 when Charles X named him Minister to Sweden.

Enrollment in a school was essential, however, if Charles was to earn the bachelor's degree, and he entered the College Sainte-Barbe in 1826. He found the students, including Victor Duruy, inclined to liberalism and hostile to the government of Charles X; and, having been favorably impressed by British parliamentary institutions, the young Montalembert counted himself a liberal. He was shocked, in contrast, to find his fellows indifferent to Christianity, many of them not even believing in God. His interest in Church and Government was excited by student arguments, and occasionally he attended the debates in the Chamber of Peers, which he found were of a "frightening mediocrity."

Having qualified for the baccalaureate in 1828, Charles was summoned by his father to Sweden. He went reluctantly, knowing that his father had little sympathy for liberalism; furthermore, considering the family's military tradition, the *Comte* would hardly approve of Charles dedicating his life to "God and His Church," which seemed to be his intention. The months in Sweden were none too happy, and were capped by Charles's sister being stricken by a fatal illness, which forced a return to France in 1829.

His melancholy became more profound as he approached his twentieth birthday. Certain that he wished to work for the faith and for liberty, he could not decide between entering the priesthood or politics. He enjoyed little social life, but spent his hours reading and attending lectures. The political and religious problems of Ireland interested him in particular (1829 was the year of Catholic Emancipation), and he was, in fact, on his way to visit Britain when the July Revolution began.

Charles rushed back to Paris, aware that his family was compromised by its support of the Bourbon dynasty. He alone had been enthusiastic for a constitutional monarchy and had felt that the king was wrong to violate the Charter in the hope of restoring absolute government. Now the Revolution, in the name of constitutional monarchy, had ruined his father's career; and Charles's brother, a page to the King, had been forced to escape the palace by leaping through a window. Accordingly, Charles was not warmly greeted by his family, who packed him off to London. He remained enthusiastic for the July Monarchy for several months until its anticlerical hue became apparent to him; then he thought more kindly of the Bourbons.

Meanwhile, Charles went from London to visit Ireland. He saw the Irish problem as a personal cause: a Catholic people subject to despotic rule. During his six weeks in Ireland, he managed to meet Daniel O'Connell, the man whose illegal election to Parliament had made him a Catholic hero. But O'Connell was indifferent to his twenty-year-old French visitor, and Charles departed greatly disappointed; "He was only a demagogue, not a great orator." His chagrin was dispelled shortly after by the news that a Liberal Catholic movement had been organized in France. He need labor no longer among the Irish.

Though the Liberal Catholic movement in France appeared in an organized form only after the Revolution of 1830, the roots of the movement went deep into the history of the Church in France. During the sixteenth century, when the authority of Rome was at its nadir, the French King secured a large measure of autonomy for the Gallican Church in the Concordat of 1516, which, in addition, increased the royal interference in hierarchical affairs. In tying Church and State more closely, the Concordat of 1516 had the ultimate effect of subjecting the Church to royal authority, clearly a retreat from the traditional medieval view that religious and secular authority ought to be separate. Nevertheless, the French bishops were pleased to be given greater authority in their dioceses and were, therefore, jealous of their "Gallican liberties"; similarly, the royal politicians, eager to strengthen royal authority, were happy to eliminate Papal influence within the kingdom.

In the eighteenth century when the authority and prestige of the French monarchy declined, the Gallican Church suffered because of its alliance with the decaying régime. Accordingly, the governments of the French Revolution dealt harshly with the Church, which had to count itself fortunate in 1801 to have its status recognized again, though by a humiliating Concordat. The French bishops received, it is true, an even greater authority in their dioceses, but the clergy really became civil servants, so great was the jurisdiction of the government over them; and Papal authority in France was more limited than it had been after 1516.

The subjection of clerical authority to the State was accompanied, in particular in the eighteenth and early nineteenth centuries, by the triumph of Rationalism over traditional Christianity. This will explain why those who wished to revitalize Christianity in France saw the problem as twofold: they had to defeat "Voltairianism" while reviving ultramontanism. Comte Joseph de Maistre initiated the revival of ultramontanism in France, arguing that the decline of Christianity during the eighteenth century was a result of Gallicanism.

After De Maistre's death in 1821, the Abbé Felicité de La Mennais became the leading ultramontanist. As early as 1814 La Mennais had written against Gallicanism in terms which suggested a medieval ideal:

> Without the Pope, no Church; without the Church, no Christianity; without Christianity, no religion or society: thus European national life has its unique source in pontifical power.

If Gallicanism was seriously hurt by the collapse of the Old Régime during the French Revolution, the second failure of the Bourbon monarchy in 1830 proved fatal to Gallicanism. The Revolution of 1830 was antilegitimist and anticlerical; in fact, there was talk among the bourgeois that the Church was finished in France because she had tied her cause too closely to Legitimacy. While the constitution recognized Catholicism as "the religion of the majority of the French," the Church was disestablished, and the coronation of Louis-Philippe was not a religious ceremony. Many of the clergy went into hiding to escape possible persecution; and a number of the bishops emigrated, still jealous of their "Gallican liberties," but recognizing that those liberties were unlikely to be supported by an anticlerical government.

The Revolution of 1830, therefore, served notice on French Catholics that they must reach a modus vivendi with modernity or risk extinction of the faith. The Gallicans were paralyzed by defeat and fear, but the ultramontanes—unattached to any one form of government—argued that a Catholic revival was dependent upon the French clergy accepting the principle of separation of Church and State. The ultramontanes, in short, saw that the medieval ideal of separation of Church and State was compatible with the nineteenth century liberal ideal of *laissez faire*. The Gallicans complained that a liberal program implied the acceptance of infidel governments, to which the ultramontanes replied that an indifference to form of government was the proper attitude and that the independence of the Church should be the goal.

In October of 1830, three of the ultramontanes, styling themselves Liberal Catholics, founded the journal *L'Avenir*, which was dedicated to "God and Liberty." The following month, Montalembert left Ireland to join these three: La Mennais, Lacordaire, and De Coux. "All that I know," he wrote to La Mennais in advance, "all that I am, I put at your feet." The policy of *L'Avenir* was basically liberal but had democratic aspects distasteful to Montalembert; nevertheless, he stood with the three founders for separation of Church and State, freedom of teaching, freedom of the press, freedom for associations, and for universal suffrage. They proposed to support the July Monarchy on condition that the government remain faithful to the spirit of the constitution and maintain religious freedom.

The social and economic policy of *L'Avenir* was more democratic than liberal, and bore the imprint of La Mennais's thought:

The question of the poor is not simply a question of economic policy; it is a question of the life and death of society, because it is a question of life or death for five-sixths of the human race; hence, more than ever one of the problems which call for a prompt solution in Europe.

Charity in the form of alms was insufficient; the Church must become the champion for social justice. Economists like Adam Smith and Simonde de Sismondi were regularly attacked for classifying only material things as wealth and forgetting the moral virtues, and for being solicitous for production of goods but indifferent to their distribution. Economics is, according to De Coux, "the theology of material interests," and he found it outrageous that these economists, whom he characterized as indifferent to human values, believed that Catholicism was the enemy of the people's well-being. The Church, he concluded, must stand ready to remedy the ills brought by the "selfish interest of the capitalists" and prevent society from suffering a terrible disaster.

In defiance of the laws which gave the state monopolistic control of education, the editors of *L'Avenir* opened a primary school in 1831, hoping to force the government to accept the principle of freedom of teaching. The régime was, of course, too anticlerical to champion legislation permitting the clergy to open primary schools, and the editors soon found themselves under arrest. Death spared the old Comte de Montalembert the spectacle of his son in court; and the latter, having paid his hundred-franc fine, left the hearing as a Peer of France.

L'Avenir had over two thousand subscribers by 1831, the majority being young clergymen. Their acceptance of the liberal principle of separation of Church and State alarmed some of the older clerical proponents of Legitimacy for whom such separation meant the loss of the budget annually provided the Church by the State. Subscriptions to the journal declined when Cardinal de Rohan and the Bishops of Chartres and Toulouse forbade the reading of *L'Avenir* in their dioceses. Fearing for the life of the journal, its editors decided to appeal to Rome for support. They expected a sympathetic reception, as their editorials had been outspokenly ultramontane.

Off to Rome, then, went La Mennais, Montalembert, and Lacordaire. But Gregory XVI, who had just ascended the Papal throne in the midst of revolt in the Papal States, had little sympathy for liberal ideas; and even had he been sympathetic, it would have been awkward for him to undercut the French hierarchy which had already made known its hostility to liberalism. In consequence, the editorial trio was coldly received and ultimately told to return to France while the liberal program was being studied. A second audience was granted them on March 1, 1832, but the presence of Cardinal de Rohan indicated defeat before the Pope had spoken a word.

An embittered La Mennais, accompanied by Montalembert, left Rome for Munich, where they met the leaders of the Bavarian Liberal Catholic movement. The Papal encyclical *Mirari vos* reached them in Munich; they were not mentioned by name, but their ideas were condemned without right of appeal. The editors of *L'Avenir* accepted the condemnation officially, and Lacordaire resigned from the journal; but La Mennais and Montalembert continued to harbor their liberal convictions, which they refrained from publishing.

In his encyclical, Gregory XVI had not criticized La Mennais's ultramontanism, but merely his liberalism. In short, Gallicanism was no longer a serious issue dividing the French clergy, which was sharply divided now over liberalism. For conservatives like Gregory XVI, liberalism was compromised by its eighteenth century philosophical origins. The notion that the natural goodness of man would become apparent in a free society seemed incompatible with the idea of Original Sin. The Liberal Catholics had never denied Original Sin and, from the Conservative point of view, were illogical in espousing a freer society which would "unleash the popular passions." Spiritual life requires authority, the Conservatives reasoned, not license.

Furthermore, the Liberals might speak of separating Church and State, of separating the spiritual from the temporal, but the Conservative Catholics did not admit that the two realms were so clearly separate. Religion and politics were enmeshed, they argued, and properly so when it came to such matters as public education and marriage. In consequence, the Conservatives believed that the Liberal program to revitalize religion by separating Church and State would have the opposite effect: the Church would simply be surrendering its rightful interest to politicians.

Gregory XVI's decision not to encourage the Poles, who, in 1831, had combined the causes of liberalism and Catholicism in a revolt against Russian rule, demonstrated the Papacy's belief in Order. The Polish cause was popular in France, however, and served to strengthen the Liberal Catholic movement. Mickiewicz's *Book of the Polish Pilgrims* was translated into French by Montalembert, who added his own preface and a *Hymn to Poland* by La Mennais in the 1833 edition. Following, La Mennais published his *Sentiments of a Believer*, an attack upon civil authority, which was censured in the encyclical *Singulari nos* in 1834. From this second condemnation, La Mennais never recovered; he lost faith in Rome while retaining his faith in Catholic doctrine. He was never excommunicated, but his career in the Church shortly came to an end, after which he wrote his name Lamennais.

Montalembert, meanwhile, had been unable to decide whether to enter the priesthood. He decided against it in 1836 after meeting Marie-Anne de Mérode, whom he married in September of that year. The Mérodes were Franco-Belgian nobility, and known for their piety and devotion to the Papacy. Four daughters were born to this happy marriage: Elisabeth, Catherine, Madeleine, and Généreuse-Thérèse, and their education became one of Montalembert's major occupations.

Education, in fact, became the chief Liberal Catholic concern after Lamennais's sad fate had suggested the inexpediency of dwelling on the issue of Church-State separation. In his *The Obligation of Catholics in the Matter of Freedom of Teaching* (1843), Montalembert urged all Catholics to demand that the government recognize the principle of freedom of teaching on grounds that the Constitution guaranteed liberty. The Liberal Catholics initiated this campaign, but the cause was agreeable to the Conservative Catholics; if the government had previously refused to permit the establishment of parochial primary schools, perhaps the government's own creed of *laissez faire* could be invoked by the Catholics to secure for clergymen the right to open parochial primary schools.

Montalembert advocated the use of political action toward

this goal, but many of the bishops—reared in the Gallican tradition of merely suggesting opinions to the government in the expectation of action—were aghast at the prospect of political organization. His support, therefore, came from the younger clergy, who, disillusioned by the Church's disastrous alliance with Legitimacy, were ready to see a Catholic Party formed. Beginning in 1844, Montalembert's Committee for the Defense of Religious Freedom organized affiliated chapters throughout the country. Members of the organization did not themselves seek parliamentary office, but candidates who agreed to champion the principle of freedom of teaching received the organization's support. In the election of 1846, one hundred and forty-six such candidates were elected to Parliament. This success, when added to the election of a liberal Pope the same year, augured well for Liberal Catholicism.

The Catholics were not embarrassed by revolution in 1848 as they had been in 1830, for they had no stake in the anticlerical July Monarchy, and Pius IX did not revere Order to the point of denying the right to rebel. In general, then, the clergy was favorable to the Revolution of 1848 and was spared the anticlerical reaction of 1830. Thus, one can affirm that the Catholics had won a round in their fight to reach a modus vivendi with modernity; the bishops were not overly enthusiastic about republican government, it is true, but neither did they feel obliged to emigrate in fear of persecution.

The Church had yet to face, however, another aspect of modernity: the harsh economic and social facts of the Industrial Revolution. Principally, of course, the Church has always been concerned with the salvation of souls, though the number of Catholic charitable organizations in the nineteenth century demonstrated that Christians were not indifferent to misery on this earth.

The Industrial Revolution was a serious challenge to the Church because it held the promise of material progress for all mankind. There were many who held that the coming material benefits would be the measure of true progress and that Christianity would perish in competition with the newer and more apparent key to salvation. Their argument was based on the assumption that human nature would improve in response to an improved environment; thus, the happy day would come when rich men would slip effortlessly through the needle's eye.

In its early days, however, industrialism seemed to produce profits for the few and, if anything, cultivated misery by concentrating the poor into squalid towns. Lamennais had earlier suggested that the Catholic obligation was to work for political and economic freedom. Salvation was not possible without freedom; crushing people politically or economically makes them brutes, not men. In this way the Liberal Catholics glimpsed a Christian argument for social reform without coming to terms with the materialism of their opponents. Freedom did not necessarily mean democracy, and certainly Montalembert did not understand freedom to mean democracy. Socialism, as economic democracy, became an anathema to most of the Catholic leaders—whether Liberal or Conservative—and in particular after the June Days, when the Socialists had excited disorder.

Of the major presidential candidates in 1848, only Cavaignac and Louis-Napoleon seemed dedicated to preserving Order; but the Catholics suspected Cavaignac of wanting free and compulsory education, which they were unwilling to sanction so long as all primary teachers were laymen. Louis-Napoleon, on the other hand, promised Montalembert that he would protect religion in France by advocating the principle of freedom to teach. He further guaranteed to protect the freedom and authority of the Pope, who, at that moment, had been chased from Rome by Italian revolutionaries. The Catholics, as a consequence, voted for Louis-Napoleon, making themselves political bedfellows of the bourgeois in the fight against socialism.

The bourgeois did not return to the clerical camp after 1848 because of a revival of faith, but because they had been taught a healthy fear of the revolutionary forces during the June Days. Church doctrine necessarily inculcated a respect for authority, which the bourgeois hoped to translate into political terms to preserve the *status quo*. Renan called them "Christians out of fear." The antisocialism of the Catholics was less selfish, if not disinterested: it may be held that the revolutionary doctrines were too materialistic to be compatible with Christianity, but Montalembert merely argued that the revolutionary doctrines would produce social chaos, which in turn would ruin religion.

When the world saw troops of the French Republic overthrow the Roman Republic in 1849 and restore Pius IX to his city, the events suggested that the French government valued Order above republicanism. And the following year, when a new education law was passed whose spirit was totally contrary to the tradition of French republicanism, the significance of the bourgeois-clerical alliance was clear: the Republic could not long survive.

The Law of March 15, 1850, bore the name of the Minister of Public Instruction, the Vicomte de Falloux. Thought a Legitimist, he had been willing to enter the government in order to devise an education law more favorable to the Catholics. Toward this end, he appointed a committee which included Thiers, Dupanloup, and Montalembert to advise him on a new law. The committee was dominated by Liberal Catholics who, in the 1840's, had been the most outspoken in denouncing the monopoly in primary education won by the anticlerical forces in the time of the French Revolution and Napoleon. (See the chapter on Duruy.)

Had there been enough clergymen in France to staff all the primary schools, Falloux's committee would undoubtedly have recommended that the lay teachers be entirely removed from the public school system on the grounds that lay teachers were "Voltairian." But as it was impractical to destroy the Université, the committee settled on a compromise designed to weaken the control of the Université over education. The law created a Higher Council for Education, which was composed of representatives from the legislative and judicial branches of the government, from the clergy, and from the administration of the Université. Secondly, educational committees were created for each department to advise the departmental councils, and the local bishop was automatically a member of the local educational committee. The law also reduced the rectoral districts in size, creating eighty-six instead of sixteen, so that they coincided with the departments: a device intended to reduce the authority of the rectors of the Université and put them on an administrative level with the local prefect and bishop. This last provision was extremely unpopular among the lay teachers and, four years later, the sixteen rectoral districts were reestablished.

The Falloux Law also proclaimed the principle of freedom of teaching in primary and secondary schools. Anyone could open a school providing he was certified by the Université or was a clergyman belonging to any sect recognized by the state. More to the point, municipal councils were again free to hire members of religious teaching orders for their local public schools, while in every town the mayor and the curé together selected the few children privileged to receive free education.

The Republicans were, of course, furious at the new education law, which they regarded as reactionary and oppressive, but Montalembert was chagrined to find many conservative Catholics opposed to the law as well. Louis Veuillot, editor of *L'Univers*, condemned the law for failing to give the Church monopolistic control of French education. Thus, the Catholics were seen to be divided as they had been during the July Monarchy; and the basic issue remained the same: whether to reach a modus vivendi with modern ideas and institutions or to remain intransigent.

Both factions of the Catholic party were unwilling, on the occasion of the *coup d'état* of 1851, to declare their loyalties immediately. Thanks to the Roman expedition and the Falloux Law, the Catholics were favorable to Louis-Napoleon, but he was surrounded by men known to be indifferent or hostile to the Church. After several days had passed and the President was seen to be firmly in the saddle, most Catholics veered toward acceptance of the *coup d'état*, rationalizing that only the President could maintain Order and recognizing that the Republicans in Parliament were unlikely to preserve the recent concessions made to the Church.

Montalembert and the Liberal Catholics were more troubled than the Conservatives by the necessity of coming to terms with Louis-Napoleon, as the *coup d'état* threatened the integrity of parliamentary government. Montalembert was among those Deputies who, on December 2nd, signed a protest against the coup. Nevertheless, he found his name on the Advisory Commission, whose membership was revealed the next day in the *Moniteur* and, in consequence, sent a protest to Morny, which was countersigned by thirteen other Deputies:

Monsieur le Ministre, We learn from the newspapers that we have been nominated to be part of an Advisory Commission, created by yesterday's decree which you countersigned. In consideration of the unjust and sad incarceration of such a great number of our colleagues and friends, we cannot accept this function.

Morny's response indicates he knew where Catholic susceptibilities lay:

My dear Montalembert, The detained deputies have been held only because they wish it so. Several times they have been offered freedom. . . . Now let me give you a bit of advice. There are in this situation only the Prince and the Reds. . . . Can you hesitate? At this moment there is fighting in the Faubourg Saint-Antoine. To refuse support to the government is a crime—to put it briefly. . . . You who have such an excellent mind, can you seriously believe that your friends are being held? I guarantee that they can emerge whenever they wish.

As Morny's note did not have the ring of despotism, Montalembert agreed to meet Louis-Napoleon on December 5th. The pressure to conform was increasing; he learned through his brother-in-law, Monseigneur de Mérode, that the Holy See approved the coup, and *L'Univers* committed the Conservative Catholics to support the régime on the 5th. At the interview, Louis-Napoleon's promises were satisfactory to Montalembert. The President guaranteed to maintain the principle of freedom of teaching, and as for universal suffrage—which the Liberals opposed—he said:

Do not worry. I regard universal suffrage as the basis of power, but not as the usual method of carrying on government. I certainly want to be baptized, but that is no reason to live forever in water.

Thus, when the Advisory Commission was constituted in its final form on December 13th, Montalembert's name appeared on the list. As a pledge of good faith, Morny ordered the prefects to see that Sundays be observed in their respective departments. In turn, both Veuillot and Montalembert urged the Catholics to support the government in the plebiscite. Nearly all the bishops followed their lead.

Montalembert's romance with the new régime was brief. On January 14, 1852, the new republican constitution made its appearance, and it was only too clear that the régime would not be truly parliamentary. Three days later Montalembert rejected his nomination to the Senate and received, as a result, the following from Louis-Napoleon:

I hope that you realize the concern I feel over your indisposition. I am troubled to learn that your sentiments towards me are no longer what they were. I do not know why this change has come about, for I hold a genuine friendship for you and would be very sorry to see something upset our good relations.

Touched by the letter, Montalembert wavered. Then he learned of the Orléans confiscation on January 23rd, and was aghast at this seizure of private property and embarrassed that the Church was designated as one of the chief benefactors of this "theft." He broke with the régime by resigning from the Advisory Commission, but retained his elective seat in the Corps législatif.

Despite the republican form of the new constitution, its spirit was authoritarian. Initiative belonged to the President alone. A law was prepared by the Ministry concerned, sent to the Council of State (men of "exceptional ability" appointed by the President) for study, and then passed on to the Corps législatif, the lower house. A legislative committee would then be appointed to examine the law; amendments could be suggested at this stage, but were subject to approval by the Council of State. In its final form, then, the law would be reported to the Corps législatif, which had the prerogative of accepting or rejecting the bill. The appointive Senate played no role in the legislative process, but acted as a check upon the constitutionality of measures passed.

Montalembert, chafed by the emasculation of the only elective body within the government—the Corps législatif—consummated his rupture with the régime on June 12, 1852. He spoke not merely to the deputies, but to Louis-Napoleon, who attended that day's session:

We are not the nation's illustrious; they are—or will be—all in the Senate, according to the Proclamation of December 2. We are not men of exceptional ability; they are all in the Council of State—again according to the Proclamation of December 2. Thus, what are we? We are nothing but a handful of honest men who have been brought from the depths of our provinces to lend support to the government by giving our stamp of approval.

The evolution of the Second Republic into the Second Empire did not disturb the Conservative Catholics, and the episcopacy, with the exception of Dupanloup, Bishop of Orléans, stood firmly behind the government and expressed little sympathy for Montalembert and his little band of Liberal Catholics. Most of the episcopacy were present for the Prince Imperial's baptism in 1856, where the Cardinal Legate, Patrizi, represented the Pope as godfather.

While Montalembert did believe in Order and authority, he refused to surrender his belief that the Church and State ought to be separate. The close alliance between the Emperor and the episcopacy, when combined with the absence of true parliamentary government, suggested the Old Régime to Montalembert. Indeed, was not the assumption of the numeral III by the Emperor a claim to legitimacy? He could not tolerate hearing the clergy eulogize Napoleon III, who was often likened to Charlemagne by those clergymen who rated political expediency above historical accuracy.

Montalembert made his position clear in a brochure written in 1852: *Catholic Interests in the Nineteenth Century*, the gist of which revealed the influence of Lamennais. Absolute political power, Montalembert wrote, is incompatible with spiritual freedom; as an absolutism will inevitably invade the spiritual realm as the only realm which remains beyond its grasp, it is the practical obligation of Catholics to champion free political institutions. Only a tiny minority of the Catholics, however, shared Montalembert's view and, in particular after the proclamation of the Second Empire, he considered resigning his seat in the Corps législatif. The Liberal Catholics successfully pleaded that it was his obligation to the Church and to France to stay in Parliament to fight against absolute power.

In its early years the Second Empire was a clerical—but not a religious—régime. Concessions made to the Church were minor, such as Morny's decree that Sundays ought to be observed; but the government not only failed to implement this particular decree, but ignored the major goals of the Church. The *Articles organiques* of 1802, which Napoleon I had tacked on the Concordat without Papal approval, were still in force; and, though not used, the government showed no interest in abolishing them to please the Church. Similarly, the *Code Napoléon* subordinated religious marriage to civil marriage, in that the law regarded a marriage as valid even though not consecrated by the Church. When the clerical forces brought this problem up for debate in the Senate (1853), they were beaten flat. Another Catholic disappointment was the failure of the government to destroy the Université, which would have left the Church in control of education. Instead, the government guarded its power to hire and fire members of the teaching profession and of the academic advisory councils. Worse, from the Catholic view, was the Law of 1854 which reestablished the sixteen rectoral districts and increased the authority of the rectors.

The principle of freedom of teaching was maintained, it is true, as was the French garrison in Rome. Some of the French clergy chose to regard the Crimean War as a religious crusade growing out of the dispute in the Holy Land and, therefore, a demonstration of the government's concern for religion; they ignored the political origin of the conflict. One gets the impression, in fact, that the alliance between Empire and clergy continued to be the matter of convenience it had been since 1851; and, not being a matter of conviction, the alliance was dependent upon the government's continued support of Papal authority.

Recognizing that the régime was not truly religious only heightened Montalembert's determination to remain in opposition. He witnessed with revulsion the public obeisance of Jacques Dupin (called Dupin the Elder) in 1853, a man of former parliamentary sympathies, who now urged Montalembert to make a similar reconciliation with the régime. The final paragraph of Montalembert's response to Dupin is noteworthy:

As for me, I recognize only two castes or classes in France and in the world: those men of courage, intelligence, and honor, whom iniquity revolts, and who believe in conscience, liberty, and the dignity of honest men; and those courtiers of fear, force, and success, who exploit and lead the masses—to the detriment of all the legitimate higher things—with the bait of material profit. Between these two castes, I have always resolved to be in the first, and I am sorry to see you . . . make a gesture towards the second. You have been one of the marshals in the parliamentary army, where I served for some time with you and whose flag remains dear to me. Under that flag I got the habit of saying what I think on every possible occasion. Thus, pardon this philippic which derives from this bad habit, and do not believe less in my friendly devotion and high esteem.

Had Montalembert merely sent this note to Dupin, the matter would have ended, but he made copies for his Liberal Catholic friends which made the rounds. Soon the government asked the Corps législatif to punish Montalembert for offenses to the Emperor, inciting hatred and suspicion of the government, and for disturbing the peace. A legislative committee was duly appointed to investigate, but it vetoed the charges. Persigny, the Minister of the Interior, refused to let the matter drop, and Montalembert had to defend himself on the grounds that he had sought to attack absolutism, not the person of the Emperor. The Corps législatif ultimately censured him by a vote of 184 to 51—with many members abstaining—and the government was satisfied.

With the bulk of the episcopacy devoted to the régime, the Liberal Catholics felt powerless to influence the course of events. Parisian salons and the Académie française proved to be their only remaining arenas. The Académie was anti-Empire, and had elected Montalembert to membership in 1852, presumably to warn Louis-Napoleon against overthrowing the Republic. Thereafter, enemies of the Empire were the successful candidates for the Académie: Bishop Dupanloup and the Legitimist Berryer were elected in 1854, the latter's election being regarded as a direct challenge to Napoleon III. Berryer refused to pay the customary call on the sovereign, claiming he had won the right to omit the call in 1840, when he had defended Louis-Napoleon before the Chamber of Peers. The imperial response was written by Mocquard, Napoleon's secretary:

The Emperor regrets that in the case of M. Berryer, the motives of the politician have transcended the duties of the academician. His presence at the Tuileries would not have caused the embarrassment which he seems to fear. From his lofty position, His Majesty would have seen only the orator and writer in the elect of the Academy, and in the adversary of the moment only the defender of yesterday.

Another Legitimist, the Vicomte de Falloux, was elected to the Académie in 1857, along with the Orleanist Duc Victor de Broglie; and in 1860 Father Lacordaire joined the august band.

To suggest that these six did not merit election to the Académie française would be unjust, but their elections did imply that the Academicians recognized hostility to Napoleon III's régime as an outward sign of literary excellence. Opposition was the Académie's *esprit de corps*, the epigram and innuendo its standard weapons. The Academicians' dilemma is reminiscent of that of the Tory poets and essayists in the eighteenth century who turned to satire in the backwash of revolutionary political developments, which they found themselves powerless to retard. The old order seemed to dissolve, while the new order seemed founded on corruption and immorality.

Here is Armand de Pontmartin writing in 1875 of the Academicians:

Now that the Empire has fallen, we can frankly avow that nothing was more childish or more senile than this monomania of furious opposition, contrary to the spirit and the origins of the Institut, and made ridiculous by the age and impotence of the fault-finders, whose violences would have been dangerous for themselves had the government really taken them seriously.

Several Liberal Catholics, including Montalembert, Falloux, and Broglie, did not limit their activity to the Académie, but took over an old Catholic journal in 1855, *Le Correspondant*, the better to do battle with Veuillot and the Conservative Catholics who supported the régime. Falloux, in particular, sensed that Napoleon III was not inclined toward despotism, and attacked Veuillot's *L'Univers* as being "more imperial than the Empire" in its frank espousal of absolutism.

Officially the government did not participate in the quarrel between the two Catholic factions, though it was glad for the support which *L'Univers* gave the régime. Actually, Napoleon III was antagonized by Veuillot's extremism, and it is ironical that His Majesty received no aid from the Liberal Catholic party, which was in many respects closer to him in spirit than was Veuillot. Indeed, after the Crimean War, when Napoleon III seemed bent on "doing something for Italy" in pursuit of his liberal principle of nation-states, Veuillot modified his enthusiasm for the Emperor. Fearing that Napoleon III might end by destroying the foundations of absolutism in France, Veuillot complained that His Majesty was turning out to be "only a perfected Louis-Philippe."

Meanwhile, Montalembert's opposition won him the distinction of being the only member of the Corps législatif who, having had official support in the 1852 election, did not again receive it in the election of 1857. Nevertheless, he stood for election in the Besançon district, which had three times before elected him to public office. He ran a poor third: 17,387 for the official candidate, 7,134 for a Republican, while Montalembert received only 4,378 votes, 15 per cent of the votes cast. Parliament had lost one of its most ardent parliamentarians.

A second humiliation followed late in 1858 after Montalembert published in *Le Correspondant* an article entitled "A debate on India in the British Parliament." While a timely piece in consideration of the recent Sepoy Mutiny, Montalembert's real aim was a comparison of the powers of the British and French Parliaments. He was sentenced to six months in prison for his criticism of the French system, but Napoleon III pardoned him on the anniversary of the *coup d'état*. As Montalembert refused the pardon, he was condemned a second time and simply released. The Emperor had no intention of imprisoning Montalembert, but explained that he was wearying of the conspiracy by the men of letters against him and that he sought to read them a lesson.

Both Catholic parties, meanwhile, had begun to watch with suspicious eye the development of Italian nationalism, fearful that the temporal power of the Papacy would be destroyed. (Other facets of the Italian Question are discussed in the chapters on Persigny, Castiglione, and Duruy.) The temporal power dated from the eighth century when Pepin the Short, having defended Pope Stephen II against the Lombards, granted the Pope territory and temporal authority in the hope of assuring the independence of the Papacy. Temporal power was a means of securing spiritual freedom, and was not an end in itself.

In the nineteenth century the temporal power of the Papacy was insignificant in the face of the great military states of Europe; but the Popes clung to their temporal power as a matter of principle. To surrender it might lead to the loss of Rome itself; furthermore, the Papacy did not accept the liberal notion that the spiritual authority ought to be separate from temporal affairs.

As Napoleon III moved toward helping the Italians realize their national ambitions in the late 1850's, it became customary for the French government to suggest that reforms were overdue in the Papal States. Pius IX, who had lost his faith in liberalism when the Italian nationalists had turned on him for failure to lead their movement, refused to sanction any changes wrought by revolutionary action in the name of modern doctrines; but he was not opposed to good government. In fact, the government of the Papal States in the time of Pius IX was moderate, and if the Pope was cautious in making reforms it must be ascribed in part to his unwillingness to appear to be knuckling under to French pressure. Pius IX understood that Napoleon's government merely sought to weaken the prestige of the Papacy in advancing the claims of Italy. Reform was not the real issue. Cardinal Antonelli, Papal Secretary of State, underscored the vulnerability of the French suggestions in a remark to the French ambassador, the Duc de Gramont: "Thus, the French people are enjoying so many liberties that they feel the need of exporting them?"

The spectacle of a dictatorship urging liberal reforms upon another state was not the only aspect of the Roman Question embarrassing to Napoleon III. He was advancing the claims of Italy, while protecting the Pope in Rome with French troops. His proposal to make the Pope the president of an Italian federation, which would have included Sardinia-Lombardy-Venetia, Parma, Modena, Tuscany, Naples, and the Papal States, was vetoed by Pius IX, who persisted in refusing to become a national leader. The plan was no more satisfactory to the Sardinian government, which wanted a united Italy under the House of Savoy.

Montalembert was furious at the events of 1859–1860, when Napoleon III aided Sardinia with troops to wrest the province of Lombardy from Austria, and went on to sanction revolutionary-inspired plebiscites which joined Parma, Modena, and Tuscany to Sardinia and despoiled the Papacy of Romagna. He published a pamphlet entitled *Pius IX and France in 1849 and in 1859*. The thesis was that in 1849, French troops had been sent to Rome as an expression of the will of the French nation, but in 1859 the national will could no longer prevail over the sovereign's will. And Montalembert was essentially correct: the last-minute enthusiasm for the War of 1859 on the part of the Parisian working class should not obscure the antagonism which the nation demonstrated when His Majesty was seen to encourage Sardinian ambitions. The Conservative Catholics, in particular, put up such a howl that the government temporarily suppressed *L'Univers* in 1860.

Yet, the French government was not indifferent to Catholic interests elsewhere. At the height of the Roman Question, French troops had been landed in Syria to restore order after 12,000 Christians had been massacred by the Moslem Druses. A similar expedition to China avenged the death of missionaries and secured for Catholic missions the right to hold land in China. Both commercial and religious interests were at stake in China, of course, but the government clearly hoped to please the French Catholics with its China policy as it did with its Mexican policy.

But as for Rome, Napoleon III expressed his desire to evacuate his troops following the annexation of Romagna by Sardinia. When the Neapolitan government refused to supply a force to replace the Roman garrison, the French Foreign Minister, Thouvenel, proposed to have Rome garrisoned by Belgian, Spanish, Bavarian, and Portuguese troops, and to have all the powers guarantee to the Pope the possession of his territory—excepting Romagna. The Pope, however, would not be part of any agreement which forced him to recognize the loss of Romagna, and Napoleon III was opposed to committing himself to guarantee the remainder of the Papal States.

An alternative was suggested by the Papacy, as eager to see the evacuation of the French troops as was the Emperor: that a Papal Army be recruited from Catholics of all nationalities. The French government refused to allow its nationals to serve in foreign armies without prior permission from Paris; nevertheless, the Pope offered the command of his force to Lamoricière, a French general hostile to the Second Empire.

Lamoricière, a Republican, had been proscribed in 1851. Subsequently he had shed his republicanism, but became an ardent Catholic, and as such, remained unfriendly to the régime. He had returned to France from exile after the amnesty of 1859, but now—in 1860—he went secretly to Rome to assume command of the Papal Army. The French Ambassador demanded that the Papacy ask the French government for authorization to hire Lamoricière, which was granted on April 5th. Mérode, Montalembert's brother-in-law, was made the Papal Minister of Arms, adding to the suggestion that the Papacy was making common cause with enemies of Napoleon III.

More eager than ever to evacuate Rome, the French reached an agreement with the Papacy in May for the evacuation of the garrison in September. Meanwhile, the Papacy speeded the recruitment of its own force and, by September, had attracted no less than 4,000 French citizens amongst others. Practically none of them bothered to secure the official permission of the French government, thus technically losing their citizenship; but the government continued to regard them as French.

But at the very moment when the French were agreeing to evacuate Rome, Garibaldi was overrunning Sicily, and in August of 1860 he crossed the straits into Naples. The French, expecting to depart in September, were forced to reinforce their Rome garrison, while the Sardinians—horrified at the thought of a clash between Garibaldi and the French—invaded the Papal provinces of Umbria and the Marches in the hope of intercepting Garibaldi. Lamoricière's little force went out to block the Sardinian advance and was smashed at Castelfidardo, permitting the Sardinians to prevent Garibaldi from assaulting Rome.

The French did nothing to evict the Sardinians or Garibaldi from Umbria, the Marches, and Naples, where plebiscites soon registered the popular desire to be annexed by Sardinia, but as Rome was now unguarded, the French stayed on. Opinion in France was largely opposed to allowing the Italians to have Rome, and as Russia threatened to require embarrassing concessions from France in exchange for supporting France in Italy, Napoleon III called a halt to Italian unification short of Rome and Venetia. The Republican minority in France accused the government of acting in contradiction to its own principles—the sovereignty of the people—in maintaining the Roman occupation, but the government was determined to await the death of Pius IX before renewing negotiations for an evacuation.

Montalembert, meanwhile, felt required by the seriousness of the Roman Question to stand for Parliament in the elections of 1863. Once again he ran in the Besançon district (Department of Doubs), but as he failed to campaign in person, the significance of his defeat was impossible to calculate. He received the enthusiastic support of the clergy, and Emile Ollivier urged the Republicans to vote for him. Despite all, the official candidate received 20,500 votes to Montalembert's 9,000. He stood for election in the Department of Côtes-du-Nord also, but here he ran far behind the winning Republican, Glais-Bizoin, and the official candidate who finished second. In general, the elections of 1863 showed that the clergy was annoyed at the government, but not sufficiently annoyed to ally with the Republicans. (See the chapter on Persigny.)

The Liberal Catholics, in the 1860's, regarded their break with the régime in 1852 as vindicated by Napoleon III's Italian policy; they struck out anew at the Conservative Catholics at a Liberal Catholic Congress held in Malines, Belgium, in 1863. Montalembert spoke in his usual vein: the less the Church is bound to any political power, the stronger she becomes in the eyes of modern society. These liberal views were repeated the following year at Malines by Dupanloup, but were heeded neither by the Papacy nor by the French government. The Pope did not believe in disestablishment, and the government had no intention of surrendering its rights under the Concordat of 1801. Instead, Montalembert was condemned by Pius IX in 1864 and his attention was called to Gregory XVI's *Mirari vos*. Most of the Liberals on *Le Correspondant* then gave up the fight and deserted Montalembert.

Meanwhile, the French and Italian governments had begun negotiations toward making a French evacuation of Rome possible. By the Convention of September 15, 1864, the two powers settled the problem of garrisoning Rome without bothering to consult the Pontifical government. The French would withdraw from Rome within two years in progressive stages—proportionate to the ability of the Papal Army to assume the defensive duties, while the Italians agreed to respect and protect the Papal States and to allow the formation of a new Papal Army. A secret clause made the treaty dependent upon the Italians transferring their capital from Turin to Florence as a symbol of their abandoning designs on Rome.

Informally, the two chief negotiators, Drouyn de Lhuys and Nigra, understood that an Italian occupation of Rome was only a matter of time after a French evacuation, but Drouyn de Lhuys asked the Italians to allow a "decent time" to elapse so as not to incriminate the French. But when the Convention was published, it proved so unpopular in Italy that the Italian government felt obliged to proclaim that it had not abandoned the hope of obtaining Rome, but had merely pledged not to take Rome by force. The French then hastily announced that they would not allow the Italians to take advantage of a "spontaneous revolution" in Rome; that they understood the Convention of September 14th to guarantee Papal independence. The clericals, however, were convinced that Napoleon III meant to abandon the Papacy.

On December 8, 1864, Pius IX published the encyclical *Quanta cura*, to which he attached a *Syllabus* of the principal errors of the time. Many of the errors were those of the Liberal Catholics, the seventy-seventh proposition for instance: "In our time, it is no longer practical to regard the Catholic religion as the unique religion of the state to the exclusion of all others." And the eightieth proposition in particular: "The Roman Pontiff can and must be reconciled to and come to terms with progress, liberalism, and modern civilization."

No one was more offended by the *Syllabus* than Napoleon III, and Catholics everywhere were astonished at the Pope's lack of political sagacity. The French government took the view that Pius IX's ideas were contrary to the ideas upon which the constitution was based, and French bishops were forbidden to publish the encyclical in their dioceses. It made little difference to the French that Pius IX published the *Syllabus* for the benefit of a small group of Liberal Catholic clergy in Sardinia, who had opposed Rome's will in regard to the temporal power and public education, for the *Syllabus* was available in countries other than Sardinia, and its strictures were too general to apply merely to Sardinia. And as for Montalembert, the *Syllabus* seemed to underline the condemnation already received that year.

Bishop Dupanloup, rather than Montalembert, made the Liberal Catholic reply to Pius IX's attack upon modernity in a pamphlet entitled *The Convention of September 15 and the Encyclical of December 8, 1864.* He first condemned the Convention in order to make his commentaries on the encyclical more palatable to the Pope. As for the encyclical, he styled it a statement of "an ideal Christian society," which was intended to warn against the abuses of modern liberalism rather than start a feud with the

entire modern world. The alacrity with which 636 Roman Catholic bishops from all parts of the world supported Dupanloup's
interpretation led the Pope to congratulate Dupanloup for explaining the encyclical's "true meaning."

Dupanloup's criticism of the Convention of September 15th,
however, made no impression on Napoleon's government, and
the first installment of the French evacuation from Rome took
place in December, 1865. The remaining troops were withdrawn
by the end of the following year and, in the meantime, the French
helped organize a Roman Legion of 1,200 men which took over
the duties of the French garrison. The clericals remained convinced that Napoleon III meant to continue his support of Italian
nationalism, particularly as he helped the Italians gain Venetia in
1866; and, of course, the Italians presumed the same thing, remembering Drouyn de Lhuys's "decent time" remark in 1864.

Garibaldi's second attempt to take Rome in 1867 gave Napoleon III the opportunity to demonstrate that he did not contem-
plate abandoning Rome to the Italians—at least not at the moment. When the Italian government failed to honor its obligations under the Convention of September 15th, ten thousand
French troops, armed with the new Chassepot rifles, were sent
for the defense of Rome. At the Battle of Mentana, the Chassepots
"worked marvels" to frustrate Garibaldi once again.

Subsequently, the distinguished member of the Opposition,
Thiers, rose in the Corps législatif to denounce Italian nationalism and to ask further guarantees that Rome be denied to the
Italians. Thiers was no partisan of the clericals, but he regarded
the Emperor's support of the principle of nation-states as inimical
to French security. His speech was well received in Parliament,
forcing Rouher, the Minister of State, to retrieve the initiative
by shouting that France would "never" allow the Papacy to be
despoiled. In a subsequent meeting of the ministers, the Emperor
twitted Rouher to the effect that in politics one does not use the
word "never."

Thiers's example is illustrative of the uneasiness felt in France
after 1866, when French hegemony seemed threatened by the
apparent unwillingness of the Emperor to check the rising star

of Prussia. Like Thiers's clericalism, the increasing clericalism of
the great majority in Parliament was not owing to a genuine
devotion to the Papacy, but to the suspicion that the reverses
suffered by the régime were attributable to the more liberal foreign and domestic policies favored by His Majesty and dating
from 1859. Born of fear, this clericalism was actually conservatism.

In preventing Garibaldi from taking Rome, and in failing to
develop the parliamentary reforms projected in 1866 (see the
chapter on Ollivier), Napoleon III seemed to bend to the clerical
will. Moreover, four leading anticlericals were absent from office
—Persigny, Morny, Thouvenel, and Prince Napoleon—giving
further credence to the popular notion that the Second Empire
was becoming clerical. On the other hand, Persigny had fallen
from office owing to inefficiency, Prince Napoleon because of
his continual indiscretions, and Morny and Thouvenel were
dead. And if the Empire had become clerical, why did the Emperor continue to sponsor Duruy's anticlerical education reforms?
And why did he announce, after the defeat of Garibaldi, that
he regarded the Convention of September 15th still in effect and
hoped for the reevacuation of French troops from Rome? In
short, he remained an anticlerical Liberal, momentarily frustrated
by the clerical conservatism about him, which seemed too formidable to risk offending; but, remembering Morny's advice to court
the intelligensia, His Majesty continued to give hints of his liberalism in the hope they would recognize his dilemma.

In the elections of 1869, the Republicans profited from the
Emperor's attempt to please everybody. The Republicans had
the longest tradition of anticlericalism and collected the votes
of anticlericals who could no longer be certain that the Empire
meant anticlericalism. And the Liberal Catholics voted against
the official candidates in the interest of parliamentary government, adding to the Republican votes in some districts. In consequence, the leading Bonapartists insisted that the Empire must
become outwardly more clerical, which meant more conservative.
As a result of the elections of 1869, then, Napoleon III reconstituted his cabinet along clerical lines; La Tour d'Auvergne, a

clerical, became the new Foreign Minister, but the fall of Duruy gave the clericals the greatest satisfaction.

The ironical side of this apparent shift toward clericalism in 1869 is that it came when Napoleon III was pondering the establishment of genuine parliamentary monarchy; but he found so little support for liberal government from those who surrounded him that he was obliged to move slowly—even in the opposite direction for a time—and ultimately to summon a leading Republican to direct the drift toward Liberal Empire.

That Republican, Emile Ollivier, was quickly elected to the Académie française in 1870, having been backed by Montalembert. Ollivier's election not only marked a reconciliation between the Académie and the régime, but suggests that Montalembert would have rallied once again to the support of Napoleon III and parliamentary government had he lived. Montalembert did not live to see Ollivier received by the Académie, and the latter—in his reception speech—paid tribute to Montalembert:

He believed that my election would have the natural effect of renewing the relations, which the Chief of State broke following the open opposition of the Académie. . . . Moreover, he thought it fitting that an institution which had desired liberty so much should demonstrate its satisfaction at the reestablishment of liberty by calling into its midst a minister of the sovereign who had heard the wishes of public opinion.

Montalembert's declining years were full of anguish. In 1865 he began to suffer from Napoleon III's ailment—kidney stones—just when he had planned a trip to the United States. Pleased by the outcome of the Civil War, he had written an article called "The Victory of the North," which won him official thanks from the President. The trip was postponed in favor of an operation, but the trouble was not remedied. In 1867 he was able to move to the Mérode manor near Brussels, Château de Rixensart, where he received a continual train of Liberal Catholic visitors. He also began studying the works of the sociologist Le Play, with whom he undertook a lengthy correspondence.

But Montalembert's anguish was mental even more than physical in these years. The Papal condemnation of liberalism not only cut the ground from under the Liberal Catholics, but made a mockery of a fundamental Liberal Catholic tenet which equated ultramontanism with liberalism. Undeniably ultramontanism had grown, owing in part to the political defeats suffered by Gallicanism in France, but also to the increasing popularity of Pius IX, whose tribulations won him widespread sympathy; but with the growth of ultramontanism came the *Syllabus* of errors and a drift toward Papal Infallibility, which, in the eyes of Liberal Catholics, was a form of the absolutism they hated.

The doctrine of Papal Infallibility had been approved by some medieval theologians but denied by the Council of Constance and omitted from the deliberations of the Council of Trent. Pius IX was often accused of reviving the doctrine as a matter of personal vanity and to assuage the pain born of the losses in temporal power, but such assertions are quite untenable. The Dogma of the Immaculate Conception, for instance, was affirmed by Pius IX in 1854 without any conciliar action, suggesting that Papal Infallibility was accepted in fact years before the temporal spoliation began and long before becoming dogma.

Rather, when Pius IX summoned a Vatican Council in 1869 for the purpose of defining the Dogma of Papal Infallibility, he sought—by taking advantage of the growth of ultramontanism— to unify and mobilize the Catholic forces to meet the challenge of modern civilization. The Liberal Catholics had supposed that religion and modernity could be reconciled; Pius IX and the Conservatives saw modernity as positivism and materialism, and there could be no reconciliation with those who denied the supernatural elements of Christianity. This cleavage between the two Catholic parties was brutally illuminated by an article in the *Civiltà Cattolica* immediately before the opening of the Vatican Council. Presumably inspired by the Papacy, the article reads: "No one is unaware that the Catholics of France are unfortunately divided into two parties: one, simply *Catholics;* the other, those who call themselves *Liberal Catholics.*" To have the Vatican imply that the Liberal Catholics were not true Catholics was a final disaster for Montalembert and his friends.

Perhaps the supreme irony of the situation from the Liberal Catholic view was the tendency of Rome, by 1869, to regard the Liberal Catholics as allied to Gallicanism. In their bitterness, many of the Liberal Catholics did, indeed, begin to suggest that if ultramontanism meant a Papal absolutism, the Gallican Church might be the only hope of liberty. On March 7, 1870, the dying Montalembert published an extreme attack upon Pius IX in the Legitimist *Gazette de France*, which implied the failure of his life and work:

Who would have expected . . . the permanent triumph of those lay theologians of absolutism who began by sacrificing all our liberties, all our principles, and all our earlier ideas to Napoleon III in order— in due course—to offer up justice and truth, reason and history, as a holocaust to the idol they are now erecting at the Vatican?

Six days later the unfortunate Montalembert was dead. His brother-in-law, Mérode, planned a Requiem Mass in Rome, which Pius IX forbade, ostensibly to prevent a possible Liberal Catholic demonstration during the sitting of the Vatican Council. In his difficulties with Pope and Emperor, Montalembert's politics were to blame—his desire to modernize both Church and State. No one challenged his piety or accused him of heresy. Even *L'Univers* proclaimed, on the day following his death, "M. de Montalembert has been, among the laymen of our time, the one who gave the greatest and the most devoted service to the Church."

IV

Jacques Offenbach

AND PARISIAN GAIETY

*God shows the little regard He has for
the riches of this world by the worth of
those to whom He has given them.*

—GILBERT RENAULT-ROULIER

In 1802, the year that a warring Europe paused to catch her breath, Isaac Offenbacher left his family home in Offenbach-am-Main, near Frankfurt, for the greener pastures of Cologne, dropping the final two letters of the family name in the interest of his career as violinist and cantor. His household was governed by poverty. Even living rent-free, thanks to the synagogue, Isaac preserved hard times through arithmetic procreation, achieving a family of ten.

Jacob, the seventh child, was born on June 20, 1819. His profession was quickly designed: a violinist at six, composer of songs at eight, and a cellist at nine. The father, elder brother Julius, and Jacob formed a trio which played at taverns and dances, but even this child labor did not provide for an increasing family. Thus it was that Isaac decided to send the two boys to Paris; he would make them independent while giving them opportunity, as he believed Paris to be the only European city where Jewish artists could make a name.

Change in residence again dictated a change in name: Julius became Jules and Jacob became Jacques. They were eighteen and fourteen respectively. The elder was immediately employed as a theater violinist, giving Jacques opportunity to study under Cherubini at the Conservatory, but the favored brother preferred theatrical life to academic, and remained at the Conservatory only one year.

He became a cellist, then, at the Opéra-Comique. Here he met Fromental Halévy, composer of *La Juive*, who consented to give Offenbach composition lessons. As Offenbach's enthusiasm to be a composer grew, he ventured to write dances in several forms: waltzes and cancans. The waltz, a respectable dance form, enjoyed great vogue in Paris, and Halévy introduced his young pupil to Jullien, a popular conductor of waltzes in the 1830's. Offenbach's first waltzes were heard at the Turkish Garden in 1836 under Jullien's direction, and at least one of them, "Winter Flowers," enjoyed success for several seasons. In 1837 he received a spanking from a critic writing in *Le Ménestrel* for having used synagogue themes in his waltz "Rebecca" and thus profaning religious melodies, but the hostile review failed to dim Offenbach's growing popularity.

Success did not bring him satisfaction. Sensing that his talent lay beyond the cellist's desk, he resigned from the Opéra-Comique and broke with the conductor Jullien. His emancipation from the orchestra pit led him directly into Parisian salons and the opportunity to prepare musical skits and fantasies. He met Friedrich von Flotow shortly after leaving the Opéra-Comique, and Flotow, a wealthy Mecklembourgeois, introduced Offenbach at the salons on his circuit. The two improvised piano-cello fantasies. Their success not only brought needed money to Offenbach, but gave him opportunity to observe the wealthy at home: the ostentation and *arrivisme* he would later satirize.

Favorable results in salons led Offenbach to the stage. In early 1839 he gave a public concert; but while his romantic waltzes were warmly applauded, his mind continually returned to cancans and comedy. Two months later he wrote several songs for a farce called *Pascal and Chambord* which ended in miserable fiasco. At twenty his hopes were dashed; he felt doomed to a life with his cello; and he resigned himself to giving lessons, writing cello exercises, and playing in salons.

But his confidence and courage slowly revived. By 1843 he was preparing a concert of his own works, which would feature a skit written for the occasion, *The Surly Monk or the Two Poltroons*. The setting was medieval: two men, meeting by chance at night on a dark street, mistake each other for Victor Hugo's frightful Quasimodo and, thus, sing happy songs to keep up their courage. Finally recognizing each other as neighbors, they go off home. This work, surprisingly enough, was well received, which left Offenbach convinced that the light and comic drama was his métier.

Shortly after, he met Herminie Mitchell and fell in love. Mitchell *père*, a London impresario, maintained a home in Paris, and though Herminie was his stepdaughter, he was as solicitous for her future happiness and welfare as if she had been his own. And a devoted father would have been doubly doubtful about Offenbach as a son-in-law: a strange-looking creature, tall and extremely thin, long hair, always agitated and trembling, and rightly styled "a knife-blade with a large nose which was always crowned by glasses and a ribbon." Furthermore, as a musician, Offenbach's financial future was questionable. To prove his worth, Offenbach made a concert tour through the provinces in 1844, but even his undeniable success did not reconcile the Mitchells. They tested him again with a round of concerts in England, including a performance before Victoria and Albert; after this triumph, only one barrier remained: his religion. Mme. Mitchell, Spanish-born, insisted on his conversion to Catholicism, and as Offenbach was indifferent to religion, he readily consented. The wedding took place on August 14, 1844. Despite having won Herminie with demonstrations of platform prowess, both Herminie and Jacques agreed that his future lay in composing for the theater and not as a virtuoso cellist. Her encouragement and strength made the lean years bearable; she did not badger him to return to the concert stage in the hope of prosperity.

If Offenbach ultimately succeeded in the world of comic opera, his exceptional talent, his wife's loyalty, and his persistence were not alone responsible. Offenbach had become completely Parisian; his tastes and pleasures were those of *les dandys*—a word newly born to usage. He dreamed of founding a "boredom insurance company." Unlike a Bach or a Berlioz, Offenbach hoped to entertain without compelling his hearers to exercise their minds.

The world of pleasure in the 1830's was expanding from salon and boudoir to the boulevard, the racetrack, and the club. In an era of rapid economic expansion, more people had money, and they demanded facilities for its squandering. The newly rich were not hampered by any traditions of responsibility or leadership: an age of rampant individualism, of self-indulgence. Here was the Marquis du Hallays-Coëtquen, student of the ballet and a collector of pornography; Lord Henry Seymour, dandy and lover of horses; Dr. Véron, one-time director of the Opera, later the owner of *Le Constitutionnel*, who directed a coterie at the Café de Paris; Roger de Veauvoir, who also held forth at the Café de Paris in his gilded vests and with his cane of rhinoceros horn; Nestor Roqueplan, the journalist—semidandy, semieccentric intellectual; Lola Montez, who danced at the Porte Saint-Martin Theater; and Thérèse Lachman, the Russian prostitute who became known as La Païva. They and their kind were neither the heart nor the soul of France, but their incredible adventures drew the limelight.

The Revolution of 1848 momentarily put an end to giddiness, and had the Republicans triumphed in the months that followed, frivolity might well have been permanently curbed. French republicanism was tinged with puritanism and had clamped Paris under blue laws in the 1790's. Uncertain of the political future, and timid by nature, Offenbach took his wife and child to Cologne, where they remained nearly a year. By 1849, when order had been clearly restored and chaos avoided, Offenbach felt it safe to return.

The Second Republic and Second Empire were a new era in name alone; the essence of the July Monarchy remained. The new spirit of the boulevards during the Monarchy was a sign that Parisians intended to live in their city, not merely work in it; the designs of Baron Haussmann during the Empire, which renovated and modernized, made the city more livable. The spirit of acquisitiveness, more sharply focused by the industrialization of the 1830's and 1840's, remained the spirit of the Empire. And Offenbach, who had not yet scored a major theatrical triumph, could work toward that goal in confidence. Frivolity had not been banished.

Meanwhile, Offenbach was driven to expediency by the pinch of poverty. In 1850 he accepted an offer of six thousand francs a year from Arsène Houssaye to take the direction of the orchestra at the Comédie-Française. Houssaye, manager of the theater, had wearied of the wretched sounds emanating from the pit, and gave Offenbach freedom to revitalize the orchestra. As Offenbach improved the orchestra, he incurred the wrath of the actors, who were unwilling to admit to the theater any excellence other than their own. Month after month, actors and musicians sabotaged each other's performances until the frail Offenbach was profoundly depressed. His depression deepened in May of 1853, when his one-act musical comedy *The Treasure at Mathurin* failed at the Opéra-Comique.

Five months later the tide turned favorably. His *Pepito* enjoyed a reasonable success at the Varieties Theater and, soon after, he completed a "dramatic Decameron" of ten dances, each one dedicated to an actress at the Comédie-Française. He also began writing for *L'Artiste,* a journal published by Arsène Houssaye, again because it brought money and not because he aspired to be a critic.

It fell to Florimond Rongé, known as Hervé, to introduce successfully the comic operas which Offenbach contemplated. Using the comic duet and the cancan, later characteristic of Offenbach, Hervé presented a one-act comic opera called *La Gargouillada* at the Palais-Royal Theater, where he was orchestra conductor. It was a parody of Italian grand opera, which brought Hervé the support of the Comte de Morny and a license to open a new theater on the Boulevard du Temple: the Concert Follies, which was renamed the New Follies in 1854. The license allowed one-act productions with two characters, which Hervé occasionally circumvented by adding a "singing corpse" to his cast.

The cancan was the scandal and the rage of the day. It derived from a dance called the *chahut,* discovered during the July Monarchy by soldiers serving in Algeria. In the form we know it today, the cancan might be styled suggestive; in the 1830's the absence of underskirts made the dance explicit. After an invasion of the Varieties Theater by a pack of *jeunesse dorée* led by Lord Henry Seymour, who interrupted the program and entertained a delighted crowd with a wild cancan, the fortune of the dance was made. Vigorous police action against the dance further ensured its popularity and longevity.

Offenbach was delighted by Hervé's success and soon took him a manuscript entitled *Oyayaïe or the Queen of the Islands.* Pleased by Offenbach's enthusiasm for the *opéra bouffe*, Hervé agreed to produce the work. It was the story of a double-bass player who, having lost his job, landed in a cannibal country. He was seized by the cannibals, stripped of all but collar, hat, tie, and shoes, and presented to Queen Oyayaïe. Sentenced to satisfy either her love or her hunger, the musician made good his escape by rowing away on his bass.

The government—to digress a moment—licensed theaters through the Ministry of the Interior in the interest of censorship. Primarily the censorship was imposed for the régime's security, but also to please the ecclesiastical authorities, whose support the government cherished. The theatrical manager who adhered to the letter of the law could expect a new license permitting longer productions with larger casts. The evidence suggests that he had to be concerned more with preventing political offenses than with offenses to the public morality.

The production was successful, and Hervé, whose assistance had made Offenbach's entry into *opéra bouffe* possible, soon became jealous of his rival. His jealousy bred ill-health, and by 1856, when Offenbach had scored several triumphs, Hervé was forced to retire temporarily from the theater. In the meantime, Offenbach had taken full advantage of the Exposition of 1855 to consolidate the position won with *Queen Oyayaïe*.

Some weeks before the opening of the Exposition, Offenbach began negotiating for a small theater near the new Palace of Industry, but the competition for the theater was intense owing to its strategic location. He appealed to the actresses to whom he had dedicated dances for support, to Prince Jerome-Napoleon, who had admired one of his dances, and to Morny. The Exposition opened without a decision having been made about the theater, but a few days later Offenbach was authorized by the Ministry of the Interior to present pantomimes and musical comedies. He named the theater the Bouffes-Parisiens, and prepared to open in three weeks.

His usual librettists were unwilling to tackle anything new on such short notice. In desperation he went to his former teacher, Fromental Halévy, who sent him on to nephew Ludovic Halévy, an attaché at the Council of State. With the latter's assistance, Offenbach opened on July 5, 1855. The program included a pantomime utilizing Rossini themes, a short bit of rural charm called *The White Night*, and a musical comedy entitled *The Two Blind Men*. Featured were two blind beggars: one a fat trombonist named Patachon, the other a skinny guitarist named Giraffier. The action consisted of a quarrel over a penny which had fallen to the street and cheating at cards in a game to decide which beggar would abandon the coveted spot on a bridge. The game ended when they heard the approaching step of a "customer" and separated to try for him. Despite the fact that the theater was tiny and supremely uncomfortable, it was sold out night after night.

In December, Offenbach moved the Bouffes-Parisiens to a larger theater on the Champs-Elysées and received a new license authorizing productions with four characters. He opened with a new musical, *Ba-Ta-Clan*, which was set in the Chinese court of a king who had twenty-seven subjects. A parody of Italian opera, *Ba-Ta-Clan* was the first example of a pet Offenbach theme: that political power was a joke and court life buffoonery. Its success was sensational, and he who had mocked grand opera and greatness itself suddenly aspired to write a serious work. He knew himself to be as yet unready, but the goal was set.

By 1857 Offenbach's output was staggering. In that year he wrote twenty operettas, five pantomimes, and several cantatas, while managing productions and conducting rehearsals. As his mastery of form increased, he was inclined to write faster cadences, and worked closely with his librettists in his desire to emphasize efficient, swift action. Vibrant rhythms were his mark, and his spicy tunes and beguiling melodies reveal his genius today as clearly as they did in 1857. A touch of Offenbach still remains the best remedy for a heavy heart.

The same year saw his company's first tour. They played to packed houses in Britain, in Berlin, and in Ems, but despite great success Offenbach was failing financially. In his enthusiasm for dazzling display, he was spending too much for costumes and décor. His response—made possible by a new license in 1858 permitting him to produce two-act plays—was to write a larger work in the hope of greater profits: *Orpheus in Hades*. *Orpheus* was written on the run with creditors in pursuit, and Offenbach was further tormented by an unusually slow production by his librettists. Finally completed in October of 1858, it achieved merely a *succès d'estime*, and Offenbach feared it would close after eighty performances.

The plot suggests that *Orpheus* was a parody on Napoleon III and the court at the Tuileries: Jupiter is shown making love to many pretty girls in the full knowledge of his jealous wife, Juno. The remaining gods all imitated the example of the master. Pluto, hoping to escape the punishment due him for the abduction of Eurydice, tries to arouse the gods against Jupiter, who, wishing to maintain his position at any cost, announces he will lead the gods to Hell, and is thereupon acclaimed by them.

The authors then introduced a character called Public Opinion who represents the social conventions of honor, fidelity, and faith. Public Opinion insists that Orpheus demand that Jupiter arrange the return of his beloved Eurydice. Thanks to a legal loophole, Jupiter forces Orpheus to renounce Eurydice and to disappear along with Public Opinion. The moral seems to be that the great and powerful can ride roughshod over Public Opinion with impunity. Finally, the Olympians of the court agree to tread on social conventions. Bending spinelessly to Jupiter's will, they espouse the dissolute life and sink into drunkenness on the road to Hell.

Six weeks after the opening, an article appeared in the *Journal des débats* by Jules Janin, who was ordinarily friendly to Offenbach's gay productions. He termed *Orpheus* "blasphemous" in accusing Offenbach of profaning "holy and glorious antiquity"; but he saved the show by qualifying it as morally outrageous. Attendance rose instantly, and *Orpheus* ran for 228 performances instead of closing after eighty. In April, 1860, the Emperor commanded a special performance which, alone, netted Offenbach 22,000 francs and a note of thanks from His Majesty for "an unforgettable evening."

To honor the success of *Orpheus*, Offenbach gave a costume

party. The invitations revealed his puckish wit. Guests were asked to wear historical costumes, but those wearing antediluvian costumes would be admitted only with special reservation. Upon payment of five francs, guests would be entitled to be called "My Prince" for the evening, "*Monsieur le Duc*" for four francs seventy-five, "My General" for three francs, "Dear Master" for two francs fifteen, and "Old Girl" for one franc. "My dear, Dear little girl, or other pickings for fifteen centimes, and assorted small terms of endearment at a just price."

On October 20, 1858, the day before *Orpheus* opened, Emma Livry made her sensational debut and inaugurated a great period of French ballet. After *Orpheus* closed, Offenbach—encouraged by his patron Morny, who was a friend of the ballet—began work on a two-set ballet, *Le Papillon*, in which Emma Livry was to star. Rehearsals began at the Opera in 1860 under Offenbach's direction, with many of the dancers, including Emma, refusing to wear costumes which had been "carteronized." An imperial decree of November 27, 1859, had commanded that all scenery and costumes used at the Opera be treated with a new solution, invented by Carteron, which made them fireproof; but as it also made costumes appear stiff and soiled, the women protested in particular.

As a result, one of the minor subjects did catch fire during a rehearsal, and though she was saved Offenbach was much upset by what he regarded as a bad omen. And so it was. Two years later, during a dress rehearsal of Auber's *La Muette de Portici*, Emma Livry's skirt caught fire from a wing-light. Horribly burned, she agonized for four months as all Paris counted the days and weeks. Her death was regarded as a national calamity, and the funeral at Notre-Dame drew a swarm of the great and small.

The passing of Emma Livry was a serious blow to French ballet. Its heydey began with her debut and ended in 1870, the year that Delibes's *Coppélia* was produced. After that, the great figures of the ballet were gone, and the rising popularity of Wagnerian opera put ballet under a cloud. The French ballet did not enjoy a renaissance until the twentieth century, when it was stimulated by the impact of Russian ballet.

In the years before 1870, Wagner was more controversial than popular in Paris. Offenbach detested his work and, in the *Carnival of Reviews* (1860), made his sentiments known. He opened the skit with Wagner, surrounded by Mozart, Gluck, and Weber, telling them that their music was fit only for dogs. Then the "musician of the future" presented two examples of his best work: a *Symphony of the Future*, whose themes he enumerated loudly as they progressed, and the *Tyrolian of the Future*, which was a burlesque of Tyrolian songs orchestrated and roared in Wagnerian fashion.

In the following spring, the presentation of *Tannhäuser* under the sponsorship of the Emperor and Princess von Metternich, the Austrian Ambassadress, produced a celebrated riot despite the support given Wagner from the crown. The gentlemen of the Jockey-Club, who patronized opera for its ballet (they preferred good legs to voices), insisted that the ballet appear in the second act of an opera, as their busy lives rarely permitted their arrival at the Opera for the first act. Wagner put the ballet of *Tannhäuser* in the first act, and for this sin the gentlemen led a demonstration which assured the opera's failure. The renown of this incident, however, has obscured the prior failures of Wagner's works in Paris, which were achieved without benefit of the Jockey-Club.

If the French ultimately began to see merit in Wagner, Offenbach never did. Nor did Wagner approve of Offenbach. He wrote of Offenbach's music that it "released the odor of manure from where all the pigs of Europe had come to wallow," and only in old age did he relent to the point of comparing Offenbach to Mozart.

Wagner aside, Offenbach was favorably disposed toward the leading composers of his day. In the case of Rossini and Meyerbeer, the regard was mutual, but Berlioz and Saint-Saëns were sharply critical of Offenbach. When Offenbach read the memoirs of Berlioz, he made many caustic marginal notes revealing that he was stung by Beriloz's hostility, but he never deviated from his belief that Berlioz was the first composer of the age. In 1854, when the Academy saw fit to pass over Berlioz in electing Clapisson, an indignant Offenbach praised Berlioz in an article in *L'Artiste*. Later, when Berlioz was elected to the Academy, Offenbach wrote, "It was merited."

After five years of outstanding music-hall successes, Offenbach was himself recognized as a composer of merit. In 1860, the year Offenbach became naturalized, the Opéra-Comique asked him to produce a new work for Christmas Eve. He presented *Barkouf*, which called for a dog on stage and music which imitated the barking of a dog; rather impolitic for a debut at the Opéra-Comique. The piece failed, and the press wrote of his "*chiennerie*" (shamelessness). A later attempt to revive *Barkouf* using a cow instead of a dog fared no better.

Successes were the rule, however, and not failures. Beginning in 1857, he went annually to Ems. The international set adored his productions, and once, in a week's time, he wrote *Lischen et Fritzchen* on a bet, which used Alsatian dialect as well as French and German. These trips gave him opportunity to take the waters for his rheumatism and gout from which he would suffer the rest of his life. Offenbach was popular in Vienna, too, which led the Imperial Opera to commission a grand opera. Having always hoped to crown his career with a serious opera, Offenbach eagerly accepted the commission. His *Rhine Fairies* was presented in February, 1864, and the Viennese press was unanimous in recommending his return to operetta. All was not lost, however, as he later salvaged the Elfs' song from this production, renaming it the Barcarole.

Offenbach's greatest success to date had been *Orpheus*. The galling failure in Vienna moved him to return to antiquity for a new theme: Helen of Troy. *La Belle Hélène* was a logical successor to *Orpheus* in that the latter was a picture of high society giving itself over to frivolity and drink, while *La Belle Hélène* suggested the resulting catastrophe. Offenbach gives us a Helen who has become bored with the unending gaiety and who seeks escape in love. Thus she becomes easy prey for her seducer:

Paris. The Greek kings are little better than imbeciles, while the augur, obviously representing the clergy, is indifferent to maintaining even the appearance of piety. The summing up is done by Orestes, who strides along a Spartan boulevard, surrounded by women, and sings:

> With these women Orestes
> Makes papa's money dance;
> Papa laughs, however, as
> It is Greece who will pay.

A majority of the critics again disapproved the profaning of the antique, but the public agreed with Henri Rochefort and Jules Vallès that *La Belle Hélène* deserved applause. It enjoyed a long run in Paris and succeeded in Berlin and Vienna as well. In fact, the successful use of classical figures made Offenbach suspect that contemporary subjects might well fail. Thus his astonishment the following year (1866) when his *La Vie parisienne* was acclaimed. His success did not derive from locale, but from his mastery of the comic opera form.

As Offenbach's fame dated from the Exposition of 1855, he sought to exploit the Exposition of 1867 in the hope of a greater triumph and needed profits. He prepared *The Grand Duchess of Gerolstein* to open coincidentally with the Exposition; a parody on absolute power, it also joked about war. The piece featured General Boum, whose bravery was equaled by his incapacity. His battle plan, presented to the Supreme War Council, was a compilation of the comic elements of real war, and he periodically fired his pistol into the air that he might take snuff by breathing the odor of gunpowder. His ignorance of the causes of the war for which he was preparing made his enthusiasm for the war ridiculous, but no more ridiculous than the actual cause: Baron Puck, councilor to the Grand Duchess, wanted a new distraction. Meanwhile, the Grand Duchess raised a gunner named Fritz to be a general, because she loved him, and then reduced him because he remained loyal to his Wanda.

Napoleon III viewed the spectacle on April 24th, twelve days after the opening, giving the audience the double fascination of the farce and His Majesty's reaction to it. He was seen to laugh and smile, but also to wind the tips of his mustache—ever the sign of his perplexity. Alexander II, coming for the Exposition, telegraphed ahead from Cologne to his ambassador in Paris to reserve him a seat. He had heard that the court of Gerolstein was a parody on the court of Russia and wished to check on it personally; but Bismarck, who saw the *Grand Duchess* a few days later, saw the locale in the petty courts of Germany, and found it hilarious.

Hortense Schneider, who played the Grand Duchess, was the most celebrated performer of the day. The public hailed her as the demolisher of all consecrated subjects, while the intelligentsia shuddered in agreement. Born in Bordeaux to a German immigrant tailor and his French wife, Hortense descended on Paris in 1855 at the age of twenty-two. She was introduced to Offenbach, who hired her after hearing her sing. For several years she was overshadowed by Lise Tautin, whom Offenbach had hired in Brussels. Tautin was most celebrated as Eurydice in *Orpheus;* in the second act her "Bacchus is King" and a particularly spritely cancan always brought down the house. But in the 1860's Hortense gained the inside track, and Lise quickly faded.

As the beautiful Helen and the Grand Duchess of Gerolstein, Hortense Schneider reigned supreme, though she was impudently challenged for a time by the pantomimist Lea Silly, who played Orestes in *La Belle Hélène*. Silly, who believed that nudity was the key to success on stage, dared to mimic the great Schneider's gestures. Audiences were delighted, but not Hortense. A quarrel of the most polished felinity began backstage and ended in an exchange of letters published by both parties in *Figaro*.

Both actresses were admired by heads of state, Schneider claiming to have found Alexander II of Russia at the stage door, but Lea Silly often boasted of her unique patron whom she met on a tour of the United States. Colonel Fisk, the New York impresario, arranged a date in Salt Lake City, where Silly's troup gave a command performance for Brigham Young. He was delighted, and wanted to convert her—in the hope that she would join his other wives.

Ismail, Khedive of Egypt, was a Schneider admirer. Taking the waters in Vichy in 1867, the Khedive longed to see her and gave his secretary orders to invite Schneider down for a visit. The secretary, who mistook the image in the Khedive's mind, wrote to Eugène Schneider, the armaments manufacturer, who supplied most of the weapons for the Egyptian Army. An equerry met Schneider at the train, escorted him to a private apartment in the Grand Hotel, which was loaded with flowers and perfumes, and invited him to bathe while awaiting the Khedive's arrival. There is not, alas, any record of the Khedive's expression upon entering the bath.

Hortense Schneider did not limit her attentions to crowned heads. For a time she was mistress to the Duc de Gramont-Caderousse, who was the unofficial leader of the *Cocodès*. The latter, a slang expression roughly equivalent to *swells*, included nearly one hundred fast-living gentlemen, mostly of aristocratic origin but with a sprinkling of officers of the Guard. Their activities encompassed gambling, racing, dueling, and making love. Rich young men of the bourgeoisie were usually unable to crash this élite, but Russian aristocrats, known in particular for their immoderation, were always welcome. The group included Baron d'Auriol, Comte d'Hérisson, Prince Demidov, Duc de Rivoli, and the Prince of Orange—called Prince Citron in Paris.

The "Ogresses" were the female counterpart of the *Cocodès*: nearly one hundred women of obscure origin who lived in a dazzling state of unrelieved luxury and who favored members of the Jockey-Club in particular. The prestige of these courtesans was so great that it was common, during the Second Empire, not only for the *demi-monde* to meet the *haute monde* socially, but for the latter to emulate the former.

Among the hundred courtesans, a select few held the limelight: Anna Deslions who sent the elect for the evening an advance notice of the cost of her gown as an index for his total bill; Giulia Barrucci who prided herself in never refusing a member of an elegant club; Marguerite Bellanger who became His Majesty's mistress in 1863; Juliette Beau who found time to play in Offenbach's *Daphnis et Chloé;* and Cora Pearl (whose name had been necessarily changed from Emma Crouch) who introduced the use of heavy makeup and was characterized by Prince Gorchakov as the last word in voluptuousness.

As the Ogresses had little to recommend them, aside from their professional perfection, the society of the Second Empire might well have been served by better models. The story is told of the Ogress who refused an invitation to stroll in the Bois de Boulogne because she had just begun reading Renan's *Life of Jesus* and was eager to see how the story ended.

The outside world regarded the corrupt shenanigans of these few as the national tendency, but the masses of the French—including the Republicans—had little sympathy for such foolery. "Paris," Henri Rochefort wrote, "which has been called the head of France, is no more than legs." Offenbach's gaiety reflected the frivolity of this "élite," and in the confusion of causes and effects he was often held responsible for their frivolity. This was patently unjust, but if he did not create frivolity he made himself its parasite. As *Orpheus* and *La Belle Hélène* reveal, he knew the penalty for indifference and irresponsibility in high places, but his moralizing was swamped by the fantastic abundance and originality of his lighthearted themes and musical ideas.

The guilt for giddiness belonged not to Offenbach but to those whose social position ought to have dictated responsible leadership rather than self-indulgence. Occasional frivolity is not a crime, but perpetual frivolity is. The society which loved *opéra bouffe* too much was fatally cushioned against reality. Brilliantly superficial, these pleasure-mad few could take up Jupiter's cry in *Orpheus:* "Let us maintain appearances, for they alone count!" The diplomat Edouard Thouvenel remarked, "The success of *Orpheus in Hades* makes me doubt the future of France," with which the writer Maxime Du Camp agreed: "To repudiate the love for the beautiful, to delight in mediocrity, to seek out the amusing at any price is to take a path from whence there is no salvation."

Offenbach's good fortune rapidly faded after 1867, his dominance in *opéra bouffe* dating between the two Expositions. Some

critics have theorized that Offenbach's decline was wrought by
the increasingly serious international situation which made frivolity unseemly; another suggests that Offenbach was outmoded
by the swing toward Liberal Empire; that is, that facing the
"realities of democracy" finished the "sense of unreality" characteristic of the Second Empire. Such notions are incorrect because they do not account for the new successes of Hervé and
Lecocq which began in 1868.

Offenbach had been working at a furious pace for many years.
By 1868 new ideas were coming hard, and the continual encroachment of rheumatism made him peevish. Thus, working
with him to perfect productions became increasingly difficult
as the quality of the raw material declined.

The outbreak of war in 1870 found Offenbach taking the
waters at Ems. He left immediately for Etretat. As the war went
unfavorably for France, Offenbach grew increasingly nervous
about Prussian accusations that he had written anti-German
songs—which was untrue. But he had, in 1862, written a hymn
entitled "God Save the Emperor," so that, after the Empire's
fall, he feared the French more than the Prussians. Deciding on a
temporary exile as in 1848, he sent his family to San Sebastian
and divided his time between Spain and Italy. His suffering was
twofold: he regretted his Prussian birth and the collapse of his
reputation in Paris. Imagine his humiliation when the returning
Prussian troops were honored with a production of *La Vie
parisienne* in Berlin!

In 1871 Offenbach went to Vienna for the production of his
Les Brigands, and in August he ventured into Paris to direct its
performance. He found himself unwelcome; simultaneously he
was accused of being an unwitting agent of Bismarck's success
(diverting the public's attention from reality) and an ardent
Bonapartist. It was true, of course, that he had been raised to
the Legion of Honor in 1861 and thus was compromised in the
eyes of many Republicans.

Politics alone, however, cannot be blamed for Offenbach's
decline. He had lost his genius for lively tunes, and his wit seemed
dulled. *Le Roi Carotte* (King Carrot) succeeded in 1872 only

because it was a spectacle, and his *Fantasio* failed miserably, as did *Le Corsaire noir* in Vienna. Recognizing that he was finished if he did not either produce spectacles featuring nudity or raise operetta to the level of true light opera in the style of Lecocq, Offenbach chose the former. He exhumed *Orpheus in Hades*, reworked it to remove the satire, and presented in February, 1873, "an exhibition of legs and décor." It was successful.

He then turned to the alternative: the light opera. He wrote *La Jolie Parfumeuse* (The Pretty Perfumer), which had over two hundred performances beginning in late 1873. Certain that he had regained his magic touch, he sank 360,000 francs into the production of *La Haine* (The Grudge). Utter failure left him with a staggering debt. Worse, new names had obscured his. By 1875 Wagner was growing in popularity, Strauss enjoyed sensational success in Paris, and Bizet had just presented his opera *Carmen*.

An offer to conduct at the Philadelphia Exposition seemed to be his salvation, and in the hope of great profits he sailed for New York in August, 1876. Enthusiastically received in New York, where he produced open-air concerts, Offenbach went on to a triumph in Philadelphia, but when it came time to sail for home (July of 1877) he was depressed by the knowledge that France was safely Republican.

All his professional life Offenbach had been ambitious to write a grand opera, but his Viennese fiasco in 1864 suggested that the dream would be unfulfilled. Yet, in 1877, he began work on another opera, because he felt the approach of death; it would be a fantastic opera in memory of his own fantastic life: *The Tales of Hoffmann*. The producers all were shy, remembering the financial losses from *La Haine*, but in the meantime a military operetta called *La Fille du tambour-major* (The Daughter of the Regiment) scored an unexpected success in 1879–1880.

Offenbach's infirmity increased. On the morning of October 4, 1880, sitting in bed with the manuscript of *The Tales of Hoffmann* before him, he suffered a heart attack which he was confident would be fatal. Death came the following morning to deprive him of the happiness of seeing his dream opera produced.

The Tales of Hoffmann opened on the following February 10th at the Opéra-Comique and won rousing applause. A similar success was achieved in Vienna, but on the second night—just before curtain time—the Ringtheater burned down, which gave rise to a superstitious fear of the opera. In consequence, many theaters have refused to produce it. More than Offenbach could have known, he had fashioned a fitting memorial: a fantastic story, vivacious music, a brilliant setting—all overshadowed by death and fear.

V

Sainte-Beuve

SULTAN OF LITERATURE

Criticism is a profession which requires healthiness more than genius.
—JEAN DE LA BRUYÈRE

From the start, Sainte-Beuve's life was a series of unsatisfactory relationships with women. Born on December 23, 1804, in Boulogne to parents who had married late, Charles-Augustin Sainte-Beuve was reared in the company of two staid, humorless widows. Mme. Sainte-Beuve had lost her husband two months before the birth of her child and was immediately joined by her widowed sister. The deceased father had been a civil servant with a fondness for Greek and Latin, but his widow had no literary interests.

Their home knew no laughter or gaiety; and to the loneliness of living with elderly women was added the loneliness of being a precocious child. The boy was studious by nature and did well in the local primary school. Furthermore, he imposed upon himself long evening and morning prayers, which became increasingly intense as he became aware of sensual pleasures. He did not understand such pleasures, and they alarmed him. That he remained in good physical health under such a régime probably derived from his fondness for the beach and for swimming in the sea.

At the age of thirteen, this boy, who had already been aroused by Latin poetry, was sent to the Lycée Charlemagne in Paris. Here the influence of François Daunou, a former member of the Convention and an atheist, was paramount, and Sainte-Beuve became attached to the republican principles of the French Revolution and to atheism. The teaching of Lamarck made its impression too, cultivating an interest in science strong enough to compete with Sainte-Beuve's interest in literature. In choosing a profession, he was torn between law and medicine, veering toward the latter ultimately because it contributed more to relieve human suffering.

The sensitivity which directed Sainte-Beuve into medicine is also revealed in his adolescent writings. At sixteen he observed that for the person of live imagination, who may sense himself touched with genius, the "most terrible period of life" is that between childhood and adulthood.

Medicine, however, never satisfied Sainte-Beuve, and his earlier interest in literature returned. He sought out a former teacher, Paul François Dubois, for advice. Dubois had been dismissed from the Université for his liberal opinions and had founded a journal called *Le Globe*. He hired Sainte-Beuve as a writer, but urged him to continue his medical studies. Sainte-Beuve always credited his medical training for giving him a taste for precision and material reality; presumably, he also became more anticlerical in this period, thanks to the increased interference by the clergy in educational questions during the Restoration, which angered the medical profession in particular.

Dubois, meanwhile, set Sainte-Beuve to following the daily progress of the Greek Revolution. *Le Globe* was a literary journal, and political reporting was forbidden it by law. Thus, Sainte-Beuve was cautioned to write only of Greek geography and literature, but the experience was useful in developing his style and tone. His tastes were soon evident: liberalism, moderation, tolerance, and propriety.

Next, Dubois gave Sainte-Beuve two volumes of Victor Hugo to review, the *Odes* and *Ballades,* and the two reviews appeared in January, 1827. The poet was then twenty-five, the critic twenty-two. He congratulated Hugo on his versification and style, noting that the lines were always grammatically correct, and suggested that Hugo was a poet of enormous talent. He warned Hugo, however, against the excessive use of imagination —against the fantastic: "In poetry, as elsewhere, nothing is so risky as power. If uncontrolled, power is abusive, and what was once original and novel becomes bizarre."

The reviews were significant, too, in that they encouraged Hugo to proceed with his divorce from the Christian Romanticism of Chateaubriand. The latter had become a Christian during the troubled times of the French Revolution, when he had suffered great privation. He came to believe in a religion of the heart, and upheld emotional conviction against the Rationalism and irreligion of the eighteenth century, which he regarded as responsible for the chaos of his time. These notions were expressed in his *Génie du Christianisme* (1802), along with his faith that Christianity was compatible with the science of modern civilization. As he favored constitutional monarchy too, Chateaubriand's political and religious ideas were regarded as orthodox by the government of Louis XVIII, and both Hugo and Lamartine had begun to write with these orthodox Restoration views.

In 1827, then, the materialistic, republican Sainte-Beuve urged Hugo to separate himself from royal politics and Christianity and to become a truly independent poet. In fact, both Hugo and Lamartine did veer away from Restoration orthodoxy by 1830; and, by becoming more independent, they became more Romantic. Hugo was grateful for the penetrating criticism given his poetry in *Le Globe* and came to thank Dubois. In this way he met Sainte-Beuve; they became great friends.

Shortly after, when Hugo moved to 11 rue Notre-Dame-des-Champs, Sainte-Beuve moved into number 19. As neighbors, they became the center of a literary circle, providing Sainte-Beuve with a social life which he had never known. Delacroix, Mérimée, Dumas, De Vigny, Lamartine, and De Musset were often present, but Sainte-Beuve was happiest when he could discuss poetry with Hugo alone. Hugo would chat about his verse construction, his rhythm, about which Sainte-Beuve wrote: "I quickly grasped new things which I heard for the first time and which, in an instant, opened a window for me on style and the composition of verse." He showed Sainte-Beuve poems no one else had yet seen, because he felt that Sainte-Beuve had a true poetic sense, revealed more in his conversation than in his reviews.

Theirs was a profitable friendship from which Sainte-Beuve derived encouragement, while Hugo basked in the admiration of the young critic whose obvious talent made his admiration flattering. Paradoxically, Hugo began his retreat from Chateaubriand's Christianity at this time, spurred on by Sainte-Beuve, who himself was feeling a growing dissatisfaction with materialism.

Hugo's drama *Hernani* was first performed in 1830 at the Théâtre-Français. The story and setting emphasized the bizarre at the expense of historical and psychological truth, but in its individualism the drama was vivid and poetic. The author's Romanticist friends came to the opening dressed in fantastic costumes to celebrate their victory over the "bourgeois," though the fisticuffs which enriched the intermissions during the evening suggested that their victory bulletins had been premature. The occasion was, nevertheless, memorable, and the Romanticists proved their vigor if nothing else.

The castigation of the "bourgeois," so frequent by the artists and the intelligentsia of the nineteenth century, can be misleading if the word *bourgeois* is merely translated as meaning "middle class." They understood *bourgeois* to mean a spirit—an attitude—rather than a class; they despised those who were acquisitive and who regarded disinterestedness as obvious folly. Acquisitiveness was an apparent characteristic of businessmen, it is true, but to suppose that they were the sole repositories of greed was to ignore a notoriously tight-fisted peasantry and the young aristocrat's traditional preference for a moneyed fiancée. More to the point, then, was the creative person's natural aversion to those who never subordinated their personal interests to exterior claims.

Sainte-Beuve fought against the bourgeois at the Battle of Hernani too, but not with the zeal of his fellow Romanticists. Several days after, he told Hugo that he had decided not to review *Hernani* in the *Revue de Paris*, whose staff he had recently joined, though he admitted that *Hernani* was a wonderful drama. He begged off by claiming to be unable to account for why it was wonderful. This was not the last time that Sainte-Beuve sacrificed his role of honest critic to personal pique.

He had fallen in love with Madame Hugo—Adèle—and suffered from the torment that his love was unrequited. His annoyance grew as the Hugo home was crowded with an enthusiastic horde of Bohemians, and he saw his beloved subjected to their uninhibited manners. The landlord soon put an end to the invasion by threatening to evict the Hugos, sparing Sainte-Beuve the necessity of fleeing the neighborhood. His unhappiness affected the Hugos, who did not understand its cause, but who were fond of him. "I am not hated," Sainte-Beuve admitted to another friend, "but my trouble and my crime are not being loved as I should like to be."

In a highly emotional state, Sainte-Beuve grew impertinent one day at *Le Globe* and was slapped with a glove by Dubois. A harmless duel in a rainstorm followed with Sainte-Beuve firing from beneath an umbrella. Subsequently, he confessed his problem to Hugo, who treated the whole matter with dignity. Hugo insisted that their friendship could continue, though he proposed to defend the integrity of his household by not permitting Sainte-Beuve to enter. The latter showed himself to be unreasonable and never forgave Hugo, continuing to covet his neighbor's wife.

Sainte-Beuve was aware that he was not physically attractive, perhaps accounting for the publicity he gave the affair. He maintained, after the break in 1831, that she had not been "unaware" of him. And, indeed, when Hugo took a mistress the following year (Juliette Drouet), Adèle began a liaison with Sainte-Beuve which lasted until 1836; and she continued to be his friend after that: his sole success in love.

During the years of their close friendship, however, Hugo did inflate Sainte-Beuve's desire to become a poet by assuring him that he could easily equal Lamartine. Sainte-Beuve's first volume (1828) was criticism, *A Description of French Poetry in the Sixteenth Century*, but the following year he published his first book of poems under the title *The Life, Poems, and Thought of Joseph Delorme*. That the work was Sainte-Beuve's, and not the recently deceased Delorme's, was generally known. In it, he advocated poetic freedom, meaning a careful avoidance of imitating masters. The volume also contained Sainte-Beuve's definition of the critical spirit, written when he was twenty-five years old:

It is the nature of the critical spirit to be quick, suggestive, versatile, and comprehensive. The critical spirit is like a large, clear stream, which winds and spreads out around the works and monuments of poetry as around the boulders, castles, vineyard-coated hills, and the luxuriant valleys which border its banks. While each one of these

rural objects remains fixed in its place, undisturbed by its neighbors
—the feudal tower indifferent to the vale and the vale unaware of
the hills—the river flows from one to the other, bathes them without
injuring them, encircles them with fresh running water, understands
them, reflects them; and when the traveller is curious to know and to
visit these varied places, it takes him in a small boat, carries him without jolts, and develops for him in an orderly fashion the sights as they
change on course.

He published a second volume of verse in 1830, *Consolations*,
which showed—despite Sainte-Beuve's advocacy of independence—the influence of the Lake poets, Wordsworth and Cole-
ridge in particular. And, in turn, Sainte-Beuve's sensualism and
his taste for the English poets influenced subsequent French
poetry, especially that of Coppée, Verlaine, and Baudelaire. Evidence of Sainte-Beuve's religious anxiety can be found in *Consolations*. His materialism left him unsatisfied; he wanted to believe,
to know God:

> Pour arriver à Toi, c'est assez de vouloir,
> Je voudrais bien, Seigneur; je veux; pourquoi ne puis-je?

Meanwhile, Sainte-Beuve was making his reputation as a critic,
and during the July Monarchy his articles began appearing in the
Revue des deux mondes. He was also known to be spiteful, lust-
ful, and particularly interested in the lives of women. Meeting
George Sand in 1833 after favorably reviewing her novel *Indiana*,
he became her literary adviser for a time. She gave him parts of
Lélia to read, the novel in which she confessed her physical impotence; Sainte-Beuve was not only impressed by the insight
and the courage of the author, but understood that she probably
hoped to develop a liaison with him. Despite his reputation, he
shrank from such a relationship with her. Sand had recently
suffered a miserable sexual fiasco with Prosper Mérimée, the
details of which had regaled the literary world. Few men could
have been expected to be eager for a liaison whose intimacies
might become the next sensation for the literati.

The literary portraits which Sainte-Beuve began publishing
in the *Revue des deux mondes* in 1832 did not prevent him from

also working on a novel. *Volupté*, his only novel, appeared in
1834. Lacking action and imagination, the book was long on
moral discussions and boring orations. Sainte-Beuve learned
from writing it that he was too scholarly to find the novel a
congenial form.

The plot of *Volupté* centered on an analysis of the passion for
vice. A priest, torn by carnal desire, fell in love with a married
woman (Sainte-Beuve and Mme. Hugo?). After great anguish,
the priest confessed his passion to the woman's husband, who
(unlike Hugo) regarded the situation as quite normal and urged
the priest to join their household. Ultimately, the husband and
wife lost their only son, which had the effect of drawing them
together and forced the departure of the erring priest. In the
end, the dying woman requested that her former lover perform
the last rites. Sainte-Beuve's moral seems to be that a man cannot
separate his life into two parts; the life of the heart and the life
of the mind must become reconciled. Otherwise, one's will is
destroyed and the intelligence squandered.

While Sainte-Beuve's search for spiritual satisfaction was not
apparent in *Volupté*, this period of his life was characterized
by his search for religion to replace the materialism of his medi-
cal-school days. As early as 1828, he grew interested in La Mennais's Liberal Catholicism, because of its attacks upon legitimate
monarchy. When La Mennais and his disciples convened at the
Oratorian College of Juilly (1830–1831), Sainte-Beuve often
joined the group and was moved by their spirituality; but he
remained an observer and was not a convert. Sainte-Beuve's later
influence upon La Mennais is questionable, but it is generally
agreed that he urged La Mennais to stand firm against the conservatism of Rome and, in 1836, arranged for the publication of
La Mennais's article "Les Affaires de Rome," which made a reconciliation between La Mennais and the Papacy impossible.

Sainte-Beuve also investigated Saint-Simonianism, called the
"new Christianity" by the founders of the cult. Saint-Simonianism was utopian socialism. The cult was organized shortly after
the death of Saint-Simon in 1825, a humanitarian—and materialistic—religion. By 1830 Sainte-Beuve often attended their meet-

ings, and Holy Father Enfantin, one of the two Saint-Simonian popes, regarded Sainte-Beuve as a probable convert. No doubt Sainte-Beuve was attracted by a cult which classed artists and writers among the useful (productive) members of society; but, like so many other members of the intelligentsia who were favorable to the humanitarian and materialistic ideals of the cult, Sainte-Beuve was repelled by the ludicrous ritual with which the cultists hoped to impress the world. And paeans to industrial production, sung in the style of Christian hymns, aroused more hilarity than piety. Nevertheless, Sainte-Beuve later avowed that Enfantin had taught him to honor and respect Industry, that art could and ought to be useful and, in consequence, that literary criticism could be construed to be beneficial for society—to be a means for perfecting society.

Saint-Simonianism, however, did not teach Sainte-Beuve to love life ("Sick you found me, and sick you left me"), and he looked still further for a satisfactory religion. Perhaps it was his anger at Rome's treatment of La Mennais that made him turn next to Jansenism. He proposed to study the history of Jansenism, and applied to the government for a post at the Ecole normale in the hope of subsidizing his research by teaching; but he was informed that he must produce the book before an appointment could be made.

He went to Switzerland, then, in 1837, with his book merely in outline, and with the aid of friends secured a teaching position in Lausanne. He thus developed the structure of the book by preparing eighty-one lectures, which were delivered over a seven-month period. His additional public lectures were popular, because such problems as predestination and grace commanded interest in this region that had known much theological controversy; but Sainte-Beuve was far less successful in the classroom. His inexperience and austerity were serious barriers for younger students.

The published results of his study of Jansenism were slow in coming. The first volume appeared in 1840, the last in 1850. He entitled the work *Port-Royal*. The study of Jansenism impressed Sainte-Beuve with the moral excellence of Christianity, but as a

Romantic, an individualist, he recoiled from the Jansenist belief in predestination, failing again to find his faith, and *Port-Royal* ended in a pessimistic key:

How limited is our vision; how quickly it becomes fixed! It resembles a pale star which ignites for a moment in the midst of an immense night. He who has taken the learning of his subject most to heart, who gave the most effort to comprehend it and felt the most pride in depicting it, feels himself powerless and beneath his task and . . . perceives that [his learning] is only the most fleeting of illusions in the heart of infinite illusion.

The first volume of *Port-Royal* helped Sainte-Beuve secure the head librarianship of the Bibliothèque Mazarine, which gave him an income independent from his newspaper articles. The book's success, in fact, led him to hope for election to the Académie française, a hope which Hugo's election in 1841 only heightened. Sainte-Beuve presented himself as a candidate in 1843, but received only seventeen of the necessary eighteen votes—Hugo not supporting him. In the following year he was a successful candidate, and his reception took place on February 25, 1845. It fell to Hugo to receive him.

Newly elected academicians were always presented to the king, and while Sainte-Beuve counted himself a Republican he agreed to the presentation. This ceremony was his sole appearance at the Tuileries during the July Monarchy. He had, in fact, no particular grievance against Louis-Philippe, but regarded him as insufficiently royal to be a king and too bourgeois to be respected long by the bourgeois. Sainte-Beuve's failure to find a satisfactory religious faith led him into skepticism, which left him increasingly indifferent to political dogmatism and less vigorous in attacking political institutions.

Nevertheless, he had never publicly disavowed his republicanism and was, therefore, outraged to be badly treated by the Republic of 1848. The revolutionary government of that year carefully examined the financial records of the previous régime, and Sainte-Beuve's was among the names claimed to have been the beneficiaries of Louis-Philippe's largesse. He protested in vain.

Unable to clear his name, he resigned from the Mazarine and accepted a professorship of French literature at Liège. The French republican press hooted his departure as if he were fleeing the country.

The situation ultimately became somewhat clearer when the financial records in question were published. In 1847 Sainte-Beuve had paid one hundred francs to have the fireplace in his room at the Académie repaired. The government recompensed him, but as the sum was acknowledged too late by the government to be included in that year's regular budget it was paid out of a secret fund. The bureaucrat examining these lists either thought the evidence suggested that Sainte-Beuve had received much more than the hundred francs or (as Sainte-Beuve believed) was an embittered author whose work had not fared well at the critic's hands.

The death of Chateaubriand on July 4, 1848, followed by that of his long-time friend Mme. Récamier ten months later, prompted Sainte-Beuve to begin a critical study of Chateaubriand. Ever since beginning the work on *Port-Royal*, Sainte-Beuve—in abandoning the poetic for the historical—had sought to reexamine his earlier judgments. Formerly, as a Republican and a materialist, Sainte-Beuve had advised Hugo to abandon Chateaubriand's Christian-Royalism; in 1849 he recognized Chateaubriand's influence on nineteenth century writers: "We are your sons, and our glory is to be called one of yours."

But Sainte-Beuve, so long the unsuccessful seeker after religious truth, refused to believe that Chateaubriand was a convinced Christian. "M. de Chateaubriand," he wrote, "was only a great actor in search—like all great actors—of a place to deploy his talent." He claimed that Chateaubriand was always ready to sacrifice truth to beauty, and had found Christianity an emotional, beautiful realm. As further evidence of Chateaubriand's dishonesty, he recalled Chateaubriand's abandonment of Charles X as opportunism. Such a judgment had an insincere ring, coming from a man who would shortly convert his Republicanism into Bonapartism. And what better description of Sainte-Beuve's own relation to Christianity than his analysis of Chateaubriand's?

Once Sainte-Beuve's year's appointment was completed in Liège, he gladly returned to France, for he had not been well received in Belgium. On October 1, 1849, he joined his fourth newspaper staff, *Le Constitutionnel,* when its publisher, Dr. Véron, offered him a weekly literary column. Thus was born the *Causeries du Lundi* (the Monday Reviews) for which Sainte-Beuve is best known. Earlier, Sainte-Beuve had held that the literary critic is inferior in quality to the poet and the novelist; ultimately he came to believe that literature's object is to know mankind better and that no one literary form is a superior key to this knowledge. Earlier, he had hoped to be remembered as a poet and a novelist; now he maintained that the choice of history, drama, the novel, or criticism was unimportant.

His critical method had taken definite form by 1849: he claimed never to separate the man from his literary work. This fondness for pyschological analysis Sainte-Beuve had already revealed in his *Literary Portraits,* published in the *Revue des deux mondes* between 1832 and 1839, and in his *Portraits of Women,* which appeared in 1844. In approaching an author's work, he studied the man's family, his children, his friends, the region from which he came. What did he think of religion? How was he affected by nature? By women? By money? Was he rich or poor, and what was his daily régime? In the case of a woman writer, was she pretty? Was she loved? And if she had been converted in religion, why?

Sainte-Beuve knew, of course, that such extensive personal information was unavailable in studying many writers of the past. He also knew that some critics judged literature esthetically and were indifferent to men and morality. But Sainte-Beuve, while not indifferent to esthetics, was eager to develop criticism into a science and, hence, his fascination for a method which, in gathering evidence from which one derived conclusions, seemed scientific.

In the course of my observations, I have sensed that the day will come when Science will be so organized that the great families of minds and their principal divisions will be recognized and known. Then, the chief characteristic of a mind being known, one will be able to deduce other characteristics from that.

In the hands of a lesser critic, Sainte-Beuve's method could become little more than a statistical report of an author's life, with the literary work itself valued merely as evidence of the author's mind and nature. Sainte-Beuve's genius lay in his ability to keep order: the details of a writer's life, or the portrait itself, were never allowed to take precedence from the piece of literature he was reviewing. Furthermore, while he might insist that all literary works have historical interest and importance, his own definition of a classic revealed his belief in the timeless quality of great art and in the fact that great works must live independently from their authors:

A true classic, as I should like to hear it defined, is an author who has enriched the human mind, increased its treasure, and caused it to advance a step; who has discovered some moral and unequivocal truth, or who revealed some eternal passion in that heart where all seemed known and discovered; who has expressed his thought, observation, or invention in any form, providing it be broad and great, refined and sensible, sane and beautiful in itself; who had spoken to everyone in his individual style, a style which is found to be also universal, a style which is new without being neologistic—simultaneously new and old—easily contemporary with all time.

Called "Uncle Beuve" by the literati of the day, Sainte-Beuve seemed to preside over the literature of the Second Empire. His career spanned three régimes, but his authority seemed consecrated with the coming of Empire. In general, the writers of the period were in reaction against Romanticism, at least against the imaginative and dramatic aspects of Romanticism. Calling themselves Realists, they retained the individualism of the Romanticists in refusing to adhere to any esthetic orthodoxy; but their art became documentary, scientific, and impersonal. Most Realists saw life as harsh and mankind as weak, and in dwelling upon the seamy, more materialistic, aspects of life they rejected any notion of an otherwordly ideal. In a sense, Realism was Romanticism secularized one more step; in fact, realism in any age is a likely companion to loss of faith.

Sainte-Beuve, who had often criticized the Romanticists for their love of the bizarre, for their optimism, and for their indif-

ference to the factual, seemed to encourage Realism. Yet he never
disavowed his own Romanticism and, as if to make his case more
complex, often seemed in search of absolute truth. Perhaps he
was a Romantic who longed not to be. He was not, as a rule,
unfair to the Romanticists, his war with Balzac, for instance,
being the result of personal rather than literary animosity. Or
in the case of Hugo, whom he had come to regard as a "barbarian
king," he refrained from an attack in deference to Mme. Hugo.

Sainte-Beuve's literary dilemma was evident in his treatment
of Flaubert's work. Before writing *Madame Bovary*, Flaubert had
toured the Levant. The sight of other peoples and customs merely
confirmed his suspicion that villainy and baseness were the only
dependable universal characteristics of mankind. Never again
could he regard himself as the unique victim of injustice or misfortune, so that, in a sense, he found his own salvation in the
universality of misery. He could not withdraw from this misery,
then, but explored and probed it. "Son and brother of distinguished physicians," wrote Sainte-Beuve in his review of *Madame
Bovary*, "M. Gustave Flaubert holds the pen as others the scal-
pel."

Sainte-Beuve objected to Flaubert's opinion that truth was
only to be found on humanity's foolish or perverse side, but
recognized that Flaubert's spirit reflected the literary vogue
of the time. Flaubert, like the Goncourt brothers, was sincere
and bold. The eagerness to capture reality meant an unwillingness to avoid any words or vulgarity which might shock more
conventional souls. Noting that the Realists were unafraid of
crudity, Sainte-Beuve asked, "But are you not looking for it?"
He accused them of deliberately ignoring any aspects of life
which might modify the brutal picture they presented, and suggested that they went out of their way to insult convention.
Sainte-Beuve's Saint-Simonian tendencies were never more evident than in his warning to the Realists that it was not enough
merely to record the vulgar and the vicious; the artist, he wrote,
must offer an ideal, which is not reality perhaps, but which will
at least be practical.

Sainte-Beuve recognized, however, the technical excellence
of *Madame Bovary* and ranked Flaubert with the best writers of

the day; but this praise was overshadowed by his criticism of Flaubert's vulgarity, because Flaubert was already under attack for "offending public morality and religion." The government made the charge, and Flaubert and his editors had to face it in court.

Madame Bovary first appeared in installments in the *Revue de Paris*, a journal generally unfriendly to the government and regarded as socialistic. Knowing their vulnerability, the editors had been uncertain as to the wisdom of publishing a book whose frankness was sure to provoke the mandarins of morality. The government was not slow to take advantage of the outcry to smite the hostile journal, and the Empress in particular was solicitous to see that the trial was not postponed. Among others, Morny protested that this was shortsighted policy; that the government ought to be courting writers rather than hauling them into court.

Flaubert defended himself skillfully. Believing that everything which existed was *true* and therefore *good*, he suggested that the society which attacked him for printing what actually existed was in an immoral position. The captive court obediently censured the book, but salved its conscience by noting the literary excellence of the work and by acquitting the defendants. The trial, of course, gave the book notoriety and sale.

Sainte-Beuve and Flaubert had not always been friendly, Flaubert having been known to express his hatred for Sainte-Beuve, but the latter received *Madame Bovary* well enough to reconcile the two. Even Sainte-Beuve's denunciation of *Salammbô*, which appeared in 1862, failed to alienate them, though causing momentary hard feelings. Again, Sainte-Beuve accused Flaubert of enlarging upon the lugubrious and atrocious side of human nature; but, unlike *Madame Bovary*, which was saved by the magnificence of its realism, *Salammbô* struck the critic as operatic. He did not deny that Flaubert had achieved effects, but styled them sadistic and bloody, revealing "a bizarre sensuality." In effect, Sainte-Beuve attacked *Salammbô* as simply not good Realism, and he likened the Carthaginian setting—despite Flaubert's attempts to achieve historical accuracy—to the imaginative settings favored by the earlier Romanticists.

Sainte-Beuve's evaluation of Flaubert was better grounded

than his estimate and treatment of Baudelaire. The latter's *Fleurs du mal* was published in 1857 in the *Revue des deux mondes*, an organ of Orleanist opinion, only six months after Flaubert's session in court. Baudelaire, too, was shortly in court for offending the public morality, but regarded his prosecution as good fortune—as good advertisement. The prosecution was mild, and while the court undertook to snip a few verses from the volume and fined Baudelaire and his publishers, the proceedings had a shabby aura and the revised edition a large sale.

By remaining silent throughout the trial, Sainte-Beuve disgraced himself in the eyes of the intelligentsia. He knew that Baudelaire revered him, that Baudelaire often acknowledged the influence of Sainte-Beuve's early poems upon his own, and they called each other "dear friend." Possibly Sainte-Beuve recognized Baudelaire's talent without understanding it and, therefore, sought a noncommittal position on Baudelaire. In 1862, for example, when Baudelaire stood for the Académie française, Sainte-Beuve published an article discussing the qualifications of the various candidates. Describing Baudelaire as the builder of ingenious poetic "follies," Sainte-Beuve hinted that perhaps Baudelaire's candidacy was intended as a joke upon the Académie. His further description of Baudelaire as conventional and polite—a pleasant person—damned him with irrelevant praise.

The two writers of the period most respected by Sainte-Beuve were Hippolyte Taine and Ernest Renan. He objected to Taine's rigid environmentalism, as a Romanticist logically would, but admired Taine as a stylist. As for Renan, Sainte-Beuve wrote, "He has an aristocratic intelligence, royal in the sense of Plato." Sainte-Beuve did not recommend Renan's *Life of Jesus* for the general reader, but urged it upon those alone who had a critical spirit; he thought the book should inculcate a respect for religion. In a subsequent article several months later (1863), he admitted his disagreement with Renan on the divinity of Christ, maintaining that Christ was obviously not human. But in suggesting that several of Renan's assertions were too bold, Sainte-Beuve did not waver in his admiration for the book.

Sainte-Beuve's relations with the leading writers of the Second

Empire were certainly affected by his speedy adherence to Napoleon III's régime, questionable in particular because of his long-time Republican and anticlerical politics. Yet, having suffered serious insult from the Republic of 1848, Sainte-Beuve had lost his faith in republicanism, and he was quick to say, in 1851, that France needed security after three years of "expedients." In addition, his loss of political faith was probably conditioned by his inability to find a satisfactory religious faith.

By the time of the Second Empire, Sainte-Beuve had become a skeptic, and the numerous times he touched on Montaigne in the *Causeries du Lundi* suggests that he felt an affinity with the most celebrated of all French skeptics. He was doubtful about the possibility of reaching absolute truth, about the limits of human intelligence, and about the superiority of any one form of government. Though he had great respect for Christianity, he was haunted by the materialism of his youth. He remained loyal to the Empire for the rest of his life, but only because he thought that Empire was the governmental form most likely to maintain order in France and that order was necessary for the development of civilization, "as savagery is always present—two steps away."

In an era when politics and religion were intertwined and writers were notably dogmatic in their political and religious views, Sainte-Beuve's skepticism was inevitably regarded as opportunism. That he rallied to a régime which was abhorred by the literati was taken as conclusive proof of his opportunism.

Sainte-Beuve's articles, during the Second Empire, not only appeared in *Le Constitutionnel*, with which he had affiliated himself in 1849, but in the *Moniteur*, the government's official journal. This attachment lent support to the charge of opportunism. In addition, he wrote for the *Revue des deux mondes* again between 1863 and 1868. But if one recalls that Sainte-Beuve had been profoundly influenced by the materialistic humanitarianism of the Saint-Simonians, then his support of Louis-Napoleon, who was the darling of the Saint-Simonians and whom Sainte-Beuve called "Saint-Simon on Horseback," seems understandable.

In 1852 he wrote an article called "Regrets," whose tone smacked of opportunism and which illustrated his spitefulness.

The article was a *salut dérisoire* to the Orleanists whose hopes for a restoration had been shattered by the *coup d'état*. He mocked the vexation of these men who had ruled France for eighteen years and laughed loudest about the censorship which deprived the Orleanists of publicity. "There are worse maladies than the loss of speech; and no misfortune is less touching than those which come to the ambitious and to fallen governments." In such bad taste were these lines that Sainte-Beuve was never forgiven them, and nobody bothered to recall that he had always —not merely in 1852—been an opponent of the Orleanists.

No one can justify censorship to authors, and Sainte-Beuve was taught this lesson at first opportunity. He was appointed to the chair of Latin poetry at the Collège de France, the government's nomination having been supported by fourteen of the fifteen professors already holding chairs. He delivered his first public lecture on March 9, 1855, and was bothered by an undercurrent of rude remarks. The second lecture produced a hubbub, which drove him from the hall, and the course was suspended. He never again gave a public lecture at the Collège de France, but held the chair until his death. The recipient of many threatening letters, he went out for a time armed with a concealed knife, but suffered no attacks. As compensation for this humiliation, the government appointed Sainte-Beuve to a professorship at the Ecole normale in 1859. He was a poor teacher, as in Lausanne, but surprised his critics by lecturing favorably on Hugo, the régime's *bêtè noire*.

Though a charitable man and given to amnesties, Napoleon III was as unforgiving of Hugo as Hugo was of Napoleon III. That Hugo had fought in the streets against the *coup d'état* of 1851 was not his crime; he was guilty of the most dangerous crime against the head of a state: ridicule. The tone of *Napoléon le petit*, written in Brussels, was implicit in its title; and *Châtiments*, also written in Brussels, avowed that the "crime of the 18th Brumaire" had not been atoned for by Waterloo or St. Helena, but by the spectacle of December 2nd:

> The horrible vision faded. In despair
> The Emperor cried out with horror in the dark,
> Lowered his eyes and raised affrighted hands.

As the Belgians were nervous about the presence of many French exiles, Hugo moved to Jersey. In 1855 he removed to Guernsey after having insulted Victoria for her alliance with Napoleon and arousing the ire of Her Majesty's Jersey subjects. He endured the leisure of exile for nineteen years.

Neither Napoleon III nor Eugénie was conversant with the fine arts, but they tried to do their duty as sovereigns by inviting artists and writers to the palace. The Empress once asked an author what she could best do for literature, and was told, "Madam, you must love it"; but as good intentions alone do not make an amateur it fell to other members of the Bonaparte family to be convincing patrons of the arts, Princess Mathilde in particular. Had Princess Mathilde married Louis-Napoleon as he had originally planned, she probably would not have cracked open his head to see what went on inside—her persistent wish during the Second Empire—but would have done much to reconcile the intelligentsia to the régime.

Sainte-Beuve met the Princess in 1844, but they did not see each other regularly until 1860. The following year she invited him to dine on Wednesdays at her home, which became his custom. Though on good terms with Victor Duruy, Mathilde backed Sainte-Beuve for the Ministry of Public Instruction in 1863, but as Duruy was the Emperor's choice Sainte-Beuve was later provided a Senate seat.

Another Bonaparte princess, Julie Marquise Roccagiovini, hoped to draw Sainte-Beuve away from Mathilde's more brilliant salon, but he remained loyal to Mathilde. In consequence, Julie spread spiteful stories about him. As a bachelor whose household was run by three women—housekeeper, cook, and maid—Sainte-Beuve was a vulnerable target for gossip; but the three did not serve as a harem, as Julie implied: only the housekeeper was his mistress. Julie also accused him of having crawled on his hands and knees to get a place in the Senate. This, too, was unfair, considering that Sainte-Beuve had refused, as a matter of principle, to review the Emperor's *History of Julius Caesar*.

Shortly after his tiff with Julie, Sainte-Beuve made plans for a dinner at which Prince Jerome-Napoleon, Mathilde's brother, was to be the guest of honor. As the Prince was soon to leave

Paris, the dates available for the dinner were few, and Sainte-Beuve finally settled on Good Friday (1868). The occasion produced a scandal, because, as most of the guests were thought to be materialist and anticlerical, the consenus was that the date had been deliberately chosen to insult religious opinion. Sainte-Beuve, of course, was not irreligious, but his anticlericalism deepened in response to the outcry his dinner provoked. In the face of the storm, Mathilde began calling at his home on Sundays as if to mock public opinion.

More trouble arose later in 1868 when the Bishop of Montpellier published an attack upon a course which had been opened at the Sorbonne for girls. Sainte-Beuve wrote an article ridiculing the bishop, which featured the lines, "He had uttered a cry of alarm—the screams of an eagle—as if it were a question of saving the capital." The editor of the *Moniteur* found the lines too bold, but Sainte-Beuve refused to strike them out; instead, he sent the article to an Opposition paper, *Le Temps*. Mathilde was indignant that Sainte-Beuve should transfer to an Opposition journal for such a petty grievance. As the two were known to be good friends, she felt his action could compromise her, for she was eager to avoid the charge of being disloyal to the Emperor.

Sainte-Beuve did not regard this transfer as disloyalty to the dynasty, and thus refused to honor Mathilde's protest. Their friendship smashed in a shower of envenomed remarks, which they both soon regretted. A kidney stone was the source of Sainte-Beuve's peevishness, and accounts in part for this action which the literati found childish and ungallant. "When you have as your friend such a good-natured creature as the princess," Flaubert wrote to George Sand, "and when this friend has given you an income of thirty thousand francs a year [the Senate], you owe her a certain consideration."

People were, of course, quick to criticize Sainte-Beuve, for the role of professional critic does not earn one many friends; criticism is the thankless art form. He was so often unflatteringly characterized—"He is a mad sheep," Buloz wrote—that one might forget the authority his words carried on matters literary during the Second Empire. The Duchesse d'Abrantès could amuse her guests by calling him Sainte-Bévue (Saint Blunder), but his opinions commanded a greater audience than her puns.

He was not a prepossessing man, and he knew it: fat cheeks, large nose, protruding cheekbones, short, and quite bald, he was far from the tall, handsome swain he longed to be. He struck some as a monk, others as a cardinal, his well shaven face, fine hands, and soft voice giving the impression of an ecclesiastic rather than a rake. His home was monastic in its frugality, though chastity was not one of its rules, and he worked hard according to a rigid schedule.

Monday through Thursday was given to intensive reading and note taking. On Friday he dictated articles to a secretary, as writer's cramp made any extensive writing impossible for him. He corrected proof on Saturday and Sunday morning and appeared in print on Monday. He rarely worked on Sunday afternoons, but often strolled along the boulevards, milling with the crowd. Dinner was usually an intellectual as well as social occasion, Princess Mathilde's Wednesdays being one example. Another was the Magny dinners, named for the restaurant where a group of writers met biweekly. Proposed by Gavarni (Guillaume Chevalier) in 1862, the Magny set originally included Sainte-Beuve, the Goncourt brothers, Chennevières, and Veyne. Flaubert, Taine, Renan, Gautier, and Saint-Victor soon became members, and other literary celebrities, like George Sand, were occasional guests. The conversation was presumed to be strictly off the record, but the Goncourts recorded much in their *Journal* despite the rule. George Sand found Sainte-Beuve the best conversationalist and the most intelligent man in the group.

Sainte-Beuve grew increasingly cantankerous during his last two years, in part the result of his kidney stone. These years coincided, too, with the régime's momentary shift toward clericalism, which deeply vexed him, as did his unfortunate break with Princess Mathilde. He never joined the Opposition or became antidynastic, merely referring to himself as "to the left of the régime" and feuding with the régime's conservative supporters. He was a silent Senator for nearly two years. Then, in 1867, as the conservative reaction set in, he made a violent speech in favor of Renan and followed it with an attack upon some superpatriots in Saint-Etienne who proposed to rid their public library of books containing advanced political, social, and economic views. He reminded the Senate that the Prisoner of Ham had socialistic opinions:

To adopt what good there is in socialism—to separate socialism from the Revolution—and to work it into the regular fabric of society has always seemed to me an original and an essential task for the Second Empire.

The Emperor, yes, Gentlemen, the Emperor (for I do not hesitate to call on the régime's highest and most liberal authority), honors M. Renan with his esteem as he honors George Sand with his friendship.

For the first time, Sainte-Beuve began to enjoy popularity, as he continued to speak in the Senate for a liberal Empire. His articles in *Le Temps* were nonpolitical, except for an open letter addressed to the editor in which he criticized the government for having been too indifferent to the hostility of the intelligentsia—the students, the academicians, the artists, and the writers. Published on September 7, 1869, the letter was his swansong. His poor health forced him to abandon a series of projected lectures at Harvard University and ended his twenty-year hope of visiting America.

In October of 1869, when it was clear that Sainte-Beuve was dying, Princess Mathilde was determined that they should become reconciled. Told of her intention, Sainte-Beuve dictated his last note to her on the twelfth in which he expreseed his great satisfaction that their friendship was to be renewed. He died the following day in great agony after an operation. According to his own instructions, his burial was civil and without discourse, but a throng came to pay him tribute. Thus perished the most notable critic of the age; and his loss was the world's, not merely that of France, for he had fulfilled his own definition of a classic— "speaking to everyone in his individual style, a style which is found to be also universal."

VI

The Countess

OF CASTIGLIONE

On woman falls the duty, in a world of brute passions, of preserving the virtues of charity and the Christian spirit. . . . When women cease to play that role, life will be the loser.

—GEORGE SAND

That irresistible beauty is the kiss of desolation is the true translation of femme fatale.

—ROGER DE MORAINE

It is reasonably certain that March 22nd was the birthday of Virginia Oldoini, but the year escapes detection. The least plausible date is 1843, which we may ignore because the lady herself provided it. Generally, writers have accepted 1840 as the date, but there is room for doubt here too. Virginia always avowed she had no birth certificate; ultimately discovered, this document carried the unflattering revelation of 1835. This would ordinarily serve as sufficient evidence were it not for a reference in a letter from mother to daughter, written on daughter's birthday, March 22, 1854: "Seventeen years ago I produced this masterpiece."

The Oldoini family, originally Genoese, lived in Florence. Marquis Philippe Oldoini early recognized his daughter's beauty and the iron will and narcissism which too often accompany great beauty. He called her Nichia, a nickname which later became Nini. There is no reason to credit her later female rivals who had a low opinion of her intelligence. She had a good mind and a knack for languages, which enabled her easily to master both English and French. Neither is there any reason to credit Virginia's snobbish insinuation that she was semiroyalty. It is true that the Marquise Oldoini was an intimate of Prince Joseph Poniatowski; but, unhappily for her social distinction, Virginia was legitimate.

The Marquise was far from an ideal mother by the standards of any age. She contributed little more than favorable remarks about her daughter's beauty; Virginia was allowed to do as she pleased, and there was ample money to satisfy her whims. Instead of learning the responsibilities which life commands, she was nurtured in an atmosphere of adulation, which grew in intensity as she matured. Offers of marriage showered in before she was fifteen, and the fame of her beauty even traveled abroad. Small wonder indeed that she developed into a tyrannical egocentric.

In 1854 Francesca Verasis, Count of Castiglione, went abroad to find a bride. At a reception in London, he confided his mission to the French Ambassador, Count Walewski (a man whose lovely wife was brilliant testimony to his taste), and was promptly advised to go to Florence where the most beautiful woman in Europe lived. Her identity made known, Castiglione went straight to the Oldoini house to request the beauty's hand in marriage. He did not inquire of her personality or character; that her beauty was celebrated sufficed.

The Marquis and Marquise Oldoini were pleased by Castiglione's offer as he was handsome and young (twenty-nine), was of high birth, and was an aide-de-camp to Victor Emmanuel II of Sardinia. In the Marquis's mind, the problem of mating a strong-willed, self-centered woman with this rather weak male who offered himself was overshadowed by the connection at the Sardinian court which the marriage would cement. Oldoini was an ambitious diplomat who yearned for responsible office abroad, and Castiglione seemed the route to royal favor.

Virginia sensed Castiglione's weakness and made no secret of the fact that she would never love him. He seemed willing to accept this as long as he could possess the most beautiful woman in Europe; the marriage was a matter of pride to him, and vanity left him no doubt that in time she would be unable to avoid loving him. Ultimately she gave way, and the alliance became a fact in 1854. If one seeks a supreme example of incompatibles joined in unhappy union, the Verasis-Oldoini match should serve. The new Countess at first thought the marriage ideal; she was persistently cold toward him, and he responded by spending lavishly on her. It was a beautiful coquette's dream come true: to receive without end and without obligation. Unfortunately, there was an end to the money, and the couple was swiftly reduced to his income from the royal household.

After the wedding they lived at the palace in Turin, where the bride received some suggestions in a letter from her mother: "I expect that by now you will have undergone what all of us have undergone with our husbands, and though it may be painful the

first time, you must be patient and careful to make him happy."
Whether or not one regards this maternal advice as sound, it
may be regarded as hopelessly tardy in shaping the daughter's
behavior. Virginia had had no practice in the consideration of
the happiness of others, and even had she wished to so contribute,
she would not have known what to do.

The marriage was, in fact, a fiasco from the start. One child,
Georges, was born in 1855, but the couple gave up familiar address shortly after and separation ultimately followed. Meanwhile, the Countess was royally treated in Turin. Victor
Emmanuel II, while not so handsome as the Countess's husband,
was vigorous, rough, and anything but shy around the ladies.
On a state visit to France, for example, he once remarked to Mme.
de Malaret that he had particularly noted that French women did
not wear the drawers customarily worn in Turin. It was often
said of the King (as of Charles II) that he was one monarch who
might rightly style himself "the Father of His People." There
remains no specific evidence of a liaison between Countess and
King, but there was an abundance of gossip.

At this time, the unification of Italy was the goal of the King's
government. Stripped of patriotic verbiage, this meant that tiny
Sardinia wished to absorb the rest of the Italian peninsula and
eradicate the frontiers of the petty Italian states. Such a gigantic
act of digestion could not be engineered by Sardinia alone, as
there were powerful opponents of Italian unification, Austria
and the Papacy in particular. Austria directly governed the
northern provinces of Lombardy and Venetia, and by protecting
the petty and unpopular despots in Modena, Parma, and Tuscany,
she indirectly ruled them too. The Pope had large temporal
possessions in central Italy, and French troops had been in Rome
since 1849 to frustrate the attempts of Italian patriots to seize
the city as a national capital.

It was apparent to Count Cavour, Prime Minister of Sardinia,
and to Victor Emmanuel II, that Italian unification would require
French sanction and military aid. Ordinarily such assistance
would not have been forthcoming, as it was hard to imagine
any French government willing to create a Mediterranean rival

and to despoil the Papacy. Yet, Cavour was incredibly lucky; the French monarch, Napoleon III, had shown himself to be a friend of Italian nationalism, both in theory and in practice.

Napoleon III had inherited his concern for the Italians from the First Empire and through the form of the Napoleonic Legend. Tradition had it that Bonapartism championed the self-determination of nationalities; furthermore, if the Austrians could be expelled from northern Italy, Louis-Napoleon would effectively smash the 1815 settlement, which had proscribed his family. Obviously, the Bonaparte dynasty was expected to profit from this policy, but there is also good reason to believe that Napoleon III was convinced of the Legend's validity. He regarded a European system of "completed nationalities" in the Wilsonian sense as the basis for international peace. In this way the Emperor was equating Bonapartism with Peace, an equation so strange for those who could remember the early years of the century that it is no wonder that Europeans mistrusted his avowed intentions.

Sardinia's task was to encourage His Majesty's Italian sympathies, and if the ordinary channels of diplomacy did not suffice, Cavour was prepared to complement diplomacy with a more ancient professional service. Perhaps the sight of the Countess of Castiglione coquetting with the King in Turin enabled Cavour to conceive the idea of sending her to Paris, where she might employ her talents for the fatherland. Or perhaps Cavour chose her—his own cousin—to perform the delicate mission to Paris as a measure of his own patriotic zeal.

Eager for adventure and bored with her husband, the Countess was ready to go. Francesca not only protested in vain, but justifiably, since he could no longer afford the extravagance of life at the French court. When it became apparent that the Countess would go to Paris with or without her husband's consent, in fact with or without her husband, poor Francesca made ruinous financial arrangements. He borrowed 400,000 francs from Prince Joseph Poniatowski, raising his accumulated debt to more than 1,500,000 francs. A gallant attempt to meet this debt by selling his Turin properties realized a paltry 70,000, forcing the Count to cede his château and agricultural lands to Poniatowski to clear the debts. Since these lands were valued at more than two million, it is not astonishing that Castiglione felt financially abused by Poniatowski. Owning the most beautiful woman in Europe had cost him his cash and most of his lands; worse, she could not be maintained on his lieutenant's pay.

Meanwhile, the Countess proceeded with her official mission, seemingly indifferent to her husband's distress. Her real regret was that she had not arrived in Paris earlier. She once remarked that had this been the case, France would have had an Italian rather than a Spanish Empress. As it was, she arrived late in 1855, dragging Francesca behind her, to find France, victorious in the Crimean War, preparing for a peace conference with Russia. Her first reception at the Tuileries came on November 24, 1855, and produced a sensation. The fame of her beauty was such that, when she was announced, the dancers paused to gape; many of the gentlemen climbed on furniture for a more favorable view, and even the music momentarily stopped. She was superbly poised, supremely confident, regarding this demonstration as a proper tribute to her obvious superiority. At the very most she was twenty, and there was no more brilliant court on the Continent! The Emperor invited her for the first waltz and passed much of the evening near her. It was an auspicious entrance into foreign affairs.

Actually, this was not the first time that Napoleon had seen the Countess of Castiglione. The Marquis Oldoini had acted as Napoleon's guardian in the earlier days of exile. Several times the young pretender had visited the Oldoinis in Italy and had even held the infant Virginia in his arms. Dare one deny that History repeats?

Whatever the Countess was to wear later on, she did not at first risk the Empress Eugénie's displeasure, but faithfully wore crinoline, a cage and petticoat hoops in the fashion set by Her Majesty. Eugénie was neither unkind nor hostile to beautiful women, recognizing her own charm as adequate defense, but she included the Countess at her "Mondays" with some reluctance because of Napoleon's obvious attraction to her.

Princess Mathilde Bonaparte, who was bitterly antagonistic to the Empress, took the cue and made a point of being warmly friendly to the Countess. Thus, Countess de Castiglione quite fortuitously won the second lady of the Empire. Louis-Napoleon had wooed and lost his cousin Mathilde in the days when all Europe regarded his throne seeking as a joke. Since Mathilde's mother shared Europe's opinion, Mathilde lost an Empire. Sadly enough, it was France's loss too, since the Princess's intelligence would have served her well as Empress. Instead, Mathilde married for what she thought was love, selecting Anatole Demidov, the Prince of San Donato. It was a short and unhappy marriage, but lasted long enough for considerable dirty linen to be washed in public. When she could not extract a princely settlement from her estranged husband, Mathilde secured the intervention of Czar Nicholas I, who had the authority to require his subject to pay the Princess an imperial pension.

Mathilde had a second opportunity to marry Louis-Napoleon after the *coup d'état* of 1851, but she refused the offer. Perhaps she was disenchanted with marriage, or possibly she was uncertain about Louis-Napoleon's future, or possibly her greatest interest was in the artistic group which had begun to gather around her. It would seem that ultimately Mathilde regretted her choice, and she could never become fond of the Empress Eugénie because of jealousy. In revenge, she carried on an open liaison with a sculptor, Count Emilien de Nieuwerkerke, which amused Paris, annoyed the Emperor, and scandalized the Empress.

The Princess and the Empress reacted in opposite ways to the fact that Countess de Castiglione came to Paris from the palace in Turin. Sardinia was not only the organizer of Italian nationalism, but had been the scene of recent anticlerical legislation. Mathilde and her brother, Prince Jerome Napoleon, were true Bonapartes in that they claimed the principles of 1789, but there was much of the *ancien régime* in Eugénie. Jerome had been elected Deputy during the Second Republic and had sat with the Mountain. He had been outspokenly opposed to sending French troops to Rome in 1849 for the defense of the Papacy, and his friendship for Louis-Napoleon was never the same afterward. True, Mathilde continued to do the honors at the Elysée Palace and at the Tuileries until there was an Empress, but she remained liberal in principle, and no doubt she welcomed Mme. de Castiglione as an Italian.

Having taken pains at first to observe the padding and puffing with which the Empress presumed to improve the female figures of France, the Countess Castiglione soon sallied forth in low-cut, clinging gowns. She wore no corsets and, in the idiom of Horace de Viel-Castel, regarded her bust as a challenge to the rest of her sex. Fancy-dress balls offered her the best opportunities for individualism and, incidentally, for the display of her physical superiority.

One of the more celebrated masked balls was given on February 17, 1856, by Count Walewski, newly Foreign Minister. La Castiglione wore the Queen of Hearts costume, presumably her own invention. Corsetless, she draped her bosom in light gauze; the skirt was raised and caught up in back in the eighteenth century fashion, showing the petticoat. Ornamental hearts were scattered over both bodice and skirt, invariably in interesting places. Her Majesty was present at the Foreign Ministry, but as a guest she could not command the Countess to disappear. Instead she congratulated the Countess on the unique costume, but added, "Your heart seems a little low."

Some time later the Countess offered the Empress another challenge which had less amusing repercussions. Invited to a court ball, she went to Leroy and demanded a coiffure identical to the one he was preparing for the Empress. Leroy, knowing full well that a crisis tantamount to civil war would erupt should he comply, absolutely refused. Castiglione, however, was not accustomed to masculine refusal, and her violent insistence ultimately prevailed over his better wisdom. The two coiffures bobbed in the same ballroom that night, and Leroy crawled before Her Majesty next morning to receive a furious dismissal. His most talented pupil, Alexandre, was appointed hairdresser in his stead, and the shocked Leroy, who had been a devoted courtier, soon sickened and died.

Meanwhile, family matters were not improving. The Count of Castiglione was restless for Turin, but his wife refused to go. Having threatened to go without her, he was eventually obliged to do so. Their separation in 1856 was permanent, though they kept up a correspondence until his accidental death in 1867. Papa Oldoini tried to save the marriage and urged conciliation, primarily to avoid scandal, but in truth he was too well aware of his daughter's power to advance his diplomatic career to risk offending her. He wrote her frequently to suggest that she use her "magic wand" on his behalf; he wanted important diplomatic posts and a steady supply of foreign decorations, particularly those with "pretty jewels." As a matter of fact she did well by him, enabling him to rise from Secretary of the Legation in Paris to Sardinian Minister to Russia (1856). With this start, he was able to maintain himself on a dignified level, and ultimately he served Italy in Lisbon for twenty years.

Many women of the Countess of Castiglione's rank, if separated from their husbands, would have felt obliged to retire from the arena of social life. To her, the absence of a husband was a convenience, an emancipation. She managed her social life with theatrical skill, making it a point to be periodically out of Paris. These trips were most frequently to Holland House in London, to Orleans House in Twickenham, to Sardinia, Dieppe, or Baden; her repeated absences created an exaggerated idea of her importance, as many observers presumed she had achieved an enormous influence in international politics.

The Congress of Paris convened early in 1856 to draw out on paper the international changes produced in desolate Crimea. Cavour was in Paris to represent Sardinia. We may doubt the Countess of Castiglione's assertion that it was her success in Paris which secured Cavour's participation. After all, Sardinian troops had been sent to the Crimea, not for any grievance against Russia, but to secure Sardinia a seat at the peace table. There is little doubt that she reveled in the grand intrigues of a major diplomatic conference, and Cavour sent word that his agents would accept any notes which she wished to send him. "I have not wanted to deprive them of the pleasure of receiving them from your pretty hands." True enough, the Countess had scored a success in Paris, but it was personal rather than political. It did not require much skill to suspect there was a notable disparity between the Countess's limited income and her lavish living. By 1857 an epigram was making the rounds: "There is no Emperor but one Emperor, and Castiglione is his prophet."

Napoleon III, who had taken an instantaneous interest in Cavour's ambassadress upon her first entrance into the Tuileries, was not a man to regard a shapely figure lightly. Perhaps he inherited his interest in the opposite sex from his mother, Hortense Beauharnais, whose liberality in such matters gave rise to much speculation about His Majesty's legitimacy. One of the perquisites of absolute power (and Napoleon III was absolute in these years) is one's irresistibility in matters of love, and the Emperor was never wasteful of his opportunities. His critics have suggested, that is, shouted from the rooftops, that his devotion to affairs of the heart often postponed his attention to affairs of state, which was no doubt true; but without seeming to make a case for sexual overindulgence, one can doubt that his policies and their results would have been very different had the Emperor labored on in laudable continence.

The gossip of 1857 was not far wrong. Napoleon made little visits to the "divine Countess" at her small home in the rue de la Pompe, and these trips could not be concealed. The secret police arranged, escorted, and protected, but at least there were no crowds to cheer him en route. The police foiled several assassination attempts near the Countess's house, none of which became as celebrated as those attempts made upon him on more seemly occasions.

Also in 1857, His Majesty invited the Countess to join the court for a number of weeks at Compiègne, his château north of Paris. This residence, built in the time of Louis XV and extended by Napoleon I, was the scene of many receptions, hunts, and theatrical productions during the Second Empire. One night, at a performance by the Comédie-Française, the Countess complained of a headache and excused herself from her box. The Emperor, aware of this oldest of female ruses, followed to her chamber to inquire after her health, and the Empress was left quite alone to face the amused and knowing eyes of the entire court.

A charitable few have doubted that Castiglione was Napoleon's favorite, to use the correct monarchical term, but all evidence points to the contrary. Her police dossier, for instance, shows a remarkable void during the months she was in favor, but is complete for the period following her retirement. Then, the Emperor was liberal in his gifts of cash and jewels. He gave her an emerald valued at 100,000 francs and a pearl necklace which brought 422,000 francs after her death. While it is true that Napoleon III was a generous man, it is safe to suppose that such magnificent gifts required extraordinary thanks. Finally, the best evidence is the Countess's Last Will and Testament, where she asked to be buried in "the Compiègne nightgown, 1857."

The diplomatic campaign waged by Cavour from 1855 on suggests that he regarded French assistance as essential and imminent. What he did not see in his patriotic insistence was the suffering which France had undergone in the Crimean War, the several disastrous harvests, the outbreaks of cholera, and serious floods in the Rhône and Loire valleys. Real food shortages, inflation, and the losses from an unpopular war created an unrest in France, which the government kept obscure through its control of the press. In short, Napoleon III did not dare provoke a second war at the moment, a war which he knew would be unpopular in Catholic France under the most favorable domestic conditions.

When Napoleon did conspire to promote a war, he was neither reacting fearfully to the Orsini attempt upon his life in 1858, as is so often suggested, nor was he merely appreciating the services rendered him by the Ambassadress from Sardinia. As a slave to the Napoleonic Legend, he had always recognized that he must "do something for Italy," and by 1858 France had recovered sufficiently to allow a new venture. Furthermore, a diplomatic campaign to reach an understanding with Russia was proceeding well, and, indeed, was crowned by an agreement in March, 1859, giving Napoleon III new strength in foreign affairs.

The war of 1859 was hatched and fought with the idea of expelling the Austrians from Lombardy and Venetia. The Franco-Sardinian armies were successful in the early engagements, though the Austrians managed an orderly withdrawal into strong defensive positions and were far from beaten. Suddenly Prussia mobilized on the northern frontiers of France, and, as the Russians did nothing to halt them, Napoleon III was obliged to end the half won war and take only Lombardy. He gave the province to Sardinia and was reviled by the Italians for his failure to liberate Venetia, a response hardly unique in the history of diplomacy, which is known for ingratitude.

The Countess of Castiglione shared her countrymen's sentiments and voiced them freely in France. This earned her close surveillance by the police, who were inclined to suspect all Italians. (All the attempts to assassinate Napoleon III were made by Italians—none by Frenchmen.) Her continued indiscretions landed her at the frontier in 1860, and she retired to her Villa Gloria at Spezia near Turin. The loss of imperial favor meant a new era for the Countess, and gentlemen who had been restrained by the Emperor's monopoly could now enter into a competition of flattering proportions for her attention.

One of the first in the amorous cortege was Prince Henri de la Tour d'Auvergne-Lauraguais, whose letters to the Countess span the years 1859–1863. During the years of his devotion, he served his country in Turin, Berlin, and London; and, if we can believe his love letters, he was desolate most of the time: "If you knew how my poor heart is broken at the thought of a separation." But their almost constant separation was a convenience to the Countess, who could expand her circle of devotees. Another young diplomat, Henri d'Ideville, serving in Turin, began visiting the Countess late in 1860 at the Villa Gloria. He did not go to make love, but to satisfy his curiosity.

D'Ideville found her quiet and cold, though friendly enough, and he wrote that her beauty was something so perfect that it aroused admiration rather than a more fundamental passion. She encouraged him to call often, so that he saw her repeatedly during 1861. He never changed his initial impression of her, however, always acknowledging her superb beauty and finding her coldness repellent. Furthermore, he suggested that she must have had remarkable inner resources and a superior intelligence to weather the exile of her villa. Not more than twenty-six years old, or perhaps only twenty-four, she was suffering the disillusionment common to all who flourish too young. She told D'Ideville that she had found herself so superior to other people in society that a calm and independent life on her hill seemed infinitely preferable. A similar assertion she once inscribed on a photograph of herself: "I am their equal in birth, their superior in beauty, their judge in intellect."

Remarks and confessions which are planted in diaries and albums may seem to be casual, but they are often revealing. The completion of questionnaires of preferences was a popular pastime in the nineteenth century, and D'Ideville happened to submit one for the Countess's entertainment. Most of her responses were in character, as a few of them will show:

What occupation?	Thinking
What pleasure?	I know none.
What passion?	Contempt
What music?	Sad
What amusement?	The fan
What season?	The spring
What country?	The desert
What virtue?	Courage
What sentiment?	Devotion
What animal repels you?	Cat
What animal attracts you?	Eagle
Most attractive historical personality?	Charlemagne
Most antagonistic figure?	The Emperor

The Countess left only one of D'Ideville's questions blank: "What moral antipathy?"

There was a remarkably persistent rumor in 1861 that the Marquis of Hertford had paid the Countess of Castiglione a million francs for the pleasure of one night. One hesitates to credit this rumor, as Hertford was a far from romantic figure. He had a collection of 250 clocks and was the sort of man who worried endlessly because he could not keep them synchronized. Furthermore, as this immensely rich nobleman was a celebrated tightwad, it is a bit hard to visualize him parting with a million francs for one evening's entertainment.

After her brief exile, the Countess was allowed to return to France in 1861, where she added Count Emilien de Nieuwerkerke to her list of callers. Nieuwerkerke, the indiscreet lover of Princess Mathilde, had been appointed Superintendent of Museums in 1853 through her patronage, but even this double obligation did not prevent him from casting about after other women. He was genuinely fond of the Countess, and their correspondence continued well into the 1880's. His letters were often graceful and humorous: "Dear Madam Nini, Do not turn your pretty back on me," he wrote in 1864; "even though I find it charming, I like the other side still more. . . ." The two were kindred spirits, always willing to flout public opinion.

The Countess had a sudden whim one Christmas eve to hear the bells of Paris from a point of vantage. She got Nieuwerkerke to take her to the roof of the Louvre, but whatever were the auditory advantages of this spot the gossips of Paris intimated that neither heard the bells. At another time, when Nieuwerkerke was escorting the Countess through the Louvre, she questioned him, a sculptor himself, about the nude statues. For what reason, she wondered, did the sculptors of antiquity endow their heroic figures so niggardly in the area of virility? The Count could not have been more embarrassed by the question than Castiglione's biographers, who have left History the poorer by recording his response as "the obvious one."

With the revenues from the imperial treasury no longer forthcoming, it is not astonishing that the Countess should have begun to include great bankers among her intimates. She was a favorite at the Rothschild House, and we find the Baron James de Rothschild, in his seventieth year, expressing his pleasure at receiving a portrait of her: "But how much more charming indeed is the original!" His son, Baron Gustave, was only a few years older than the Countess, and it is presumed that he was better able to enjoy the family investments in her. One of the Rothschild friends and business associates, a banker named Ignace Bauer, also fell for the fatal beauty. The affair was inconvenienced by Bauer's almost continual residence in Madrid, where he served Italy as Consul General. This harried soul was of literary bent. He sent her masses of letters to supplement his brief visits to Paris. A wealthy man, he made her important loans, but he never lived under the illusion that she loved him, and compared his lot with those of Romeo and Abélard.

If Bauer was sure that she was "the beautiful Countess who loves nobody," he did entertain the hope that she might marry him. For several years, she persistently refused to promise anything in the event her husband could be removed from the scene, and finally, in 1865, Bauer married another woman. Castiglione's immediate response was to accuse him of desertion; perhaps his own suggestion of Romeo and Abélard had given her ideas that a noteworthy sacrifice ought to be made to her beauty.

Another banker, Charles Laffitte, fell in love with the Countess in 1861. His loans to her ultimately reached 450,000 francs. Though about sixty years of age, he must have been rather new at the game, since he expected to be repaid. The Countess was able to reduce this debt to 250,000 by 1866, but financial squabbling stained the beauty of their friendship: "Here, my dear Nichia, are a hundred thousand francs. Allow me to request as a favor, not as a condition, that you not go to the Tuileries this evening." And then a few days later he writes: "You asked me to give you 100,000 francs for twenty-four hours. . . . More than twelve days have elapsed, and not only have you returned nothing, but you have said and written some very unfriendly things. . . . I am not your lover; I am not your banker; you do not treat me as a friend. What am I then?" He gave the answer himself in 1866: "For a long time I have not counted on affection. I ask no more than simple equity."

In 1863 the newspapers were full of stories that the Countess of Castiglione had appeared nearly nude at a Tuileries ball, costumed, if that is the word, as Salammbô. (Flaubert's novel had appeared the previous year.) Her husband, who ordinarily never believed the stories he heard about her and considered her perfectly faithful, was in this case outraged that she should have linked his family name with a scandalous proceeding. In time, however, the actual facts of the Salammbô affair were clarified.

The costume ball was held at the Tuileries on February 9, 1863, and the Countess went garbed as the Queen of Etruria. It was a proper costume with very little décolleté, and the Countess noted in her diary that the simplicity of her gown was favorably compared with those of the other women who went as flies, midges, and butterflies. There was one exception. A Mme. Rimsky-Korsakov, usually given to daring costumes, came in a light veil, which passed for Salammbô's veil of Tanit, and shortly after was invited by the Empress Eugénie to leave the Tuileries.

It is understandable that the newspapers believed and printed the story, substituting the Countess's name for that of Mme. Rimsky-Korsakov. The deed fitted the reputation. The Countess's anger over the mistake was compounded by an encounter she had with the Russian woman before the latter's expulsion from the palace. Sizing up the Queen of Etruria, Mme. Rimsky-Korsakov said, "A pretty costume, but that of a deposed queen."

The furious Countess appealed to the Empress, and complaints against the press were referred to Persigny, then Minister of Interior. He acknowledged that he was shocked by the "treachery" of the press, and promised that suitable corrections would be forthcoming. He could not approve, however, the Countess's request that an announcement be made that the guilty newspapers had been banned from France at the Empress's instigation.

The Salammbô affair was not the last or least of Mme. Rimsky-Korsakov's indiscretions. Two years later at Biarritz, when the Villa Eugénie was crowded with guests—including Bismarck—she paraded along the beach in a bathing suit which left little to the imagination. The windows of the Villa glinted with the focusing of fieldglasses, as *Madame* skillfully improved the effect by keeping her suit wet. The Empress was much annoyed by this display and insisted that less revealing costumes be worn henceforth.

If the gentlemen of France found the Countess of Castiglione fascinating, it did not follow that their wives were equally enthusiastic. Nor would it be fair to insist that the women were merely jealous of her beauty. The Countess did her best to be a troublesome guest. She accepted invitations with ungraceful indifference, made it a point to arrive late, and was usually sulky for the remainder of the evening. She had a genius for giving insulting excuses to explain her tardiness, such as that she had been to the races.

Many of the women of the time were accustomed to keeping albums in which their guests might jot down verses or poetic thoughts. The Countess modified this custom to suit her own tastes. Her album was entitled *Book of Testimonials*. She was not interested in any poetic souvenir, but preferred a formal statement of her own glory. Adolphe Thiers, Prince Jerome-Napoleon, Count Nieuwerkerke, and Lord Cowley (the British Ambassador) were among the contributors. The following example was signed by Antoine Berryer, a leading Royalist:

I hereby certify for all present and future generations that neither the noble carriage of the Countess of Castiglione, nor her wondrously perfect beauty, her radiant youth, her unique position in the world, her glorious mouth, nor her eyes, shining or sad, express the whole of that wit, intellect, goodness, tenderness, and rare intuition which she possesses.

Though the Count and Countess of Castiglione were separated in 1856, their correspondence did not lag. The aggrieved husband, in Turin, drew up a list of his complaints which he dispatched to her. Among the motives for the separation he included her refusal "to submit to the natural duties of marriage on the pretext that she did not wish to become pregnant a second time, which obliged the husband to make ridiculous and tiring scenes to obtain what was legitimately owed him." He also seems to have been annoyed that she regarded him as an imbecile who was good for nothing, an opinion she made no effort to conceal in the presence of others. He did not like her "complete lack of religion," finding it difficult to get her to go to mass on Sundays.

Furthermore, he thought she gave way to excessive rage without sufficient provocation and that her expenditures for clothes were not in keeping with his fortune. Her conduct in public, he continued, was hardly praiseworthy; though perhaps innocent, her little flirtations did not always have that appearance and were an embarrassment to him.

The Count's grievances were followed by an ultimatum:

May 26, 1857: ". . . You will try to modify your ideas to bring them more into harmony with your position of wife and mother. You will avoid treating me with this indifference which wounds me. You will consult me before acting. . . . If, on the contrary, you persist in your present attitude, our separation shall remain irrevocable."

The Countess did not quail; indeed, 1857 was a year of notable success for her, and the Count must have realized that he had lost her. Even so, the correspondence went on:

July 31, 1858: ". . . The day will come when your fatal beauty will have disappeared and the flatterers will be rarer. Perhaps you will then understand the unworthy manner with which you have obeyed the oath you made me before God and how, for four years, you have neglected your wifely duties while making me the most unhappy of men."

If the Countess had made precious little effort to fulfill her domestic obligation earlier, there was certainly no chance that she would submit to the matrimonial leash just as the Italian Question was becoming paramount in European affairs. She never lived with her husband again, and saw him for the last time in the spring of 1867, when she went to Turin for the wedding of Amadeo, Duke of Aosta, and the Princess Marie del Pozzo della Cisterna. The Count of Castiglione accompanied Victor Emmanuel, the father of the groom. Except that the wedding brought the Count and Countess together for the last time, the attendant devastation certainly merits some note.

To begin with, the bride's wardrobe mistress hanged herself instead of the bridal gown: a thoughtless act which necessitated the finding of another gown for the superstitious Princess. The colonel who was to lead the procession from the palace to the church fell from his horse with sunstroke, causing delay until a new officer arrived. The third contretemps was the failure of the palace gates to open. The gatekeeper was found dead in a large pool of blood, and a substitute had to be recruited to open the gates.

The ceremony itself was not spoiled by anyone's dying, but shortly afterward the best man contributed to the excitement by firing a pistol at his head. The procession proceeded toward the railway station, where the bridal party was to entrain, when suddenly the official who had drawn up the marriage contract succumbed to an apoplectic fit. At the station, the overzealous stationmaster fell beneath the wheels of the approaching bridal train, whereupon the King, thoroughly frightened, refused to allow anyone to board the train. Instead, the party returned to the carriages to drive back to the palace. The Count of Castiglione trotted alongside the bridal carriage, when suddenly he either fell or was thrown from his horse. The carriage wheels passed over him, crushing his new Order of the Annonciade into his chest and wounding him beyond hope. The House of Savoy considered the day an unhappy omen for the dynasty, and the whole affair was hushed up.

It is hard to imagine the Countess of Castiglione going into anything but the most superficial mourning for her husband. The real misfortune was the paltry inheritance left her. She suspected, however, that her late husband had secured property in Egypt, where he had been in 1864, and she got Ferdinand de Lesseps, builder of the Suez Canal, to arrange an interview for her with Ismail, Viceroy of Egypt. Conveniently enough, the Viceroy was in Paris for the Exposition of 1867. De Lesseps arranged the interview as bidden, but warned the Countess that he had been informed that her husband had received nothing more than a snuffbox and a pipe-case. The collision of these two notorious spendthrifts ended with the Countess getting nothing. "Your King," she wrote to De Lesseps, "is not only unfriendly and impolite, but is inclined to dishonesty. You can make my sentiments known to him."

Widowhood had no visible effect on the Countess of Castiglione. It neither softened her heart nor curtailed her affairs. A new lover came into her life in 1868, the diplomat and writer Baron Imbert de Saint-Amand, whose passion burned fiercely for the next five years. Whether she be "wicked or good," he wrote to her, "selfish or devoted, I love you with all my heart, before, during, after, yesterday, today, tomorrow, always, and I shall never 'unlove' you. . . . But when I was kissing you, there was so much indifference and boredom in your face."

Her answer? "Loving very much is not the same thing as loving." But as men will, he continued this cruel torture for years until she was too bored even to be flattered by his suffering. "Since you wish it," he wrote, "let us henceforth be strangers one to another; let us not be enemies but retain the only good thing which remains when all else vanishes: the memory." He might have his sentiments for all she cared. Her greatest happiness, she told him, derived from her independent position, and this she intended to keep.

In 1870 the war with Prussia broke out, destroying the France which the Countess had known for nearly fifteen years. She happened to be in Italy during the war and was one of the few of her compatriots who remembered Italy's great obligation to France. Blinded by the old illusion of her diplomatic importance, she sought to intercede with Bismarck to secure a generous peace for France. She argued that since Prussia had incontestably won the military honors, the only additional profit which might be secured by Prussia would come from a conciliatory peace settlement. She meant that a reasonable peace might prevent "an implacable hatred which would be allied to vengeance" from rising in France. There is no evidence that Bismarck took her seriously.

The Republic put Mme. de Castiglione out of style; the new régime merely hastened the inevitable, as her beauty had already begun to fade. Old age seemed to approach her prematurely, but she hated the thought. She tried to take revenge on the laws of nature by conspiring against the Republic. Sadly for her, she could no longer successfully employ her body to make a kingdom. The Duc d'Aumale, son of Louis-Philippe, who carried on a liaison with the Countess both before and after the fall of the Empire, declined to be pushed by her toward a dictatorship. His nephew, Robert, Duc de Chartres, was similarly willing to pay court to her, but refused her collaboration in politics. But, as the years went by, their personal attentions decreased, which was worse for her than the failure to manufacture an Orleans restoration.

In despair, the Countess rarely appeared in public view. The death of her son, Georges, in 1879, was another severe blow. Only twenty-four, he was serving in the Italian Embassy in Madrid at the time of his death. They had never lived closely together, since his presence had made her embarrassingly old, but General Estancelin believed that Georges was the only person she ever really loved. The difficulty was, of course, that she was fonder of herself. She was genuinely attracted to General Louis Estancelin, with whom she plotted an Orleanist restoration, but while he was a loyal friend for over forty years, he never became her lover. Probably he recognized and resisted the subjection the latter role required, though he remained devoted and constant in his attentions.

The Countess's retirement from public life quickly developed into virtual seclusion. In 1877 she moved into a ground-floor apartment on the Place Vendôme to wait out her days; she would have been about forty at the time. Occasionally she emerged at odd hours, driving to the various properties she owned in Paris, peering into windows but never venturing foot into rooms where she had lived. Neither were there mirrors on the walls at home. The apartment was kept heavily shuttered, and there were no bells. She recognized no family after Georges's death, though actually there were relatives in Italy.

Her reluctance to realize any cash from her properties or her fabulous jewels left her short of money, and she regarded herself as destitute. It was the first time in her life that she saw her true self; she was destitute, because she had only jewels and properties. The Rothschilds provided a small monthly pension, and she was consistent in its mismanagement. To the illusion of pauperism she added, like many egocentrics, the illusion of sickness, and in later years passed a great share of her time in bed. At that point her chief occupation was a continual reworking of her Last Will and Testament. In 1894 the building on the Place Vendôme changed hands, and the Countess was obliged to move. Her last residence was in the rue Cambon. Here she took her gold and purple wedding bed, which had come from the Villa in Spezia, and which she had stubbornly refused to sell.

Death came in 1899, either in her sixty-third or sixty-fifth year. In reality, she had departed long before, as much a victim of her superficial qualities as her myriad of admirers had been. Her Last Will and Testament provided for the disposal of many valuable documents in her possession, but its chief concern was the details of her funeral and burial, faithfully mirroring her narcissism. As a subject of the King of Italy, she left her papers to be disposed of at the discretion of the Italian Embassy in Paris, expressly forbidding the French to touch a thing. The speed with which the Embassy agents investigated her papers, destroying many, suggested that the Countess was in the possession of documents which would have edified the French.

The details of the funeral speak for themselves: "The Compiègne nightgown, 1857, of cambric and lace; the black velvet and white plush dressing-gown (at 14 rue Cambon). On my neck, the pearl necklace of nine ropes, six white and three black— the necklace which I have worn every day. . . . The pillow . . . in cross-stitch embroidery in white floss-silk, lined with violet satin, with four corners, bouquets of pansies embroidered by my son as a child, at the Café Anglais in Paris; a violet cord around it and four tassels . . .

"The two dogs from 26 Place Vendôme (stuffed) will be placed at my feet during the last night, as I wish the vigil to be kept by my dead dogs, whom I named Sandouga and Kasino. Also put them in the coffin . . . one under each foot. Besides my pets, I want their little music box, *The Wave*, which used to start them dancing a waltz. . . . I want them beautifully dressed, blue and violet winter-coat with my monogram and their names, and their collars of pink flowers and cypress."

The Countess wanted her passing to go unnoticed by the newspapers, and instructed her lawyers to pay the press for silence. The burial place, too, was to be kept secret. Actually, she was buried without display in Père Lachaise, and no great monument adorned the grave. The simplest granite slab was left to mark the end. Quite unwittingly many of us epitomize our lives in some casual reference or idle phrase. When the Countess wrote in her journal, "Where there is no love, there is nothing in the long run," she unknowingly offered herself as proof.

VII

Louis Pasteur

AND THE BACTERIAL REVOLUTION

> *That common basis of all beautiful and true work, that divine fire, that indefinable breath which inspires Science, Literature, and Art, we have found in you, Sir: it is genius.*
>
> —RENAN

> *Science should not concern itself in any way with the philosophical consequences of its discoveries.*
>
> —PASTEUR

Pasteur's birth and early years were not attended by signs of genius or prophecies of success. Born December 27, 1822, in the town of Dôle (Jura), Louis Pasteur was the son of a tanner. The latter, though lightly schooled, had learned to speak with warmly patriotic accent after his conscription in 1811 and had served with merit in the Peninsular Campaign. Raised to be a Chevalier in the Legion of Honor in 1814, the brave young sergeant served during the remaining months of Napoleon's régime, only to be discharged by Louis XVIII's government as Bonapartist. Back then to the tannery with its six days of obscure labor, followed by a seventh day largely spent strutting the byroads with the Legion's ribbon in full view. Shortly after Louis's birth, the tanner moved his family to Marnoz and then to Arbois.

Here Louis began his primary education. The teachers found him unusually slow, indecisive, quiet, inclined to dream, and his mediocre work suggested that he would never achieve the tanner's ambition for him—to be a professor at Collège d'Arbois. He demonstrated a talent for sketching, however, and spent his time painting the local landscape and the portraits of his relatives. But Father was persistent and, in 1838, Louis was sent to the Lycée Saint-Louis in Paris for secondary training. There he suffered the bitterness of exile until, consumed by nostalgia, he was fetched by his father, who was too kind to permit the suffering to continue.

Back in Arbois he returned to painting, but the humiliation of his failure in Paris cast its shadow on the painting, which soon became associated with his shame. Moreover, the striking kindness of his family (for he was never berated for his failure) inspired him to achieve a success pleasing to them, and he seems to have veered toward science as the field where prestige was most likely to be won. He returned to school after several months in Arbois, but this time to the Collège royal de Besançon, only thirty miles from home.

Pasteur received the Bachelor of Arts degree in August, 1840, and hoped to go on to the Ecole normale to prepare for secondary teaching. Meanwhile, however, a sudden enrollment increase at Besançon opened a new instructorship in mathematics, and he was offered the position in recognition of his personal and moral qualities and despite the fact that he had not had a brilliant academic record. During the months that he taught mathematics, he began preparing himself to take examinations for the Bachelor of Science degree, but a simultaneous outburst of interest in literature may partly account for the poor showing he made when examined by the Dijon faculty in 1842. He was granted the degree and even permitted to take entrance examinations for the Ecole normale, but the results were so poor that he returned to the Lycée Saint-Louis for a few months' preparation before entering the Ecole normale in 1843.

Here his interest in science was sharpened. His enthusiasm, tenacity, and tendency to work too hard pleased his mentors as much as it distressed his family. The professors regarded Pasteur as better fitted for the laboratory than for the classroom and, accordingly, when he had finished his course work in 1846, begged the Minister of Public Instruction to give Pasteur an assistantship in chemistry at the Ecole normale and to cancel plans to send him as a professor to the Lycée de Tournon. The assistantship allowed Pasteur to continue work on his doctorate, while he aided Auguste Laurent, a professor from the Bordeaux faculty, in laboratory work on crystals.

After Pasteur received the doctorate, the Ministry of Public Instruction sent him to teach at the Lycée de Dijon, just at a moment when he was engrossed in his study on crystals. Longing for the laboratory, he resented the amount of time required to prepare his courses, but after a few months the intervention of his Ecole normale teachers secured him a transfer to the Strasbourg faculty with the title of assistant in chemistry.

He had been in Strasbourg only several weeks (1849) when he

began negotiating for the hand of the rector's daughter, Marie Laurent. His resources were similar to most young academicians': no money, but a doctorate and a university position. Furthermore, he had a reputation for integrity, and the previous year he had read a paper before the Académie des sciences growing out of his studies in crystallography, which won him important praise. His future seemed bright, so that when Pasteur's father came from Arbois to make the formal proposal of marriage, it was accepted by the Laurents.

Pasteur's associates were unanimous in qualifying his marriage in 1849 as supremely successful. Raised in an academic family, Marie could accept her husband's love for learning without resentment. She was prepared for his long hours in the laboratory, for his absent-mindedness, and to give uncomplaining aid when overwork led him into exhaustion or illness. Some of the credit for his brilliant career clearly belongs to her. Four daughters and a son were born within the next thirteen years, but between 1859 and 1866, three of the girls succumbed. "My poor Marie," he wrote after the third death, "our dear children are dying one after the other."

Pasteur continued at Strasbourg the work he had begun as a graduate student at the Ecole normale. He had observed that the crystals of tartaric acid had tiny facets which had escaped the attention of the most famous crystallographers of the day. This observation led Pasteur to the discovery of two distinct acids. Having checked Pasteur's discovery, Biot, who held the chair of chemistry at the Collège de France, reported the find to the Académie des sciences. Then, in a letter to Pasteur, the old scholar expressed his faith in the young chemist's future: "At my age, one lives only in the interest one takes in those one loves. You are one of the small number who can provide such food for my mind." In 1852, when it was suggested to Pasteur that he might become a corresponding member of the Académie in physics, Biot advised against it on the grounds that Pasteur's creative genius lay in chemistry. The advice was taken. And the following year, when Pasteur finally succeeded in obtaining paratartaric (racemic) acid from tartaric acid, Biot used his influence to obtain the cross of Chevalier of the Legion of Honor for Pasteur.

The Pharmaceutical Society of Paris similarly honored Pasteur with a prize of 1,500 francs. He used nearly half the money to buy equipment for his laboratory in Strasbourg, for at that time the state provided only 1,200 francs a year for all his classroom and laboratory expenses—including the salary of his laboratory assistant.

Pasteur's growing reputation won him a promotion in 1854 (he was thirty-two) to be Professor and Dean of the Science Faculty at Lille. His initial lecture at Lille contained the following words:

Without theory, practice is but routine born of habit. Theory alone can bring forth and develop the spirit of invention. It is especially essential that you not share the opinion of those narrow minds who disdain everything in science which has no immediate application.

Yet, for all his devotion to theory, Pasteur was willing to derive practical results from theory and to develop theory from facts secured from practical researches, and often took his students to factories and foundries in search of problems in applied science. While at Lille, he tested manures at the request of the Departmental Council of Nord, and he went to the aid of a Lille manufacturer who was having difficulty producing beetroot alcohol. This study, which involved fermentation, led him directly into the field where he was to make his greatest original contribution to knowledge—to discoveries upon which all his later triumphs were to hinge.

In the 1850's most chemists regarded fermentations and putrefactions as resulting from chemical changes, and rejected the notion that living organisms were responsible. Pasteur isolated the tiny globules which he found in sour milk in order to watch the lactic fermentation develop. He saw a multiplying such as he had seen in beer yeast, clearly a phenomenon related to life, and reported his findings to the Lille Scientific Society in 1857 and to the Académie des sciences later the same year. His report concluded: "The reduction of sugar into alcohol and carbonic acid is correlative to a phenomenon of life, to an organization of globules." This work won Pasteur the Academy's prize for experimental physiology in 1860.

His continuing work on fermentations led him inevitably to challenge the heterogenesists—those who believed in spontaneous generation. Heterogenesis was accepted generally in 1860, even though men like the Reverend M. J. Berkeley had more than a decade earlier discredited heterogenesis in accounting for the appearance of fungi on plants. Now that Pasteur was convinced that fermentation and putrefactions depended upon the growth of living organisms, he had to demonstrate from whence these organisms came. If he could show that they were in the air (and having read the Abbé Spallanzani, Needham, Buffon, Schwann, and Helmholtz, he suspected this to be the case), he would be well along the road which led to ruin of the theory of spontaneous generation.

Pasteur began the microscopic examination of the air in 1860; he found spores and germs. Theorizing that even the most putrescible liquids would remain pure if, after boiling, they were kept free of the dusts in the air, and realizing that the higher he went the purer the air would be, Pasteur went high into the Alps with his phials to "bottle air" as he called it. These experiments verified his belief that putrescible liquids would remain pure indefinitely if isolated from the germs in the air; putrefaction did not occur spontaneously.

In conjunction with the brilliant physiologist Claude Bernard, Pasteur organized another experiment. They took blood from a dog and, careful of its purity, sealed it in a glass phial. The phial was placed in an oven heated to 30 degrees Centigrade and was allowed to remain there from March 3 to April 20, 1862. The blood suffered no putrefaction. Urine treated the same way gave the same result.

The heterogenesists were by no means ready to concede that Pasteur was right. One group determined to verify Pasteur's Alpine experiment. They went high in the Pyrenees above Bagnères-de-Luchon opening and shutting their phials, but upon their descent they found alteration in every phial. Their conclusion: that air at any altitude was equally favorable to organic genesis. Pasteur's evaluation of their experiments: that they had been careless in controlling their phials of putrescible material.

Joly and Musset demanded that the Académie des sciences appoint a commission to examine the evidence, a move which Pasteur welcomed. The commission agreed on a date in March of 1864, but when the moment arrived the heterogenesists asked for a postponement on the grounds that the cold weather might affect the tests. Their request was granted; but later, when meteorological conditions seemed favorable for a test, the heterogenesists temporized by arguing over details of the test and ended by repudiating the commission. Their performance did their cause little good.

Meanwhile, Pasteur began to put his ideas on fermentations to practical purpose. He suspected that the sourness, acidity, and bitterness of some wines might be caused by fermentations which could develop in bottled wine under certain conditions, and was encouraged by the Emperor to seek a remedy in the interest of the wine industry. He found that by keeping the wine at a temperature between fifty and sixty degrees Centigrade for a few minutes, the vitality of the "parasites" could be destroyed without altering the quality of the wine. Firmly corked to prevent further contamination from the air, the bottles preserved the wine from deterioration.

Pasteur presented these ideas in 1864, but the viniculturists were reluctant to adopt new methods. The Emperor urged the acceptance of Pasteur's suggestions, rightly arguing that the export market for French wine would be greatly expanded if the spoilage could be reduced. His Majesty's opinion could not compete, however, with that of the gourmets, who were unanimous in their firm faith that heating wine would prevent it from mellowing with age. Pasteur had already demonstrated that mellowness was not associated with fermentation, but came from oxidation, which, if anything, would be enhanced by the brief heating rather than hindered. In time, of course, the wine industry adopted "pasteurization" as a standard procedure; meanwhile,

Pasteur was awarded a grand-prize medal for his work on wines at the Exposition of 1867.

In the same year Pasteur was more than ever conscious of the wretched state of laboratory resources in France, as he was chosen by the Minister of Public Instruction, Victor Duruy, to be one of a group which would show France's role in the intellectual world at the Exposition of 1867. He produced a study entitled *Report on the Progress and Achievements of General Physiology in France*, which ended with a plea: "French physiology demands only that which can easily be given; genius has never been lacking."

The dearth of facilities was appalling. Even in the greatest centers of learning, equipment was far below minimum needs. Claude Bernard worked in a cellar at the Collège de France and was the author of the remark that "laboratories are the tombs of scientists." Adolphe Wurtz had an attic in the Dupuytren Museum, while J. B. Dumas scorned the trap reserved for him at the Sorbonne and turned his home into a laboratory at his own expense. Pasteur's own facilities at the Ecole normale, where he had been since 1857, were equally inadequate. Clearly, opportunities for research were sadly inferior to those in Britain and Germany.

Yet, Science had traditionally had an honored name in France and was really part of French civilization. The cultivated lady of the eighteenth century was presumably as at home in the audience of the distinguished lecturer on Newtonian physics as in a gallery gazing at a Watteau. She may have understood neither, but both were seemly uses of her time. But this tendency to make science a part of culture contributed to making French science theoretical rather than practical, mathematical rather than experimental. In short, the dearth of laboratory facilities in the nineteenth century for experimentation did not necessarily reflect lack of interest in science. Pasteur and his friends who complained about inadequate facilities for experimentation were in the secondary tradition of French science.

It is astonishing that these experimental scientists tarried so long before appealing to Napoleon III for funds. His Majesty had dabbled in chemistry when a prisoner at Ham and, as Emperor, took keen interest in the invention of new weapons for the Army. Furthermore, scientists were often invited to Compiègne, where the Emperor could never resist drawing them aside for a chat. Claude Bernard found himself obliged to lecture the Emperor for two hours on physiology, and reported that his imperial pupil had been fascinated. On another occasion, Pasteur spent a whole evening explaining his ideas on molecular dissymmetry and fermentation, following which the Emperor sent to Paris for a microscope and some samples of diseased wine. A second lesson was held the following afternoon with both Their Majesties present, and at five o'clock, when the Empress received guests for tea, she subjected them to a short lecture from Pasteur.

Only in 1867, when Pasteur was compiling his report for the Exposition, did he appeal to the Emperor for scientific equipment. His work on fermentations and microscopic organisms, Pasteur explained, was leading him into new studies on infectious diseases and on the nature of putrefaction, and he needed a large laboratory with several small adjacent buildings for experiments which required isolation. Napoleon III responded at once by ordering Duruy to assist Pasteur through the Ministry of Public Instruction, and Duruy, who was only too glad to advance science, proposed to build the facilities which Pasteur had requested in the garden of the Ecole normale. But Duruy, who invariably had difficulty raising funds for his educational projects, found the Finance Minister and the members of the Corps législatif indifferent to Pasteur's requirements.

In annoyance, Pasteur wrote a letter to the *Moniteur*, the official journal, protesting the blindness of those who would vote credits for a glittering opera house but found nothing for a modest laboratory. He compared the funds available for research in Britain, Germany, Russia, and the United States with those in France and said what Wurtz would repeat some months later: that national strength was dependent upon the importance placed on the things of the mind. The editor of the *Moniteur* feared to print this attack upon the government, but the letter was shown to the Emperor, who took the matter up with Duruy early in

1868. They agreed that Pasteur's ideas ought to be made public, but for the sake of form it would be better for him to publish them in a pamphlet rather than in the *Moniteur*.

Meanwhile, His Majesty invited a number of scientists—Pasteur, Milne-Edwards, Claude Bernard, and Henri Sainte-Claire Deville—to meet with Rouher, Duruy, and Marshal Vaillant in the Emperor's study. Napoleon directed the discussion around the problem of attracting young men into pure science at a time when industry could easily pull them into applied science. They agreed that the state must create new assistantships in institutions like the Ecole polytechnique to encourage students to take research training and to go into teaching. Furthermore, money must be found for research (the Ecole des hautes études, more fully discussed in the chapter on Duruy, was founded in July of 1868), and Pasteur was promised action on the facilities he had requested. Duruy was able in 1868 to provide a small sum to begin their construction, and additional money was given by the Emperor out of his household budget.

Pasteur had stayed at Lille, where he began his work on fermentations, only three years. In 1857, feeling that he had revitalized the science faculty there, he let it be known in Paris that a similar rejuvenation was in order at the Ecole normale. The Minister of Public Instruction agreed, and transferred Pasteur from Lille to Paris. The Ecole normale possessed only one laboratory, and it was occupied by Sainte-Claire Deville, whom Pasteur refused to disturb. Instead, he devised his own laboratory in the attic and proceeded with his work.

The same year, a vacancy occurred in the Académie des sciences. Several of Pasteur's friends urged him to stand for election, which he did, though confident he would be beaten. His fear was confirmed, and he was only elected to the Académie in 1862 when Senarmont's seat fell vacant. By then, Pasteur's work was better known; but, even so, he received only thirty-six of the sixty votes. In the meantime he had the pleasure of seeing his old friend Biot, who had been a member of the Académie des sciences for fifty-four years, received by the Académie française. It was a triumph for this man of science who had always taught that scientists should be literate. "Their science," he said in his reception speech, "was not the more apparent through their want of literary culture."

Pasteur, meanwhile, having demonstrated to his own satisfaction that fermentation is a process of life rather than death, and that life does not generate spontaneously, was prepared to believe that diseases in animals and in man result from the growth of microorganisms within the host. Furthermore, if the organisms which ruined wines could be controlled, why not the organisms causing animal diseases? But however logical it was for Pasteur to drift from fermentations into the germ theory of disease, he cannot be credited with inventing the latter theory. M. J. Berkeley in Britain and Anton de Bary in France, among others, had concluded that diseases are caused by living microorganisms, but their work has been overshadowed by Pasteur's because they worked on the diseases of plants.

Nor was Pasteur the first to see bacteria, for Leeuwenhoek had seen bacteria through his microscope as early as 1683. Yet the knowledge of bacteria—up to Pasteur's time—had lagged behind the knowledge of the microorganisms associated with plant diseases, perhaps because the bacteria belonged to a "second order of smallness." Pasteur recognized that destructiveness was not related to size and, in his work on silkworms, offered support for the view that animal disease, too, is caused by a parasite.

The old scientist J. B. Dumas, a Senator in 1865, brought the silkworm epidemic to Pasteur's attention and begged him to work on the problem. The disease had made its first appearance in 1845 during the reign of Louis-Philippe, when the silkworm industry was worth one hundred million francs a year. Now, in 1865, Pasteur was aghast at the sight of the poverty in the Cévennes district and its deserted mulberry plantations. The tiny pepper-like spots on the silkworms had appeared first here, spreading then to Spain, Italy, Greece, Turkey, and China. By 1865 healthy seed (eggs) was available in Japan alone.

A serious outbreak of cholera in the same year momentarily occupied Pasteur's attention. With Bernard and Sainte-Claire Deville, he tried to find a cure for this dread disease, but their experiments were unsuccessful. In the late autumn the epidemic subsided, and Pasteur returned to consider the silkworm problem. The Ministry of Agriculture financed a five-month study under his direction, and Duruy, as Minister of Public Instruction, provided academic leaves of absence for professors selected by Pasteur as his assistants.

They settled down to observe the silkworm's metamorphosis, noting that the black spots first appeared in the chrysalis stage. Their first conclusion was that the problem could be handled by hastening the maturity of a few cocoons in a given nursery by raising the temperature. The new moths would reveal the condition of the lot, and infected moths meant the destruction of the batch of cocoons. Healthy seed, meanwhile, was presented to Napoleon III by the Japanese government and in turn was distributed to the sericulturists in the southern departments. The scientists hoped that the use of healthy seed and the destruction of infected cocoons would combine to wipe out the disease.

Their disappointment was great when the carefully controlled development of healthy worms did not completely eliminate the difficulty. They began the examination of dying worms, which, being spot-free presumably should have been disease-free. Only then did Pasteur and his associates discover the presence of foreign, microscopic bodies in the worms: they were dealing with an infectious disease which could attack the worms, the eggs, the chrysalises, and the moths. They identified the malady as the wilt disease, sometimes called the flacherie disease.

Pasteur then emphasized that it was not enough to check the chrysalises, but that contaminated eggs must also be destroyed. He suggested the following method of control: when the moths from apparently healthy chrysalises emerge from their cocoons, separate the females from the males as soon as mating has taken place. Each female moth is to be placed on a square of linen where she will lay her eggs, following which she is to be pinned to the same linen, where she dies. When completely dried, she is then moistened and pounded into a paste for observation under a microscope, and if the microscope reveals the least trace of the disease corpuscles that batch of eggs must be destroyed—burned.

In the late spring of 1868, Pasteur returned to the south of France to observe the results of his work. Those sericulturists who had accepted Pasteur's diagnosis of the disease and who were applying his proscribed treatment were having success. The majority of sericulturists, however, had the provincial's distrust of anything newfangled, and suffered accordingly. Their reluctance to adopt the new methods was exploited by the seed merchants, who slandered the Pasteur cure because it was injurious to their business.

Eighteen sixty-eight was, in fact, the beginning of a time of troubles for Pasteur. In the midst of his anxiety resulting from the conservatism of the sericulturists, he found a student revolt on his hands at the Ecole normale. The trouble began when the unquenchable Sainte-Beuve lectured the indifferent Senate on freedom of thought and literary expression. The students of the Ecole normale, through one of their number, congratulated Sainte-Beuve, and the congratulatory message was published. As Université regulations prohibited students from engaging in political action, the student who had written the letter was expelled, whereupon his fellows demonstrated in his support. The government replied by reorganizing the institution, removing the director as well as the students. Pasteur was transferred to the Sorbonne as Professor of Chemistry. Duruy was upset that Pasteur had been at all involved and, himself approving the students' position, he saved the expelled student by placing him as a teacher in the Collège de Sens.

Then in October of 1868, shortly after Pasteur had read a treatise by an Italian scientist to the Académie des sciences which seemed to verify his views on the silkworm, Pasteur was stricken with a cerebral hemorrhage. "I am sorry to die," he said to Sainte-Claire Deville; "I wanted to do much more for my country." But he did not die. All scientific Paris waited day by day for news of his improvement, and a messenger came daily from the palace for information. As his mind remained clear, he dictated further thoughts on the silkworm problem. Ultimately he became aware that the government had halted the work on his laboratory in the expectations of his death, and his bitterness was apparent.

Hearing of it, Napoleon III wrote to Duruy; "He has been much affected by this circumstance, which seems to point to his non-recovery. I beg you to issue orders that the work begun should be continued."

As the weeks went past, Pasteur was able to get about slowly and to receive callers, but the stroke left him partially paralyzed on the left side. The forearm was bent and contracted, the fingers locked into the hand and could not be opened, and he dragged a stiff left leg in a slow, difficult walk. Three months after the stroke, he insisted on going south again to oversee the work on silkworms; and though he suffered a fall which retarded his recovery, Pasteur was heartened to find his theories confirmed by a good crop of silkworms in 1869.

Pasteur, confident that he had demonstrated the correctness of his method of controlling the silkworm disease, was confounded by the failure of the sericulturists to rally instantly to the truth. In his annoyance, he found a new ally in Paris, Marshal Vaillant, who had become interested in the silkworm problem and had organized his own silkworm nursery in the heart of the city. Because Vaillant was eager to give Pasteur further opportunity to prove himself he arranged for Pasteur to go to an imperial estate near Trieste called the Villa Vicentina. This estate, originally belonging to Elisa Bonaparte and her daughter, Princess Bacciocchi, had been willed to the Prince Imperial. The property was planted with vines and mulberry, but disease had ruined the silkworms.

Napoleon III gave the half paralyzed Pasteur permission to occupy the estate for the double purpose of convalescence and of revitalizing the silkworms. He arrived in November of 1869 and immediately introduced his method of controlling the hatching of eggs. The results were spectacular: the property, which had not shown a profit for ten years, earned 22,000 francs in the first year that Pasteur's method was used.

But Pasteur continued to be troubled. In 1870 it was the war and the sight of young students enlisting for service—including his own eighteen-year-old son and Duruy's three sons—which affected Pasteur profoundly. Upon the insistence of his family, he went to the old family home in Arbois during the war, and there he brooded over the news from the front. The defeat, however it stung him, was no surprise, for he had foreseen disaster arising from a half-century's neglect of science and learning, from the failure to invigorate and expand the public schools.

In January, 1871, Pasteur read that the Prussians had bombarded the Museum of Natural History in the course of their siege of Paris. Despairing and angry, he wrote to the Dean of the Medical Faculty at Bonn, expressed his respect for the faculty, but asked permission to return his doctorate in medicine which had been granted him by Bonn in 1868. It was his protest against the "barbarism of the German Emperor." The answer from Bonn was an expression of the Faculty's "complete contempt" for Pasteur, who had insulted the German nation as personified by the "sacred Emperor."

Perhaps it was Pasteur's postwar bitterness which led him to aid the French beer industry, generally recognized as inferior to that of Germany. He demonstrated that beer could be preserved by a method similar to that used to preserve wine. By heating bottled beer to a temperature of fifty or fifty-five degrees Centigrade, the development of disease fermentations could be avoided. The adjective *pasteurized* was coined by the bottlers of beer, though the process was first used by the wine industry.

Despite the increasing acceptance of Pasteur's views on fermentations by the beer and wine industries of France, many scientists still refused to accept the principle of biogenesis, and the Académie des sciences debates were seldom free from anger and antagonism. Pasteur's own good humor, his usual tolerance of contrary opinions, and his innate kindness began to wear thin after 1870 in the face of what appeared to him to be a perverse determination to ignore the demonstrated truth of his position. If the brewers accepted the notion that ferments are organisms which cannot be born spontaneously, why not his colleagues in the Académie?

But if Pasteur lost his temper in debate, he did not lose his compassion for humanity. Moreover, the loss of three daughters to disease encouraged him to work in that realm where his ex-

periments on fermentations and the silkworm disease were
logically leading him. And perhaps the most sickening aspect of
the war for Pasteur was his certain knowledge that many of the
wounded died because of the medical scientists' refusal to accept
a germ theory of disease. He began regretting that he was a
chemist and not a physician, for chemists were held in low esteem
by the medical profession. Who then would lead the blind? The
answer came to him as a surprise: his election to the Academy of
Medicine in 1873.

He found himself, of course, amid the alien corn. A brave
physician named Villemin, who dared to rise in the Academy of
Medicine to state that tuberculosis was a disease which reproduced itself and could not be produced any other way—a specific,
contagious, and inoculable disease—was hooted down by the
distinguished assembly. If the physicians could not learn from one
of their own, a chemist could hardly expect to be heard. Then,
in February, 1874, came a letter from Joseph Lister to prove that
Pasteur was not without honor in Britain:

> Allow me to take this opportunity to tender you my most cordial
> thanks for having demonstrated to me, by your brilliant researches,
> the truth of the germ theory of putrefaction, and thus furnished me
> with the principle upon which alone the antiseptic system can be
> carried out.

Pasteur was not, of course, without honor in his own country.
The assistance he had given to the wine, beer, and silk industries
was recognized and appreciated, and in 1874, when Pasteur decided to relinquish his post at the Sorbonne because of his paralysis, a bill was presented in Parliament to provide him with an
annuity for life equal to his salary at the Sorbonne. This pension
(12,000 francs) was voted by an overwhelming majority. Nine
years later, Parliament by unanimous vote raised the pension to
25,000 francs, to be payable also to Pasteur's widow and children.

Meanwhile, Pasteur began to experiment in the realm of animal
disease, where others were already at work. The microbe causing
chicken cholera had been recognized in 1869 by several men
sympathetic to Pasteur's theories. He obtained a culture of their

microbes in the hope of finding some way to protect chickens against the disease. Pasteur knew, of course, of Jenner's use of cowpox vaccine in order to immunize against smallpox, but in that treatment a benign disease was induced in order to protect against a serious disease. Pasteur began to inoculate hens from a new culture of chicken cholera microbes; they all died quickly. Then he noticed that hens inoculated from an older culture of the microbes became ill—but they recovered. If reinoculated with a new culture, they showed resistance to the disease. Pasteur quickly recognized the analogy with Jenner's earlier work: immunity from a dread disease could be achieved by inoculating with a vaccine made from the attenuated microbes of the *same disease*. This discovery was a major contribution to medical knowledge.

Pasteur began work on anthrax in 1877, a disease which killed hundreds of sheep annually in France and which often spread to other animals and even to men. Other scientists, Davaine in particular, had found anthrax bacteria in the blood of dying sheep, but had failed to prove conclusively that these bacteria were the cause of the sheep's death. Pasteur first found that it was possible to develop a culture of the bacteria from one drop of a dead animal's blood and that the bacteria were capable of rapid reproduction. He then demonstrated that some of the earlier experiments had failed because blood had not been taken from sheep newly dead. In such instances the blood would contain not merely the anthrax bacteria, but also putrefactive bacteria; and this blood, if inoculated into a rabbit, would kill the rabbit efficiently enough—but from the growth of the putrefactive bacteria in the blood. The putrefactive bacteria, as they grew in the bloodstream, destroyed the anthrax bacteria. The experimenter would then be confounded by the absence of anthrax bacteria in the rabbit, when he knew full well that the blood of the dying sheep had contained them. Accordingly, Pasteur was careful to take blood only from newly dead sheep, and in this blood examination revealed the presence of the anthrax bacteria alone.

As for the development of a vaccine against anthrax, a

Toulouse veterinarian named Toussaint announced a discovery in 1880. He claimed that if blood containing the anthrax bacteria was either filtered to remove the bacteria or heated to fifty-five degrees Centigrade for ten minutes to kill the bacteria, the blood itself would become an effective vaccine. Pasteur was highly skeptical, because he could not understand how such a vaccine could produce an immunity. He tested Toussaint's work and found it unsatisfactory.

Pasteur then proceeded along the track that had brought him success in treating chicken cholera. The problem was to develop a method of attenuating the virulence of the anthrax bacteria. Early in 1881 he announced to the Académie des sciences that he and his assistants had discovered a formula for controlling the virulence of the bacteria: by keeping the bacteria in a broth at a higher temperature than was normal for development, their virulence decreased day by day—making possible a vaccine of controllable virulence. In his report, Pasteur also noted that the weakened bacteria could be restored to their original virulence through successive cultures in small animals.

The Society of French Agriculturists awarded Pasteur a medal in 1881, but their confidence in him was not shared by many scientists. A few, like the physician Sédillot, not only recognized the soundness of the germ theory of disease, but understood that the theory was forcing a medical revolution. The notion that diseases generated spontaneously was no more tenable than the idea that ferments generated spontaneously, but it met similar resistance. It was Sédillot, incidentally, who suggested the word *microbe* to describe disease germs, and when Rossignol, an editor of the *Veterinary Press*, wished to ridicule the whole germ theory of disease he used the word *microbiolatry*.

Confident that Pasteur was wrong, Rossignol demanded that the anthrax vaccine be given a public demonstration. A demonstration was arranged by the Agricultural Society of Melun for April, 1882. Pasteur was given sixty sheep by the Society for the experiment. He began by inoculating twenty-five of the sheep, giving them a second shot after two weeks. Then, on May 31st, the twenty-five were given an inoculation of virulent vaccine, as were twenty-five sheep which had received no prior inoculations of the attenuated vaccine.

A rendezvous was set for June 2nd, when the results would be known. Pasteur, usually confident and calm, suffered a momentary siege of anxiety. He did not lose faith in his theory, but realized that the tests might not have been properly controlled. On the morning of June 2nd, however, a throng of farmers and scientists found the twenty-five sheep prepared by Pasteur for the test healthy and normal; but the other twenty-five, which had not received the attenuated vaccine, were dead or dying. Even Rossignol congratulated Pasteur for his "stunning success." Already a Chevalier in the Legion of Honor, Pasteur was now raised to be a Knight Grand Cross in the Legion of Honor, but he accepted the honor only on condition that his collaborators, Chamberland and Roux, be made Chevaliers.

Pasteur did not initiate the germ theory of disease. Properly speaking, the development of the chicken cholera vaccine was one of Pasteur's two critical innovations. The other was his demonstration of biogenesis. The method used in obtaining the chicken cholera vaccine served as a model for the discovery of the subsequent vaccines; and this work was based on the germ theory of disease, which in turn was based on the concept of biogenesis. Developing the vaccines against chicken cholera, anthrax, and the rouget disease in 1882, of course helped to force the medical profession to accept the germ theory of disease. After Pasteur's demonstrations and his vigorous lectures before the Académie, only the willfully blind could fail to see that a revolution in medicine had taken place.

When Pasteur had demonstrated that spontaneous generation was not necessary to explain what happened in his experiments, why did so many scientists persist in defending heterogenesis? One can suggest that the doctrine of spontaneous generation had a significance for its believers which transcended chemistry and biology. The materialists of the nineteenth century rarely shrank from embracing ideas hurtful to the Church or to religion, but even Darwin's theory of evolution—so distressing to proponents of literal interpretation of the Scriptures—could not provide any ultimate aid and comfort to the materialists. In itself, Evolution did not deny or disprove some sort of First Cause, but the notion of spontaneous generation was clearly subversive to the idea of Divine interference. When Thomas Henry Huxley, the zoologist and evolutionist, announced in 1870 that he could not point to any instance when an organism had been produced without parents, the heterogenesists were further undermined—and from an unexpected quarter.

Most French scientists in the mid-nineteenth century were materialists; therefore, the doctrine of spontaneous generation seemed both logical and desirable to them, and their minds were not prepared to accept the newer notion of biogenesis. Pasteur, on the other hand, was a Christian. Consciously or otherwise, he was hostile to the idea of spontaneous generation.

Questions asked of Pasteur—and his answers—reveal that non-scientific considerations were at stake. He was asked, for example, from whence had come the first germ. He replied that this was a mystery which was beyond the realm of science, because it concerned the origin of all life. Nor could he prove that spontaneous generation had not taken place sometime in the prehistorical past, which gave the heterogenesists some satisfaction; but he continued to assert two points: that he was solely concerned with phenomena which Science can demonstrate, and that the fermentations which took place in his phials derived from biogenesis and not from spontaneous generation.

Pasteur's importance, however, does not rest on his innovations alone. He believed in biogenesis before he had demonstrated the soundness of biogenesis in the laboratory; similarly, he understood that biogenesis was the key to attacking disease successfully. This was the real measure of his genius. His laboratory work remains a supreme example of the experimental method. His experiments were directed toward proving theories he held before the experiments began, and he was not a blank slate, so to speak, objectively piling up data in a laboratory in the expectation that the data would coalesce into a discovery.

In his later years Pasteur became increasingly obsessed with a desire to conquer hydrophobia, a disease which inspired a particular horror in him and which Renan had hopefully predicted that Pasteur would conquer. He failed to find the microbe which produced rabies in dogs, but he became convinced that a mad dog's brain was a better source than its saliva for obtaining the microbes. He then began to cultivate the unseen microbes in the brains of live rabbits, until he produced a microbe whose virulence was greater than that found in the usual rabid dog.

Next, Pasteur turned his attention to attenuating the virulence of the microbes. He found that by drying a bit of a rabbit's medulla kept in a glass phial at a constant temperature of twenty-three degrees Centigrade, the microbe's virulence disappeared in two weeks. If the medulla was then crushed and mixed with water, it provided a vaccine which gave dogs immunity to rabies. A commission was formed in 1884 by the Ministry of Public Instruction to test Pasteur's discovery, and it verified his results.

The work was not complete, however, as it was impractical to try immunizing all the dogs in France, whose estimated number was 100,000 in Paris alone with another two and a half million in the provinces. Pasteur wanted a vaccine which would protect people after they had been bitten by rabid dogs, as it was probable that many dogs would escape immunization. But how did one test vaccine on human beings? Pasteur proposed to the Emperor of Brazil, who had expressed great interest in Pasteur's researches, that perhaps criminals condemned to death might be induced to volunteer for experiments. It happened, however, that the decision to inoculate a human being was forced upon Pasteur before he had become reconciled to the idea.

In 1885 a nine-year-old Alsatian boy, Joseph Meister, was bitten badly by a rabid dog. His mother brought him to Pasteur for treatment. Pasteur, of course, did not know whether the vaccine which gave dogs immunity to rabies would protect the child—or even a dog—if administered after a bite. He consulted with other scientists and physicians, and the consensus was that, as the child was doomed in any event, Pasteur should proceed with the inoculations. The first inoculation was made with the two-week-old matter from the rabbit's medulla which had entirely lost its virulence. The subsequent shots—and there were twelve—were steadily increased in virulence. Pasteur suffered terrible anxiety during the treatment until it became clear that the boy would survive.

The battle against hydrophobia had been won, though, as some patients were brought to Pasteur too late to be saved, the treatment's efficacy was challenged for a time by a few physicians. In gratitude for Pasteur's work, the Comte de Laubespin pledged 40,000 francs in his desire to establish a hydrophobia control center in Paris: the Institut Pasteur. A gift of 43,000 francs came from Alsace-Lorraine, little Joseph Meister being one of the subscribers. Then the Russian government gave 100,000 francs in gratitude for the treatment Pasteur had given nineteen Russian peasants who had been bitten by a rabid wolf. They had been brought to Paris from the province of Smolensk so that two weeks had transpired before treatment began; three were beyond help, but Pasteur saved sixteen. In addition to the money for the Institut, the Czar presented Pasteur with the Cross of the Order of St. Anne.

Though one remembers Pasteur for his triumphs in scientific research, he often thought of himself as a teacher, and worried about the inadequate public school system. At his earlier teaching posts, he was not regarded as a skillful teacher, but by the time he got to Lille his lectures were considerably more polished. That he resented the time lost to the laboratory there is no doubt, but he also recognized the importance of good teaching. His desire to serve education better led him to stand for the Senate (1876) in the Department of Jura. The departmental electoral college, however, paid him the compliment of suggesting that France could not afford to lose so valuable a citizen to the Senate. Receiving sixty-two of the 650 electoral votes, he ran last in a field of five.

More appropriately, he was elected to the Académie française in 1881. From his eighteenth year Pasteur had maintained an interest in French literary matters. Even during his busy years at the Ecole normale, he never missed a lecture by Sainte-Beuve and once was heard to remark that in Science the mind alone is necessary, but that in Literature "both the mind and heart intervene, accounting for its [Literature's] superiority in leading the general train of thought." He owed his election, of course, to the literary excellence of the volumes describing his research and not to his love of literature.

At the Académie française, Pasteur took the chair of Littré, a Positivist whose philosophy had always been distasteful to Pasteur. Years earlier, Sainte-Beuve and Pasteur had discussed supporting a young scientist, Charles Robin, for a seat in the Académie des sciences. Robin was known as a disciple of Auguste Comte, and Pasteur remarked that, having himself read "a few absurd passages" from Comte, he hoped that Robin's scientific work would not be influenced by his philosophical prejudices. Pasteur summed up his opposition to Positivism in his introductory speech at the Académie: "Positivism does not take into account the most important of positive notions—that of the Infinite."

Pasteur's last honor came on his seventieth birthday, December 27, 1892. Delegates from learned academies and societies—both French and foreign—joined with the diplomatic corps in the Sorbonne theater to greet the distinguished scholar. He entered the theater on the arm of President Sadi Carnot and, amidst an ovation from the audience, was embraced by the English surgeon Joseph Lister. Pasteur's emotion was so great that he could not respond to the audience, and his brief speech was read by his son.

Pasteur was loved for more than his contributions to knowledge. He was known for his gratitude for his family's kind indulgence when he was a shy, uncertain adolescent, for his devotion to his old teachers and his academic friends, and for his kindly nature which had always made him unwilling to engage in academic quarrels or answer his critics. Later in life, it is true, he became a more aggressive publicist for his ideas, but only because his humanitarianism overcame his natural reticence. Each day counted in his campaign to end human suffering. His sensitivity was such that hospitals filled him with horror, and for all his scientific disinterestedness he was usually ill after post-mortem examinations, so much did he hate the sight of corpses. In this light, the attacks of the antivivisectionists upon Pasteur were particularly vicious, because they implied that he took pleasure in the injections and operations. No one could have taken less pleasure in them than he; they were an unpleasant necessity in the interest of mankind.

Pasteur had suffered partial paralysis since 1868, but only in the last several years of his life was his speech affected. An attack of uremia in late 1894 was nearly fatal, but he recovered to survive another eleven months. He died on September 28, 1895, surrounded by family and disciples, but completely paralyzed and mute at the end. He was given a state funeral at Notre-Dame, and only one address, by Raymond Poincaré, the Minister of Public Instruction, was allowed. The body was placed in a tomb at the Institut Pasteur, and over the entrance to the tomb one finds the words: "Blessed is he who bears a god within himself, an ideal of beauty which he obeys: the ideal of art, the ideal of science, the ideal of the fatherland, the ideal of the virtues of the Gospel."

VIII

Victor Duruy

AND LIBERAL EDUCATION

*I think that all religious ideas are merely
symbolical; but I think the same of the
ideas of science and even of the senses: so
that the way is cleared for faith, in deciding which set of symbols one will
trust.*

—GEORGE SANTAYANA

The man who was to become one of Napoleon III's most able and controversial ministers was born on September 10, 1811, in Gobelins, the celebrated tapestry quarter in Paris. The Duruy family had lived in Gobelins since the reign of Louis XIV, when Colbert had induced them to move from Arras in his effort to stimulate the Parisian tapestry industry. In the sixteenth and seventeenth centuries, the family had been Protestant, though by Victor's time this tradition had been lost. For generations after Colbert, the boys of the family learned their fathers' skills, and at the age of twelve Victor began his apprenticeship.

The previous year, however, he had been sent to study with a man named Hénon, who was an outspoken liberal, a Bonapartist, and an anticlerical, who taught young Duruy that the Bourbon Restoration was really a victory for the Church and for those rather feeble souls who required religious escape. This lesson harmonized with sentiments expressed at the Duruy home and was readily accepted by the boy. But Hénon also gave him a taste for books, leaving him miscast as an apprentice. A family friend, an economist at the Collège Sainte-Barbe, intervened, and in 1824 Duruy was enrolled at the Collège, even though inadequately prepared. To the end of his days, Duruy was conscious of his family's sacrifice. They were poor, so poor that Victor could not have travel money to go home on vacation days. And they sorrowed at seeing the family tradition broken, as there had been only one other defection since the seventeenth century—an uncle who had served Napoleon I rather than art.

Owing to his industry, Duruy surmounted his slow start at the Collège and soon did well in Greek, Latin, and history. He graduated in 1830 (just in time to see the Bourbon monarchy overthrown in July), and on August 1st he began his entrance tests for admission to the Ecole normale, where he hoped to become a history professor. The examination results were not known for six weeks, and Duruy was determined to enter military service in Algeria should he fail. But he passed and thus spent the next three years under Michelet, Burnouf, Jouffroy, and Ampère. He was certified in history in September of 1833 and appointed the next month to a professorship at the Collège de Reims.

This appointment did not make Duruy a college professor in the American sense, but a teacher in a secondary school. French educational terminology is often confusing and requires explanation. Primary education in France is roughly equal to our first eight grades. Secondary education, the next six years, includes our high school and junior college training, and these schools are designated as either *collèges* or *lycées*. The graduate of the secondary school may then proceed to a professional school on the university level, as in the case of Duruy at the Ecole normale.

In the time of the First Empire—and in the anticlerical spirit of the eighteenth century and the French Revolution—Napoleon I created the Université de France, which was the public school faculty, and which taught in the name of the state in primary, secondary, and professional schools. The Minister of Public Instruction was, therefore, automatically head of the Université. Catholic teaching orders did exist, of course, but they were obliged to limit their work to parochial schools. Under the Bourbon Restoration governments, there was real danger that the Université would be abolished and the Church put in control of public education, but as anticlericalism was strong the Restoration governments were obliged to bide their time.

Duruy found Reims isolated and provincial, but he loved the teaching. Upon his arrival, he discovered that a philosophy professor had been nourishing a running battle with a physics professor on the subject of miracles. In his classes he avoided political and religious issues, which he regarded as transitory matters and, therefore, foreign to the verities which ought to constitute scholarly instruction. In addition, he thought that teachers, as state officials, ought not to serve political or religious factions. Less than six months after his arrival at Reims, Duruy was promoted to a school in Paris, Henri IV. Two of the King's sons, the Ducs d'Aumale and de Montpensier, were enrolled, and the school needed a better history instructor. He began his work on March 1, 1834, and soon found the Duc d'Aumale to be a superior student. Duruy gave him extra work at the Tuileries in the winter and at Neuilly in the summer. In this way he came to know the royal family and to admire in particular the Duc d'Orléans. Later in life, Duruy said that he was convinced that the Duc d'Orléans, had he lived past 1842, would never have sanctioned the domestic policies which brought down the House of Orléans in 1848. We get a glimpse of Duruy's philosophy when he says that the Duc knew

that society is a collection of constantly renewing individuals, that ideas modify, interests change, that nothing on earth is immutable, that yesterday's policy cannot always be tomorrow's. History reveals that evolution is the law of the social world.

During the second year at Henri IV, Duruy began writing books for a distinguished member of the Institut de France, for which he received half the royalties, and he began work on his own *Roman History*. He spent ten years in the preparation of the first two volumes of this work, which appeared in 1843–1844. They were well received by the academic world and brought Duruy to the attention of the Comte de Salvandy, then Minister of Public Instruction. Salvandy was always eager to promote promising professors, and he arranged to have Duruy decorated by the state. Furthermore, he had Duruy promoted to be the second-ranking history professor at Saint-Louis (1845).

Duruy believed that all men ought to take stock of themselves and their beliefs midway in life. In his own case, he was thirty-six when he set himself to the task and began by writing a motto: "All intellectual life has truth and justice as a goal." He then proceeded to depict a philosophy which is a curious mixture of eighteenth century rationalism, skepticism, and classical idealism.

Recognizing man's physical limitations, he suggested in an essay that there are also limits to human intelligence, and concluded that man's intelligence by itself is insufficient to know

God. Moreover, "man would even be more than God if he could analyze and define Him." Despite the futility of searching for God, Duruy noted that Western man had been retarded until the sixteenth century when he had awakened to more profitable research. "How long have the devil, astrology, alchemy, magic, and religions—with their conceptions of the divine, their miracles, and their mysteries—kept peoples and science in bondage?"

Like many of his contemporaries, Duruy equated religion and fear. Man is born quite defenseless and is surrounded by frightening objects and phenomena; "he trembles and prays." To prayer he soon adds the sacrifice; "thus, he creates a cult." Finally, men of superior knowledge range themselves between the crowd and the fearsome: "the priesthood." But happily for modern men in the scientific age, reason explains all phenomena and man ceases to be fearful. Explains all except God, of course, but He is not a proper subject for human reasoning as He is beyond understanding.

Duruy felt his views were summarized in a line from Corneille: "Tend to your own work and leave the gods alone." But while he might say with Montaigne, "What do I know?" he would contradict himself by asserting that everything in the universe has its law, and "laws suppose a legislator. . . . It is essential to recognize God as a Prime Mover and supreme organizer, but . . . He reigns and does not govern." Man's proper work, wrote Duruy, is to strive for a human ideal on earth, where man is the supreme being. The ideal will vary according to time and place; and, significantly enough, he wrote, "Morality is a thing which increases in proportion as intellectual life grows." Salvation was, it would seem, to be achieved on earth through education.

More precisely, human progress would depend upon education. Duruy felt that humanity had not surpassed the Greeks or Hebrews in morality, nor Homer, Pericles, Plato, Aristotle, or Molière in intelligence, nor the physical strength of the Greeks and Romans. Progress, then, was dependent, in his view, upon making "knowledge, morality, taste, and well-being the property of a greater number. Man has been given powers; it is our duty to develop them." This was an honorable ideal and one which

Duruy spent his life promoting. If, in his enthusiasm for education, he was prone to equate literacy with culture, we must
remember that his notion of what constituted an education was
a rigorous introduction to the history, philosophy, science, and
fine arts of Western civilization.

As Duruy was by choice a historian, it is natural that his self-
appraisal suggested a philosophy of history. He thought that
historians ought to be most concerned with the ideas and motives
which have guided the world, as they give us the truest apprecia-
tion of past societies. Furthermore, this approach makes us feel
keenly how much of the past there is in the present. "The ideas
of yesterday," he wrote, "are a useful rein on today's ideas in
that they prevent us from plunging too swiftly toward those of
the future." Obviously Duruy was not reactionary, nor was he
enthusiastic for novelty just for the sake of change.

He believed that society is subject to the same "leveling law" as
the physical world. Mountains wear down and their debris fills up
the valleys. Similarly, he said, aristocracies slowly melt back into
the people, while slaves rise toward more freedom. Echoing an
Hegelian idea, Duruy noted that every forward step in mankind's
existence had been toward freedom, and that in the nineteenth
century it was no longer a question of smashing bastilles but of
bringing a higher standard of living to everyone. He was quick
to add that though it was right to bring greater ease to everyone, it would "mutilate human nature" to establish any sort of
economic or social equality, for Nature, if she did not create
slaves, did not make men equal in mind or body.

Rather than work to make the proletariat disappear, Duruy
favored reducing its size, just as Science works to reduce physical ills without ever expecting to see them entirely removed. As
property is the accumulation of the fruits of man's labor, it is
a legitimate extension of individual freedom. "To touch one
would be to destroy the other." This was his answer to the socialist doctrines of the day which, he claimed, were incompatible
with the laws of nature.

At the same time, Duruy knew that an industrializing France
faced serious social questions which would require concessions by

those who "possessed" and moderation by those who wished to possess, and his recommendation for the future was only common sense given the circumstances: "Henceforth, let the bourgeois consider the workers as one of the means to his own good fortune and allow them to earn a greater share of the profits." The vision of women and children dying of hunger on the doorsteps of sumptuous houses haunted Duruy, and he thought it high time that the people of means be instructed in their charitable obligations at the same time that they learned of their own true interests.

The February Revolution of 1848 occurred shortly after Duruy had completed his philosophical résumé. He was hostile to the "unwholesome utopianism" of many of the Republicans and angry that Louis-Philippe's ministers, Guizot in particular, had not known how to prevent the uprising. When it came to the presidential elections, he voted for General Cavaignac as an honest man who had saved France from further radicalism during the June Days. Poor Cavaignac, of course, was swamped by a heavy majority for Louis-Napoleon.

Soon after the elections Duruy completed work on the third and fourth volumes of his *Roman History*. The earlier volumes had appeared in 1843–1844, but he was hesitant to publish the later volumes owing to the fact that he openly sided with the Roman Empire against what he called the "false Republic." He had characterized the latter as an oligarchy of one hundred families who gnawed on the bones of sixty million men. Fearing to encourage a new Caesar, the one he had voted against in 1848 (historians commonly suffer the illusion that their works will be influential), Duruy put his manuscript in a drawer from which it did not emerge until 1872.

In the second year of the Republic, 1849, there was an opening in history at the Ecole normale, and Duruy expected the appointment. But Falloux, a Legitimist, was the Minister of Public Instruction, and Duruy's liberalism made him unacceptable. Despite this disappointment, Duruy decided to promote a project which he had anticipated beginning upon his arrival at the Ecole normale. Long annoyed at the uncritical, styleless, boring history texts used in the schools, he recruited thirty professors and outlined sixty volumes which would survey the history of civilized man. The plan, which included histories of literature, the arts, and the sciences, was entitled: *Universal History Published by a Society of Professors and Learned Men, Under the Direction of M. Victor Duruy*.

In addition to directing the project, Duruy agreed to produce one volume on Greek history and two volumes on French history. His *Greek History* appeared in 1851 and won him a scolding by the administration of the Université. The Ministry of Public Instruction was dominated by men of conservative opinion, and they held that Duruy was wrong in preferring Athens to Sparta. Here is Duruy's summary of the Ministry's position: "Sparta, representing the principle of authority, must be exalted; Athens, having had the bad taste to grant too much liberty, must be condemned by History, despite Pericles's century."

Duruy's position as a member of the Université continued to be uneasy as he opposed the *coup d'état* of 1851 and voted against Louis-Napoleon in the plebiscite which amended the constitution. But Duruy did not feel obliged to resign his teaching post, for though he was a state official he had always believed that his professional work transcended daily politics. He was determined to stay on as long as no one prevented him from giving his opinion or forced him to say what he did not think. Perhaps it is a commentary on the dictatorship of Napoleon III—for the Republic gave way to Empire in 1852—that Duruy never felt himself censored.

There were, to be sure, academic quarrels with political overtones. Duruy was known to be liberal and anticlerical, and, being partisan himself, was therefore subject to partisan reviews of his books. His two-volume *History of France* was published in 1853, and it was no surprise that it received a bad review in *L'Univers*, the conservative Catholic journal. The review was written by the Abbé Brulebois, who scored Duruy for the "rashness and inaccuracy" of his interpretations and insisted on the suppression of several passages, notably one relative to the Civil Constitution of the Clergy.

If this response had been foreseen, Duruy was considerably less prepared to have the official journal of the Ministry of Public Instruction take its cue from the Abbé Brulebois and suggest that corrections were in order. This official criticism was never sent directly to Duruy, and he was aware that the government did not plan to pursue the matter. The incident was, in fact, an illustration of the government's policy of simultaneously pleasing all the major factions in the nation.

The new Emperor was eager to prove one of the main theses in the Napoleonic Legend: that the Bonapartes alone were above faction and hence could govern in the general interest. In the case of Duruy's books, the government had thrown the Catholics a sop by appearing to adopt the line suggested in *L'Univers* and expected to satisfy the liberals by never moving in the direction of censorship or suppression. Behind such a smoke screen of appearances, the Emperor promoted his real policies, and whether the policies were noble or infamous, wise or stupid, such a governing technique must inevitably produce confusion, misunderstanding, and lack of confidence.

Duruy, however, could not be placated by the failure of the government to censor or suppress his texts, as he had received publicity injurious to his professional reputation. It was bad enough, he wrote to the Université administration, to have received only one promotion in twenty-three years of laborious service. Was he now to tolerate a sort of excommunication for the pleasure of the conservative Catholics, "who will always be —no matter what they do—the enemies of the government?" In response, the Ministry assigned an inspector general named Laferrière, a man of moderate Catholic views, to examine Duruy's book. Laferrière thought well of the book and suggested only a few alterations—all of them "nuances and not points of doctrine."

Duruy, quite naturally, expected to be vindicated, but he waited in vain for the ministerial pronouncement. The following year, 1854, he called on the Minister, then Fortoul, and discovered some misunderstanding. It is possible that Fortoul never bothered to read Laferrière's report or had just been shown the negative sections. After some confusion, Duruy was assured that the report had indeed been favorable, whereupon Duruy promised he would comply with Laferrière's suggestions in his next edition. After something under two years, he had cleared his reputation and could continue teaching with a peaceful conscience.

Indeed, it seems likely that Duruy would have completed his days in professorial obscurity had it not been for an aggrieved Marshal of France who required the services of a historian. Marshal Randon was removed as Governor of Algeria in 1859 to make room for Prince Jerome-Napoleon, who took a new title: Minister of Colonies. The Prince, a strong supporter of Napoleon's Italian policy, was thus officially thanked, and Randon, who had never been enthusiastic for the Empire, paid the price. (He had resigned the Ministry of War in 1851 to avoid participation in the *coup d'état.*)

Shortly afterward the Emperor discovered that Marshal Vaillant's preparations for the coming war against Austria were inadequate, revealing him a poor administrator; having a spare marshal, Napoleon removed Vaillant and named Randon the Minister of War. Even so, Randon did not consider his record in Algeria vindicated, and he hoped to flatten the government with a literary salvo. Duruy and Randon were introduced, and Duruy, who knew the futility of paper wars against the impersonal agencies of government, persuaded the Marshal to surrender the idea of polemics in favor of an account of his record in Algeria. Duruy would write the pamphlet, Randon would furnish the source materials, and it would be signed by one of the Marshal's aides. As a simple historical task, Duruy was glad to set the record straight, and he noted in his *Mémoires* that he received no compensation—as if to prove that he had written history.

One day when Randon was waiting on the Emperor, he noticed Duruy's *Roman History* on the Emperor's desk. When Napoleon entered, Randon remarked that he knew the author. Napoleon then asked Randon to arrange an audience for the following day. If one will remember that this was 1859, the year in which His Majesty pondered the most critical foreign and domestic decisions of his reign, and will then visualize him sphinx-like in a chair, smoking cigarette after cigarette with his mind riveted on Julius

Caesar, one will get a characteristic picture of the man. He lived a double life: he had to govern, to meet the exigencies of his supreme political position, and yet he felt compelled to persist in his life-long habit of developing the rationale for caesarean democracy. That he had become Caesar was not enough; he was also, as Duke Ernest of Saxe-Coburg remarked, a German savant. The two roles are not always compatible.

It is difficult to say how long Napoleon III had seriously contemplated writing a history of Julius Caesar. Maxime Du Camp tells us that one week before the *coup d'état* of 1851, Morny arranged for Napoleon to see photographs which Du Camp had taken in Egypt and the Near East. In retrospect, Du Camp noted that Napoleon had been especially interested in monuments and ruins relating to Caesar, and there is evidence that Napoleon thought of the project while still a prisoner in Ham. Now, in 1859, he was at work, and he sat down in his study to chat with Duruy in a manner so informal that Duruy forgot his host's rank and held forth on the insecurity of the Roman emperors:

> I claimed that the first Caesar, while founding royalty, had not established a monarchy. The emperors did not have the support of the noble and priestly classes of monarchical states, nor were they supported by the institutions of free societies. Thus, they were exposed to ambitious schemers. In order to seize sovereign power—to become a god on earth—only one chest needs to be pierced, and from Augustus to Constantine, it was pierced forty times.

Once outside, Duruy began to question the tact of his remark about the forty assassinated Emperors and concluded he had been a better citizen than a courtier. Marshal Randon later assured him, however, that the Emperor had reported him an intelligent man, adding that he had not agreed with Duruy on all points.

In January of 1860, Duruy was summoned by Gustave Rouland, who had been Minister of Public Instruction since 1856. The Council of State was about to discuss the Roman Question (see the chapter on the Duc de Persigny), and Rouland wanted some notes on the subject in order to seem informed. He gave Duruy four days to prepare a memorandum, which, when completed, recommended the following solution: to limit the Papacy to the Vatican, the Pope to receive ambassadors from the Christian nations, and a civil list to be provided by all Catholic countries, each paying in proportion to its population. Duruy noted that, thus constituted, the Papacy would benefit "by being despoiled of its governmental troubles, despoiled of the cheaper, less spiritual, aspects of government."

Several days later, Rouland ordered Duruy to publish his ideas, suggesting that they had received imperial approval. He was granted four more days to polish the memorandum into literature, but in the meantime the plebiscite in Romagna produced union with Sardinia, and the brochure became dated. It was published under another name to avoid any association with the Université. The Emperor had first assumed that the ideas had been Rouland's, and it is not clear who informed His Majesty of the true author.

In 1861, however, a senior inspector generalship fell vacant, and when Rouland nominated an old man of merit, Professor Chéruel, Napoleon ordered Duruy's name substituted. Rouland immediately suspected that Duruy was undermining him at the Tuileries. To smooth over the situation, Duruy offered to accept a lesser position at the Ecole normale, which carried with it an inspector generalship at the Academy of Paris, the Sorbonne. The inspector generalship was regarded as a sinecure by the Ministry and was handed out to make the professorship at the Ecole normale more attractive financially. This will explain why the Minister was surprised to receive a schedule of reforms for the Sorbonne, which Duruy compiled in 1861, and why nothing came of his proposals.

In July, Marshal Randon again approached Duruy, requesting that he review the curricula in military schools. Duruy spent a week at La Flèche, and his recommendations were quite acceptable to the Ministry of War and were deemed applicable to Saint-Cyr as well. Once again Rouland's jealousy was aroused, and he accused Duruy of insulting the Army. Marshal Randon, thoroughly annoyed at such pettiness, ordered that Duruy be sent a letter of commendation for the "active, devoted, and disinterested part" he had taken in furthering the necessary reforms. Thus armed, Duruy fired back at Rouland:

I have been offering you, M. le Ministre, a friendly, resolute, and active cooperation. . . . When one has spent one's life—as I have—in looking for what is right for others, it is quite proper to seek it for oneself.

In February of 1862, Duruy was nominated to a newly vacated inspector generalship, and coming after his tiff with Rouland, there was no doubt that the Emperor had interfered. The new post required Duruy to be absent from Paris four months out of the year and meant that he had to give up his chair at the Ecole normale. Coincidentally, however, the Ministry of War created a chair of history at the Ecole polytechnique as one of the curriculum reforms, and Duruy was offered the position with the understanding that his courses could be arranged to suit his inspection schedule.

He proposed to avoid the usual survey course in French history and to offer the students a course in the history of traditional European problems. Noting that these students would have already had three or four years of French history in *lycée*, he suggested that it would be to the national interest to provide them with a broader education worthy of their eventual positions of influence. Furthermore, a study of traditional problems should lead to a consideration of recent events and even current problems. It was part of Duruy's philosophy of education that formal instruction in contemporary affairs could help to heal the factionalism left by the French Revolution, to produce what he called a "reunification" of the French in putting country above party.

Fragments of Duruy's opening lecture at the Ecole polytechnique express his educational philosophy:

What an immense realm is that where imagination and thought are queen, where the poet and artist search for beauty, the moralist for justice, and the historian for truth. It includes your realm, Gentlemen, and it goes farther; for beyond the nebulae—whose distances you calculate—lie the unfathomable depths of infinity, which are penetrated by the mind's eye alone, and that other infinity for which your

Laplace has no use—God. . . . The Humanities do not give man an increased power over matter but give him greater justice, purify his heart, raise his spirit, captivate his imagination and taste, and, finally, make him a man. . . .

Extreme division of labor produces marvels in industry and science, but only a few gifted people escape the dangers of narrow specialization, and the system acts to reduce the value of man. Even the most fruitful land becomes exhausted by bearing the same crop. Rotation conserves and promotes the original vigor. . . .

Two and two are four in mathematics, but not always in life, in art, or in morality. Outside the exact sciences, truth is often a mixture of the true and the false. . . . Greek architecture, the world's best, represents the triumph of the straight line. Yet, do you Gentlemen know one of the reasons for the powerful impression which the bare Parthenon—dismantled and ruined—still produces? Not one of its lines is rigorously straight; not one of its surfaces is rigorously flat.

In short, Duruy told his audience that education means learning what it is to be a man among men, and he warned them against an indifference to individual responsibility. His study of history had taught him that every fault, every error, every crime had been punished, though he noted that justice had often confused our notions of individual responsibility:

If it has been said, "Sow the wind and reap the whirlwind," it is true that the one who gathers the miserable harvest is not always the reprehensible sower. . . . In the organic world, nature cares not for the individual; let him live, prosper, or fail. She reserves all her solicitude for the species. There is an analogous law in the moral world. The individual is neither immediately nor always rewarded or punished, but society unfailingly is.

Meanwhile Duruy began his inspection trips. At Lorient, he found the naval cadets studying only technical subjects, and an admiral seriously objected to the narrow curriculum on the grounds that it had never prepared him for the actual duties of a naval officer.

In my entire career, I have not had to use one-hundredth of the mathematics that they took so much trouble to teach me. But constantly I have had reports to write, memoranda to draw up, men to lead, important administrative matters to resolve, and even to carry on negotiations. Newton's binomial has been perfectly useless for all that, and I should have been lost twenty times had I not undertaken the general education of my mind after my schooling.

Duruy was reasonably certain that his recommendations to Rouland—that the Army educational reforms be copied—were never passed on to the Navy.

At Coutances, a town in Manche, Duruy watched a boy who was twice the size of his classmates struggle hopelessly with his Greek and Latin recitation. His father had done well enough in butter and cows to allow the boy to take advantage of public education. As Duruy watched the unhappy boy, he realized that the state was wrong in trying to provide the same instruction for all children. While never supposing for a minute that vocational training was true education, Duruy understood the state's obligation to provide special schools for those not able to benefit from the traditional courses. This boy would ultimately return to the farm provided, to use Duruy's remark, with no other agricultural instruction than a smattering of Greek roots. He did not forget the incident, but put it aside for the moment.

Duruy had to do more than criticize curricula and visit classrooms. Bursars' books, dormitories, and kitchens were his realm also, and it was only now that he realized the deplorable state of scientific equipment available in the schools. On top of this, Napoleon III, after more than two years of silence, wrote on February 27, 1862, to ask what proof existed for the following statement:

I submit that the greatness of a man's genius can be measured by the duration of the influence which survives him, that is, the influence of ideas which he has made triumphant and which still prevail long after he has ceased to exist.

Duruy answered that the proposition was incontestable and that, in the case of Caesar, one could see his influence on all subsequent Roman government. The ultimate collapse of the Roman Empire, he suggested, was caused by the failure of the later emperors to complete the reform of taxes and provincial administration begun by Caesar and to centralize the Empire. The death of the Empire was not caused by bad morals, fiscal problems, soldiers, or slaves, he wrote, but by bad politics, a poor constitution of power, and faulty organization of the state. "Caesar would have known how to prevent this."

His Majesty had completed a draft of his two volumes on Caesar and was working on the Preface when he sent Duruy the above question. The Preface deserves attention, for in none of Napoleon III's written work is there such specific evidence of his sincere belief in the Napoleonic Legend. He writes of Caesar but slips into generalities about superior men:

When the extraordinary facts attest to an eminent genius, what is more contrary to good sense than to assign him all the passions and sentiments of mediocrity? What is more false than not to recognize the preeminence of these privileged beings who appear from time to time in history as beacons, scattering the shadows of their epoch and lighting the future? In addition, to deny this preeminence would be an injury to humanity.

The Preface ends with a frank admission of the writer's purpose:

My goal is to prove that when Providence creates men such as Caesar, Charlemagne, and Napoleon, it is to trace out the path which the peoples must follow, to mark a new era with the impact of their genius, and to fulfill several centuries' work in a few years. Happy are the peoples who understand them and follow them! Misfortune to those who misunderstand them and resist. They are like the Jews: they crucify their Messiah. . . .

Napoleon's ostracism by Europe has not prevented the resurgence of Empire, though we are far from the resolution of great problems, the appeasement of passions, and the legitimate satisfactions given to the peoples by the First Empire!

Every day since 1815, this prophecy by the captive of St. Helena has been verified: "How many struggles, how much blood, how many years will still be required until the good which I desire for humanity can be realized!"

Palace of the Tuileries, March 20, 1862.

The next communication from the Emperor was an invitation to spend a week at Compiègne in November, but Duruy was frightened at the prospect and invented excuses. Then came a message from Mocquard, Napoleon's secretary, asking Duruy to recommend someone as an assistant. Mocquard was getting old and was in poor health, but as Duruy inferred that he was being asked to recommend a scholar, he volunteered his own services from four to seven o'clock each day. It appeared that Mocquard had nothing but secretarial work to be done, and as Napoleon quickly escorted Duruy out of Mocquard's office it is evident that the imperial author had chosen this subterfuge to gain some professional criticism. Duruy was presented with the draft of the *History of Julius Caesar* and his opinion required.

As anyone who has had occasion to criticize a manuscript can attest, Duruy had been assigned a necessary—if often thankless—task. And when the manuscript was the property of the Emperor, in a nation where teachers were civil servants, Duruy might have been excused for likening the volumes to Thucydides. The astonishing thing was that Napoleon III, still respected by Europe as the vanquisher of Russia and Austria, was a friendly, gentle, quiet man. He allowed complete freedom of language in his presence, so that Duruy dared give the criticism his professional integrity demanded.

He found in the first volume, for example, the following sentence: "One can legitimately violate legality when society is running to ruin and a heroic remedy is indispensable." It was clearly a paraphrase of a sentence which had appeared in Napoleon III's proclamation to the French on the morrow of the *coup d'état* of 1851. Duruy advised omitting the sentence: "One does things like that, but it is best not to recall their memory." And he protested against the theory of providential men, which he found in the Preface, on the grounds that it made "God an accomplice in realms where He does not mingle."

Duruy spent a few hours a week at the Tuileries for nearly three months and then left for his annual inspection tour. He did not write to Napoleon, preferring to be as obscure as possible. For the Emperor had made Mocquard a Senator, a certain indication that Mocquard was preparing to retire and that a new secretary would be recruited. Duruy feared himself to be a candidate, and thus we may gauge his surprise to receive a telegram from the Ministry in Paris: "It appears that you are our Minister." Duruy—in Moulins—thought it an error, but when the Prefect of Allier rushed in to congratulate him, Duruy knew it to be true.

In deciding to accept the office, Duruy tells us that he did so with a clear conscience. The Emperor knew that he had opposed the *coup d'état*, that he was a liberal and an anticlerical, and even the quality of his historical work. His nomination specifically mentioned that henceforth the Ministry of Cults would be separate from the Ministry of Public Instruction, and Duruy believed this to be another liberal sign. Perhaps, in taking office, he could support the development of a truly liberal government. Furthermore, Napoleon III was offering him free rein within the Ministry (he never received any specific instructions from the Emperor), and the recent inspection trips had suggested many necessary reforms. His appointment as Minister was dated June 23, 1863.

Rouland, now former Minister, was furious, and regarded Duruy's appointment as clear evidence that Duruy had been sabotaging him at court. To prove his good faith, Duruy helped Rouland to get the governorship of the Bank of France, but Rouland never got over his bitterness. There were others, however, who were pleased by the appointment, if somewhat startled, for Duruy had no political influence, no official ambition, and he was not well known even in academic circles. His colleagues rated him a substantial scholar, but not a brilliant one. Yet, the professors can be excused if they were delighted to see one of their own rise to head the Université, a post almost always held by a politician. For once, academic problems would take precedence over politics; for once, the Minister would be an able champion of public education, as he had devoted his life to its basic principles.

Duruy's educational program and the opposition which it aroused must be studied with two points in mind. The first is that France had never had an uncontested tradition of the separation of State and Church; indeed, traditionally they were united, and hence state-supported education and religious training were not widely regarded as incompatible. The second factor is that the secular spirit characteristic of modern life—which made the separation of Church and State, religion and education, inevitable —had been gathering momentum since the later Middle Ages, as the intelligentsia increasingly lost faith in a religious ideal and in Revelation as the means to the most profound truths.

As this evolution progressed, science became more physical and less metaphysical, and the quest for heavenly salvation gave way to demands for a more pleasant existence on this earth. By the late eighteenth century, the secular forces became politically dominant in France, and when Napoleon I established the Université, putting education in the hands of laymen, he defined the battle lines between the old and the new. In the nineteenth century, and in particular during Duruy's régime, the clerical forces fought a rearguard action in defense of the old definitions of a good life and of salvation. When Maxime Du Camp wrote that "education is indeed the salvation of humanity," he was echoing Duruy's views, for the latter believed that religion had little ameliorating effect on the general morality of mankind.

Having received no formal instructions from the Emperor, Duruy wrote to Napoleon on August 6, 1863, outlining the principles which he intended to pursue. First of all, primary education must become obligatory for all as a logical consequence of universal suffrage, and the early years must be sufficiently rich to encourage students to proceed to secondary schools.

Next, the secondary schools must always work "to develop the mind and purify the taste of our future industrial population" before they teach the practical use of the hands. Third, there should be a special classical secondary education available to the children of the wealthier classes, who, owing to birth or fortune, will fill the professions. "Let us assure them the greatest and most fertile cultivation of the mind through letters, science, philosophy, and history. . . . The people rise; let the bourgeoisie not stand still." Finally, there was the problem of educating girls, whose training had been left to the clergy.

When Duruy took office in 1863, the resources for French education were deplorable. Primary schools were universally inadequate, and more than a thousand communities had none at all. Secondary schools catered to the upper classes alone; there had been virtually no attempt to meet the educational requirements of an industrializing era. On the university level, the quality of teaching had progressively declined, except in medicine and law, until a professor's success was measured in his platform performance rather than his learning. He generally lectured once a week on minor points of his special interest, and it was no wonder that students were rarely made to feel the thrill of academic investigation. And should a student develop scholarly tastes, a shortage of equipment in the schools hampered his advancement. If literacy does not necessarily indicate culture, it at least suggests educational opportunity, and as late as 1857 one-third of the men called up for military service could not read or write.

Why had French education come to such a point? If a people who had traditionally esteemed the things of the mind, and who had always been in the vanguard of creative thought, were negligent in keeping their educational system vigorous, it is evidence that they were not sufficiently occupied with meeting the problems of the moment and the future. Once again we see the mark of the French Revolution, which, failing to regulate the political, social, and financial problems paralyzing late eighteenth century France, lived on to transfix the nineteenth. Such is the heritage of any great upheaval which unsettles the traditional values and ideals holding a community together. There can be only limited forward movement until the wounds are healed and the community spirit resolidified. That so much Bonapartist propaganda had attempted to equate Bonapartism with the national interest and all other parties with selfish or limited interests reveals that the disunion was recognized and caused alarm.

It is significant that there was a strong current of patriotism in Duruy. If he wanted reform of the educational system, it was because "the greatness of France is my religion," and aside from his views on religion which made him hostile to the Church, Duruy was her enemy because he considered her indifferent to

French nationalism. One of the less well known patriotic and anticlerical aspects of Duruy's program was his attempt to propagate the French language in regions where a local dialect prevailed. In Brittany, Alsace, Lorraine, the Basque country, and Flanders, the clergy persisted in teaching the catechism in the local dialect, and when the Bishop of Cambrai defended the practice by saying that French was the vehicle of all bad ideas, the issue was clearly defined. It was a *Kulturkampf* a decade before Bismarck's, but it never became the paramount educational issue of Duruy's administration.

His work was made more complicated by the Falloux Law of 1850, which is more fully discussed in the chapter on Montalembert. It is ironical that the reaction against the Napoleonic Université was legislated, not under the Bourbon Restoration, but during the Second Republic. The Law of 1850 permitted clergymen to teach in public primary schools, so that it was no longer enough for the anticlericals to increase the number of students attending public schools. They had to weed the clergymen from public education and replace them with laymen.

There were two religious orders devoted to primary education: the Congregation of the Brothers of the Christian Doctrine, dating from the seventeenth century, and the Congregation of the Brothers of Mary, which had been authorized by the government in 1825. By 1860 they taught about 20 per cent of the primary students in France, nearly 500,000 pupils. Oddly enough—as rural France was regarded as the Catholic stronghold—the Brothers were predominant in many industrial centers, excepting Paris and Le Creusot. The Law of 1850 had given municipal councils the right to hire either clerics or laymen as teachers, and in the industrial centers the employer-dominated councils usually favored hiring the Brothers. It was not their solicitude for Christian teaching that dictated the choice, but the fact that the Church was opposed to socialism.

If Duruy was given a free hand by Napoleon III to expand popular education, the imperial mandate did not cut down the formidable opposition to the reforms which Duruy envisioned. Convinced that there was a tie between an enlightened mind and salvation, Duruy insisted that primary education must be free and become every child's *right*—the family's obligation. Second, he would abolish religious instruction from all state schools. Abolition would have meant a certain exodus from the schools, unless Duruy were able to legislate compulsory education in the public schools. If the Church did not share Duruy's faith in the remedial possibilities of literacy, it was nevertheless an embarrassment to be apparently arguing for illiteracy when the issue was really religious instruction.

French intellectuals, having for the most part lost faith, were amused at the discomfiture of the Church. They did not, however, necessarily rally to Duruy's support, as many of them were Republican. Since 1860, when the Empire began to veer toward liberalism, the government became more conscious of the need to reconcile the intelligentsia. The latter kept aloof, however, as the government did not make a clean break between Church and State. It would be an error to suppose that all anticlericals were antigovernment, but the alliance of republicanism and anticlericalism was traditional. In short, many anticlericals were delighted with Duruy's program but held back from an enthusiastic support.

Then Guizot, an Orleanist and a Protestant, spoke out against compulsory primary education. According to him, to make it obligatory for a father to send his child to school was a tyrannical demand; it was a violation of the *laissez-faire* doctrine and, hence, threatened the liberty of the individual. Worse, it could lead to the destruction of the family by reducing the parental authority.

These arguments were eagerly adopted by most conservatives, even though they represented the liberal tradition of *laissez faire*, for conservatives and liberals were as one when confronted with the Jacobin part of Bonapartism. The great majority of the Ministers and the members of Parliament were decidedly conservative. They had voted for Napoleon III because they feared revolutionary movements, and if they valued education for themselves they feared a learned proletariat. With such an opposition, the Emperor forced Duruy to move slowly. It was typical of Napoleon III that he met opposition with postponement. His views were part of an inviolable doctrine, which could not be surrendered, and he employed the remedy of time to make unpopular policies more palatable.

The popularity of compulsory education was questionable, though Duruy always assured the Emperor that it would be well received. Recent studies suggest that workers in the industrialized centers and rural areas were reluctant to send their children to school, as the demands of farm and factory came first. The greed of the parents did not alone produce this attitude; some employers hired parents only on condition that their children be available to work during periods of increased production.

It is ironical that those who argued that compulsory education would destroy the family were themselves contributing to its destruction. Workers' children had traditionally received what little education they got from their mothers. When mothers went to the factories, there was no time for teaching. Even if the children were sent to primary schools, their attendance was conditioned by the seasonal demands of manufacturing. Finally, if industrialization did not increase poverty, it brought out the evils of a concentrated population. Factory conditions promoted debauchery, and more often than not a debauched worker meant a neglected child.

Only the workers in the smaller towns were, as a group, enthusiastic for free and compulsory education. The worker who labored in a small shop took better care of his children and, in fact, often had fewer of them to guarantee that they would have the benefit of an education. Furthermore, he was less subject to night work than the factory workers and could take advantage of evening courses for adults. Employers, who feared an educated laboring force, were known to keep employees late into the evenings to prevent their attendance at these courses, which were sponsored by the Université. Such employers represented the dominant tendency in French capitalism during the Second Empire: the new, feverish industrialists who cared for nothing but increased production and sales.

But it is also possible during the Second Empire to see a second disposition among a smaller group of industrialists. They had recovered from the initial fever of expansion and began to consider their employees as professionals, often concluding that the improvement of the employee would ultimately boost production. This group of industrialists gave Duruy support, urged more vocational training, and sometimes even established night schools for their employees. It was probably not a coincidence that this group of employers favoring an increase in educational facilities were often either Saint-Simonian or Protestant. The Saint-Simonian cult was industrial utopianism, and the Calvinist branches of Protestantism, from their earliest days, had valued literacy for the purpose of Bible reading. Furthermore, the Protestants and Saint-Simonians hoped Duruy could remove religious instruction from the schools.

It is only right to emphasize that few employers fell into this second category of a more enlightened labor policy. There was a group of Protestant industrialists in Alsace, who campaigned for compulsory primary education; the spinning-mill owners of Condé-sur-Noireau (Calvados), all Protestant, championed the cause of lay teaching in the schools; classes for adults were established at the Schneider Works in Le Creusot and by Pierre Dorian for his workers in Pont-Salomon (Haute-Loire). Both Schneider and Dorian were Saint-Simonians. Their support, however, was insufficient to permit Duruy and the Emperor to ignore the heavy opposition to educational reform.

Meanwhile, Duruy was obliged to nominate professors to several vacant chairs, and his appointments were applauded or condemned according to the dictates of religious and political affiliation. He inherited the Renan problem from Rouland's administration. Ernest Renan was Professor of Hebrew at the Collège de France, and stated during his first lecture that Jesus was a man and not divine. Since he had previously published this opinion, his belief was no surprise, but Rouland had secured Renan's word that he would not use his classroom as an arena for bouts of dogma. He had been appointed to teach language and literature alone, and when he crossed the frontier into religion the Catholic outburst was instantaneous. It was another example

of the government's attempt to walk a path which would please all parties, and which ended by pleasing no one. The Council of Ministers agreed that Renan must resign, and Duruy had to fill the empty chair.

He was embarrassed by the situation, to say the least. It was disagreeable to succumb to the wishes of the Catholics, and yet Duruy had always opposed bringing religious arguments into the schools. He found himself obliged to concur in Renan's dismissal while sharing Renan's opinions, and in the hope of achieving a compromise he offered Renan a position at the Imperial Library. The professor refused the gesture by writing—and publishing—a letter to Duruy which contained the words of St. Peter to Simon the Sorcerer: "Thy money perish with thee." The Catholics proposed their own candidate to fill Renan's chair, but Duruy had the last word. He appointed Salomon Munk, a Jew and a leading Hebrew scholar.

The second controversial professor was Hippolyte Taine. He believed that all things are determined by a sequence of causes which are entirely independent of man's will; furthermore, he regarded as valid only positive, observable facts, and rejected speculation. Taine's determinism and positivism were illustrative of the Realism of his time, and his appointment to Saint-Cyr in 1863 and to the Ecole des beaux-arts in 1864 only increased Catholic anger.

If the Church rightly calculated the degree of irreligion among the intellectuals, the distinction between irreligion and anticlericalism was often lost in the heat of polemics. The most prominent Republican newspapers and Deputies—men like Jules Simon and Jules Favre—professed great respect for Christianity, but as anticlericals they were attacked as irreligious. The loudest Catholic voices, like the most offensive of the anticlericals, were the extremists. Each side put its worst foot forward, giving the educational battle the appearance of a choice between atheism and medievalism. When the Bishop of Montauban could write that "minds are being corrupted by detestable modern doctrines," and when the Bishop of Orléans could announce that the re-

cent floods and cholera epidemics were punishments sent to halt the progress of irreligion, they merely confirmed suspicions that the Church was an anachronism.

The *Syllabus errorum*, published by Pius IX on December 8, 1864, likewise injured the educational cause of the French Catholics. Among the many "errors" of the nineteenth century— nationalism, naturalism, socialism, communism, and freemasonry —the Pope proclaimed that "it is an error to believe that the Roman Pontiff can and ought to reconcile himself to, and agree with, progress, liberalism, and contemporary civilization." He proclaimed Church control of education and science, the independence of the Church from any State interference, upheld the temporal power of the Papacy, and specifically condemned lay teaching. The Pope's ideas, whatever their merit, were impolitic. Napoleon III was offended, but at the moment he was equally annoyed at the primary patron of the anticlericals, Prince Jerome-Napoleon.

Jerome had always been an embarrassment to Napoleon III and was periodically in and out of favor. He had a complicated personality and was a bundle of contradictions. In public life, he had an almost infallible feeling for the inappropriate remark, and the wonder is that Napoleon III continually forgave him. He was sent to Ajaccio (Corsica) in 1864 to represent the government at an unveiling of a monument to Napoleon I and his four brothers. Among other things, he criticized the temporal power of the Pope and announced his support for the Poles, who were being crushed in an unsuccessful revolt against the Russians. Finally, he suggested that

the establishment of democracy is the problem for the future. Everywhere, the aristocracies are falling. It belongs to France, the great nation, to promote this necessary development, as she, through her genius, is always the innovating nation.

Jerome received a public rebuke for this aggressive speech and resigned as Vice President of the Privy Council.

In full knowledge that the Ministers were solidly against him, Duruy sent Napoleon the draft of his free and compulsory ed-

ucation recommendation in February, 1865. Duruy was then allowed to present his report to a joint session of the Council of Ministers and the Privy Council, and when Rouher, the Minister of State, tried to sidetrack the discussion to a commercial treaty project, the Emperor cut him short and Duruy's report was accepted in an amended form.

He was aware that some of the ministerial opposition came from men who were relatively indifferent to the principles involved, but who feared the expense of providing free education. They assumed that levying new taxes on the towns would be unpopular, and to defray the expenses from the government's budget would create an uncomfortable deficit. Duruy argued that if Fould, the Minister of Finance, could find money for war, he could find it for education, and if popularity was the measure one might consider that "France spends twenty-five million for a Prefecture, fifty or sixty million for an Opera, and can manage only seven or eight million for the education of her people."

Duruy asked for a budget of nineteen million as a start. Instead of directly taxing the towns for the increased amount, he suggested that the towns raise only six or seven million levied against all their taxpayers; that the departmental councils be asked to raise another five or six million, the tax to be prorated according to income; and, finally, that the government allocate eight or nine million.

In accepting an amended version of Duruy's report, the Council actually admitted the principle of free and compulsory education without providing for its universal application, and in any event the report was not yet a law. The towns were to be granted the initiative in establishing free education, and if Duruy had not won a complete victory he interpreted the gain as satisfactory in view of the opposition. Thus, he did not resign from the Ministry, as some of his opponents presumed he would, and contented himself with the compromise.

It took over a year for the Council of State to transform Duruy's amended report into a law. It was sent to the Corps législatif for approval on June 22, 1866, where it passed unanimously. The law required all communities of more than five hun-

dred inhabitants to maintain a primary school for girls, as the Law of 1833 had provided for boys. In communities where no primary school for girls existed except for a parochial school, the law permitted the parochial school to be regarded as semi-public if the community concurred. The nuns would derive the benefit of public support and would be subject to the inspectors general of the Université.

The law did not, however, modify the academic requirements for teachers; those provisions of the Falloux Law of 1850 which permitted clerical teachers to be certified without having had courses in philosophy and rhetoric were still in effect. From the point of view of Duruy and the Université, however, the most important clause in the Law of 1866 was the one which gave communities the right to establish free education by the simple device of augmenting the local school appropriation by three centimes. This action would immediately obligate the department and the government to lend further aid.

At the time of its adoption, the Law of 1866 was called both a defeat and a victory for Duruy, depending upon the predisposition of the commentators. Duruy recognized the law to be a step in the direction he wanted to go and now felt free to devote more attention to other reforms. For one thing, he had been alert to every opportunity to replace conservative bureaucrats in the Ministry of Public Instruction with men more favorable to lay teaching. Within the Ministry there was an Imperial Council on Public Instruction. Five bishops customarily sat in this Council, and by 1866 Duruy had succeeded in obtaining five bishops who were regarded as liberal. In trying to infuse the Ministry of Public Instruction with a liberal spirit, Duruy felt obliged to reassure the Emperor that the Université could not be criticized for any serious religious or political bias. The Catholics had always insinuated that a liberal teaching body would not be loyal to the Empire; Duruy not only disagreed but accused the Catholics of fostering Legitimist principles in parochial schools.

It is apparent that the liberal program of lay instruction in the public schools was compromised by a too enthusiastic support from radical groups. In 1865, for instance, a number of French

students attended an antireligion congress in Liège. Returning to France, they organized the International Society of Free-thinkers. Members took three vows: that they would not have a priest in attendance at a birth, a marriage, or a death. Civil inter-ments were to be occasions for "lodge meetings." The movement spread, though not receiving any support from the moderate republican press, and provided the Catholics with an extreme example of secularism.

In the following year, 1866, Jean Macé organized the Teach-ing League in the hope of promoting lay teaching. He quickly gathered more than five thousand adherents, Sainte-Beuve and Emile Ollivier being the most prominent patrons, and only after some months was the League revealed to have been Masonic in inspiration.

Meanwhile, Duruy had been promoting reforms in secondary education. One of his earliest decrees, June 29, 1863, restored the teaching of philosophy in the secondary schools; philosophy had been generally omitted from the curriculum after 1850. A second decree, on September 24, 1863, ordered that recent history be added to the curriculum, and a week later Duruy published a circular urging an emphasis on modern languages. These decrees illustrate one of Duruy's main contentions: that French secondary education was neither adjusting to the increasing complexity of modern life nor facing realistically the compromises in curric-ulum which the mass education of democratic life was beginning to require. Aside from these decrees in 1863, Duruy proposed on October 2nd that the entire secondary school organization be studied in the hope of dividing secondary education into two independent programs. The memory of the farm boy in Cou-tances, struggling with his Greek conjugations, was still fresh in Duruy's mind.

Himself a classicist, Duruy did not deprecate the value of the traditional classical education. The true role of the humani-ties, he wrote, is not to teach men to speak Greek nor to make chemists or historians, "but to enable students to learn to think and act as men." But since the graduates of secondary schools were likely to become the leaders in their communities, Duruy was dismayed to see how little they knew of modern civilization. In short, he insisted that the new classical secondary curriculum be augmented with the history of politics, economics, science, and the arts. Secondly, he urged the establishment of a new curriculum—called Special Secondary Education—to provide a more vocational type of training for students not able to benefit from the classical curriculum.

Unlike the classical secondary curriculum, which was standard throughout France, Duruy proposed to vary the curricula in the special secondary schools in order to account for regional agricultural and industrial requirements. He wanted to include courses in modern civilization and modern language "to preserve the literary and scientific honor of France," so that vocational courses really displaced only the classical studies of the traditional curriculum.

The opposition to the reform came from all sides, though the Emperor was again in Duruy's camp. Many members of the Université were unwilling to recognize the legitimacy of any curriculum which dropped Latin and Greek. The Finance Minister, naturally, opposed any expansion which might unsettle the budget, and the Minister of Public Works objected on the grounds that the project was an encroachment upon his sphere. Duruy told Rouher that the project need not be feared as an innovation, since it had been considered desirable by Richelieu in 1625 and by Rolland in 1768. A fourth Minister revealed his own lack of faith in the Second Empire by saying that courses in modern history would be dangerous for the government, while a member of the parliamentary opposition said that such courses would simply eulogize the Empire. Duruy's answer was that a study of modern history was the proper antidote to factionalism in France, "which is fanned by all parties and by antinational groups like the Church."

The battle of opinions and interests went on for nearly two years. Finally, on April 21, 1865, the Corps législatif voted unanimous approval of the secondary education reforms—but did not provide one cent to inaugurate them. As in the later case of primary education, Duruy had to be satisfied with having gained a principle, which he knew would ultimately lead to action. To have demanded cash would have brought certain defeat for the principle.

The next project was to provide teachers for the special secondary schools. The Ecole normale supérieure, founded in 1810, trained teachers for classical secondary education, while the écoles normales primaires, created after 1830, produced teachers for primary schools. On August 1, 1865, Duruy proposed to the Emperor that the government accept an offer by the town of Cluny to give its Benedictine abbey to the state, along with a subsidy of 70,000 francs, for a new Ecole normale spéciale, and to accept an offer of 100,000 francs from the Department of Saône-et-Loire to adapt the abbey for educational use. Secondly, he proposed a drastic consolidation of the eighty-four écoles normales primaires in the interest of economy. The Emperor gave enthusiatic approval despite Rouher's objection.

The school opened in Cluny in November of 1866 and operated without any government funds. The Ministry of Public Instruction provided scholarships for twenty students, and at Duruy's suggestion seventy departmental councils voted another ninety scholarships between them. Several railroad companies sponsored students, and gifts of money and books flowed in from private sources. Every official in the new school was required to do some teaching, including the director, Ferdinand Roux, and the excellent morale and enthusiasm convinced Duruy that Cluny could become the leading school of applied science in Europe.

In great confidence, he began the establishment of special secondary schools, but he had not calculated the true depths of the academic world's hostility to the idea of vocational training. While the Corps législatif was sufficiently impressed with Cluny's future to vote a 200,000 franc budget in 1868, the school's days were numbered. With the fall of the Second Empire, Cluny lost its autonomy and became a skeleton in the academic closet. After 1871 Cluny suffered a slow death with teachers and students who had failed in classical secondary schools—an academic Devil's Island—and finally perished in 1891.

Beginning in 1864, Duruy's budget provided 50,000 francs

for adult education courses, most of which were devoted to reducing illiteracy. The Ministry of Public Instruction had no accurate figures on illiteracy in France and used the statistics provided by the Army. In 1848, for example, roughly 35 per cent of the recruits could not read or write; one year after the beginning of adult education courses the Army figures showed illiteracy reduced to 26 per cent. Enrollment increased swiftly in these courses from 7,500 in 1865 to 20,000 in 1866; but the Council of Ministers did not share the popular enthusiasm. No additional funds were voted, and Duruy tells us that French teachers simply donated their time, often paying for paper and books themselves to promote the adult courses. Their efforts were rewarded at the Exposition of 1867, when the International Jury awarded the teachers of France a gold medal for the adult courses. In consequence, Napoleon III decreed that every teacher was entitled to wear a small purple ribbon to signify the honor. This concession presumably did not upset the sacred calculations of the Finance Minister.

But as teachers do not live by purple ribbons alone, Duruy worked to improve their financial status. His decree of September 4, 1863, stipulated that the Ministry of Public Instruction would henceforth supply furniture to teachers going to new posts. Accused of trying to buy teachers' votes for the government, Duruy explained the measure as an attempt to avoid making teachers contract difficult debts when first becoming established in a new community. It was fruitless, of course, to appeal to the reason of an Opposition which simultaneously urged the government to aid teachers and characterized every assistance granted as blackmail.

Pensions for teachers were hopelessly inadequate. In the 1860's, a minimum of one franc a day was considered essential to buy the necessities of life, and teachers' pensions were then averaging 100 francs a year. Thirty years of service were required to make one eligible for a pension, and the teacher must have reached sixty before payment began—an age at which it was difficult to find any supplementary work. In comparison, soldiers could retire at forty-eight, after a minimum service of twenty-eight years, and receive at least 365 francs a year.

A law of 1853 had provided for a gradual increase in teachers' pensions until they reached the soldiers' level in 1884. But that was still twenty years in the future, and Duruy wanted funds to bridge the gap. Furthermore, he wanted a teacher to be eligible for a pension at fifty-five instead of sixty. As usual, the Finance Minister was able to demonstrate his inability to raise the required money, and even though Napoleon III favored Duruy's cause the pensions always fell victim to more pressing needs. It is interesting, in the light of later reckoning about the defeat in 1870, that in 1868–1869, the Opposition favored cutting the Army in half to provide the credits necessary for teachers' pensions.

Duruy, however, did not favor cutting the military establishment; he favored modernizing it. Like Napoleon III, Duruy believed that the Army chiefs were too conservative in their views, and he deplored the absence of trained reserves. Because the professional army system did not provide universal military training, Duruy proposed, in 1867, to develop a physical education program in the schools. The increased pressures on the nervous system brought by modern civilization, he argued, require compensatory physical exercise, and the usual exercises could be supplemented with military-type activities: fencing with foil and wooden bayonets; military drill and basic infantry training.

Duruy was no more successful in his hopes for physical education than he had been in his efforts for pensions. In 1865–1866, he had been able to get certain reforms in primary and secondary education accepted in principle; the resistance to innovation steadily increased after the Austro-Prussian War of 1866. The resurgence of conservatism within the Council of Ministers and Parliament was essentially caused by the recent setbacks France had suffered in her foreign policies. The drift toward Liberal Empire, to which Napoleon III was philosophically committed owing to his interpretation of the Napoleonic Legend, was being compromised by foreign policy failures—the policies them-

selves being generally pursued in His Majesty's efforts to adhere
to the Legend.

In this time of troubles, Minister and Deputies harkened back
to the victories and the prestige of the 1850's and remembered
that the Emperor had had dictatorial powers in those years. It
was this resurgence of conservatism, and not a revival of clericalism, which increasingly hampered Duruy and which made
Napoleon III's groping for Liberal Empire unpopular among
his immediate associates.

Despite all, Duruy began, in 1867, a program which won him
the most violent criticism of his term in office: the expansion
of educational facilities for girls. He hoped to implement the
Law of 1866 by organizing 10,000 primary schools for girls;
furthermore, he proposed secondary courses for girls—both regular and special—and to permit mothers to accompany daughters
to class as guardians of morality. Instructions to organize these
courses were sent out to the sixteen rectors on October 30,
1867. (For purposes of Université administration, France was
divided into sixteen districts, each headed by a rector.)

In extending public secondary education to girls, Duruy found
himself abandoned by even the liberal clergy, but the most violent attacks came from Rome and from the Bishop of Orléans,
Dupanloup. The latter published a brochure on November 16th
entitled *Monsieur Duruy and the Education of Girls*. His thesis
was that it was dangerous for the morality and religion of the
young to be subjected to the influence of lay instructors. This attack came three weeks after the Battle of Mentana, where French
troops had defended the temporal authority of the Papacy by
defeating Garibaldi. When the official Papal journal *L'Osserva-
tore Romano* demanded Duruy's dismissal as a condition all
Catholics should require before giving Napoleon's government
support in the next elections, it was only too apparent that there
was no gratitude in Rome for the protection French troops had
been providing. The Emperor lost his temper and gave Duruy
free reign to defend himself, while the Empress enrolled her
two nieces in the new courses to be offered at the Sorbonne.

Duruy took prompt action. Secondary courses were publicly proclaimed in Orléans, Dupanloup's diocese, on November 21st, in the presence of the prefect of Loiret and under the patronage of the mayor. Duruy's message to the two officials was blunt: "The sophisms and the violence of your irascible prelate have not stopped you. I congratulate and thank you." The second blow to the Bishop was the enrollment of fifty-seven Orléans girls in the courses; it was the largest enrollment achieved in any of the provincial cities in the northern half of France.

Dupanloup then shifted his ground somewhat, and in subsequent pamphlets he stressed the rights of the Church rather than the issue of morality. Understanding the growing conservatism in the government, he tried to demonstrate that Duruy was ally of the Republicans and, hence, an attack upon Duruy was not an attack upon the Emperor or the imperial government. The argument was not very impressive in view of the imperial couple's recent patronage of the new courses at the Sorbonne.

On the other hand, there is no doubt that the Catholic outburst severely limited the success of the program. Many local officials were reluctant to open classes which would inevitably produce quarrels, and in many towns it was impossible to get students. The Université, increasingly anticlerical and proud of Duruy's energetic leadership, was generally ready to support this innovation, though some teachers were torn by the necessity of defying their bishops. Aside from the 57 girls enrolled in Orléans, there were 49 at Rouen, 30 at Amiens and Valenciennes, 24 at Tours, 23 at Dieppe, 15 at Saint-Quentin and Versailles, and 9 at Beauvais. In the southern half of France, 75 girls enrolled at Bordeaux, 62 in Marseille, 40 at Lyons, 33 at Toulon, and 16 at Limoges. The greatest success was in Saint-Etienne, where an anticlerical municipal council voted funds to make the courses free. The enrollment was 179. It seemed that the bishops had prevailed, but in reality Duruy had forced the acceptance of a new principle. As Saint-Etienne showed, when money was supplied to back up the principle there would be willing students.

The state of higher education in France during this period was incredible, and suggests once again the failure of the French, in the nineteenth century, to make a wholehearted adjustment of their institutions to meet both the competition of their neighbors and the requirements of an industrializing age. The universities had practically ceased to be centers of learning and, with the exception of Paris, Strasbourg, and Montpellier, had been declining since the sixteenth century. The University of Paris had schools of theology, science, letters, law, medicine, and pharmacy, and during the Second Empire enrolled about six thousand students a year.

As the universities decayed, learning was continued in the great monasteries and in the academies. It was useful, of course, to group learned men together and have them subsidized by Church and State, but the academies and monasteries did not directly train students in the traditional university fashion. Similarly, the Observatory, the Collège de France, and the Museum had faculties who did not enroll students or grant degrees.

In 1794, during the French Revolution, the government began to provide facilities for higher education by creating specialized institutions, and this precedent was followed by subsequent régimes. Thus the Ecole polytechnique for engineering, the Ecole normale supérieure for training secondary teachers, the Conservatoire des arts et métiers for business, the Ecole des chartes for archivists, the Ecole des beaux-arts for fine arts, the Ecole d'architecture, and the Ecole des mines. There were others, too, but the total enrollment in these schools was small. In 1867, when the enrollment at the Military Academy of Saint-Cyr was 301, the Ecole centrale, the industrial school, had 233 students and the Ecole polytechnique only 145.

Duruy sent Charles-Adolphe Wurtz, a chemist and a member of the Académie des sciences, to study the principal German universities and their scientific establishments in particular. His report, ultimately published in 1870, showed that learning in both Catholic and Protestant universities was encourged and well financed, and he suggested that it was high time for the French to spend the sums necessary to revive the universities:

It is a problem of the first order, for the intellectual life of a nation feeds the sources of its material power, and a nation's rank depends upon the ascendancy given to the things of the mind as much as upon the number and valor of its defenders.

In 1868, however, Ministers and Deputies were too concerned with the increasing tensions of foreign policy and the dangerous isolation of France to bother about academic questions. They did not understand what men like Wurtz knew: that handsome armies can become useless if a nation's leadership suffers from an intellectual mandarinism. Increasing military budgets and multiplying treaties will not in themselves guarantee the quality and vigor of a nation's resources. Speaking at the Ecole pratique de médecine in 1864, Duruy had said, "The budget must give way to Science and not Science to the budget," but he was shouting down a well. The sixteen provincial universities of twentieth century France were not formally organized until 1896.

Meanwhile, Duruy found an inexpensive substitute, the Ecole des hautes études, which he discussed with the Emperor and Hortense Cornu. Mme. Cornu had been a childhood friend of Napoleon and had faithfully supplied him with books during the years in Ham. They had shared liberal opinions, which had led to their estrangement after the *coup d'état* of 1851, but a reconciliation had taken place in March of 1862 when she became convinced that Napoleon was sincerely attempting to produce a liberal Empire. She became one of Duruy's staunchest supporters, and it is not clear whether the idea for the Ecole des hautes études was originally hers or Duruy's.

The new school was not an institution in the usual sense, but a foundation financed through the Ministry of Public Instruction. The various state-supported schools of higher education established faculty committees which corresponded with the Council for the Ecole des hautes études. The Council, thus informed of the most pressing financial needs of the various schools, could feed them money from the limited budget provided by the Corps législatif. Because scientific equipment and research laboratories had become the neglected children of French academic life, Duruy stressed the need to give them priority in the allocation of funds. The Council was free to subsidize worthwhile individual projects and to pay for publications; and individuals and institutions receiving money were expected to promote the spirit of learning by increasing the number of lectures open to the general public.

The Ecole des hautes études was created by Duruy's decree of July 31, 1868. Earlier in the month, the Corps législatif had provided 50,000 francs for research facilities, and Duruy was promised that the government would attempt to double the amount in 1869, as well as find 80,000 francs for instructional laboratories in the public schools. He also wanted to create a meteorological observatory on the Plateau of Montsouris (where Baron Haussmann was developing a park) in the hope of making meteorology into a science useful to the Navy and to agriculture. Haussmann agreed to cooperate. The City of Paris bought a house on the Plateau belonging to the Bey of Tunis for 120,000 francs and rented it to the Ministry of Public Instruction for one franc a year.

Duruy made his last appearance at the Council of Ministers on July 12, 1869. The government was to be reconstituted (see the chapter on Emile Ollivier), and Napoleon asked for the immediate resignation of three Ministers: Rouher, Minister of State; Baroche, Minister of Justice; and Vuitry, President of the Council of State. The remaining Ministers were asked to stay in office until their successors were able to assume their duties. Five days later, Duruy received the following note from His Majesty:

MY DEAR M. DURUY,

I am obliged by the present situation to remove a minister who has my confidence and who rendered great service to public education.

If politics has no feelings, the sovereign has, and he is anxious to express his regrets to you. I have asked M. Bourbeau, a Deputy, to replace you. I hope to see you one of these days so that you can tell me what I can do to demonstrate my sincere friendship.

NAPOLEON

In consequence, Duruy gave his prepared speech of farewell to his associates in the Ministry of Public Instruction and began to pack his bags for an extensive trip. His vacation took him to Egypt, Constantinople, Greece, and Italy, and everywhere he signed the registers as Senator Duruy, the new office conferred upon him by Napoleon III as a reward for services to France.

As the Senate was not truly a legislative body but served as a check upon the constitutionality of legislation, the work of Senators was not arduous. It was a convenience for the government to have an exclusive club to which it might retire notable public figures, providing them with a handsome pension for life. And to this small gerontocracy, one must add the French marshals and cardinals who were automatically members of the Senate by right of rank. In short, the Senate was not simmering with liberalism, and Duruy found himself surrounded by hostility. A lesser man would have surrendered at this point and slunk into the depths of his senatorial chair, but Duruy had one more battle to fight.

The Falloux Law of 1850 provided for academic freedom in the primary and secondary schools but not in higher education. On the surface a liberal measure, this academic freedom had been inserted by Falloux and Montalembert to protect the clergymen whom the law permitted to teach in public primary schools. In 1863 Duruy had proposed to extend this liberty to higher education and had been solidly opposed by those who had championed the principle in 1850. They argued that professors in higher education were inclined to teach revolutionary and materialistic doctrines.

In the spring of 1868, a journalist named Girault petitioned the Senate to recommend the principle of academic freedom on the university level. He wanted in particular to guarantee some medical professors the right to debate the merits of materialism. A sick Sainte-Beuve rose in defense of the petition, and in the certainty that it would fail he denounced the hypocrisy of upper French society for being clerical but unchristian. As foreseen, the petition was beaten eighty to forty-three.

Duruy reopened the question on June 28, 1870, this time as a Senator. He began by revealing how little the state actually invested in its professors of higher education; six hundred men, who maintained the literary and scientific honor of France, cost

the state between 50,000 and 60,000 francs in 1869. The remainder
of their salaries came from students' tuition. It was time, he suggested, for the government to consider its responsibilities to these
learned men and stop trying to subject scholarly institutions and
ideas to parliamentary supervision. He told the Senators what his
own professional experience had taught him: that the real check
belongs within the profession itself, and that the standards of a
profession are more rigid than any law. But this time his effort
was too late; in six weeks the Empire was gone.

Duruy now had the leisure to prepare his final two volumes of
the *Roman History* for the publisher. They appeared in 1872. He
began to assemble notes for his *Mémoires* and to reconsider the
Emperor under whom he had served for six years. His Majesty
was certainly guilty of mistakes: the *coup d'état* of 1851 was "unnecessary" and led to absolute power, an anachronism in the nineteenth century, and he believed that the lavish court belonged to
another era. But even a complete list of mistakes, Duruy wrote,
"will not permit posterity to be as unjust to Napoleon III as his
immediate successors have been."

He recalled Napoleon's speech of November 5, 1863, opening
the new Parliament, in which he proposed an international congress to arbitrate the differences between nations. It was the old
project of Henri IV and not a fantastic vision of a hallucinated
dreamer. Duruy recognized that Napoleon III did dream, but he
claimed that dreaming was often the "necessary condition to arrive at an ideal." He believed the Emperor's well known generosity and kindness to be genuine and not a matter of political
expediency. Indeed, as both Duruy and Dr. Barthez, the Prince
Imperial's physician, have testified, the Emperor was kind to a
point of weakness. He detested the shrewd dealing at the market
place—so characteristic of his régime—but feigned to ignore it
to repay those who had helped him. He was forever needing advances on his civil list, because he gave money away too generously, and if he provided well for Eugénie's future, he himself
could only pay half the usual rent at Chistlehurst when in exile.
"How often I saw him arrive at the Council of Ministers with
projects for assistance to the weak and needy!" And if only the

Army had paid more attention to the Emperor's military ideas in the 1860's, Duruy thought, the complexion of the war could have been considerably changed.

Meanwhile, Duruy began to reap the honors which his labors as historian and Minister so richly deserved. In 1873 he was elected to the Académie des inscriptions et belles-lettres; in 1879 to the Académie des sciences morales et politiques; and finally to the Académie francaise in 1884. His long retirement, for he did not die until 1894, gave him the pleasure of seeing his educational innovations develop into generally accepted practices, and one can envision his smile in 1880 when France opened her first regular *lycée* for girls. Speaking at a dinner in his honor four years later, Duruy remarked that "the good one has done is the best baggage one takes in leaving life." By this reckoning, Victor Duruy departed heavily laden.

IX

Gustave Courbet

REALISM, AND THE ART WARS
OF THE SECOND EMPIRE

*One of the happiest facets of the creative life is that
we are remembered for our works and not for ourselves.*

—ROGER DE MORAINE

Courbet was born on June 10, 1819, at Ornans in the Department of the Doubs. The family had ancient roots in the Franche-Comté and were landed and well-to-do. Through his mother's line, the radical and anticlerical Oudots, Gustave may have acquired his sympathy for the Revolution, but his father, Régis Courbet, dabbled at inventions rather than politics. During his long life, Régis produced an impressive number of unusable farm implements, but his good humor allowed him to survive his neighbors' jibes as well as to bear the vanity of his eldest son.

Gustave's chief pastime as a child was the composition of songs with which he regaled all without discrimination. In fact, this youthful talent could not be avoided, as he bellowed his songs through doors and walls, shattering sanctuaries and disturbing the peace. At the age of twelve Gustave was enrolled at the local seminary, which accepted both lay and clerical pupils. Despite a wretched record during his six years at the school, his conceit remained undiminished. A wild, noisy, gauche young man, he much preferred the countryside to the classroom. If his academic record was poor, his religious record was worse. This rebellious boy confessed extraordinary sins, and the priests refused him absolution. Finally Cardinal de Rohan of Besançon solved the problem by discovering Gustave reading from a list of sins at confession. Thus, this child—who would remain unchanged in his attitude toward religion—made his first communion, which was administered by a Prince of the Church.

The only part of the curriculum at Ornans which had interested Gustave was the study of art, but when it came time to leave the seminary—in his eighteenth year—the boy was informed by his sensible and practical parent that he was to take prelaw training at the Collège royal in Besançon. He was completely miserable in Besançon until, as a compassionate concession, his father allowed him to be a day student. This made it possible for him to live away from school, and he utilized his new freedom by seeking the company of painters.

Courbet was particularly attracted to two brothers, Arthaud and Edouard Baille, and they began taking him to the Besançon Ecole des beaux-arts. The teacher was Charles Flajoulot, a disciple of Louis David, and Courbet was taught to draw from life. In the second year at Besançon, Courbet was joined by Maximilian Buchon, an old friend from seminary days. Buchon fancied himself a poet and claimed to be a Realist. In the meantime the Courbet family was beginning to realize the futility of the law course, and after Gustave had spent three years in Besançon they allowed him to move to Paris. It was 1840, and he was twenty-one.

His first Parisian school was directed by a Baron von Steuben, a remarkable choice because Courbet hated supervision and discipline above all. He quickly changed to the Atelier suisse on the Ile de la Cité, where models were supplied, but nothing more. The absence of instruction suited Courbet, but his family was suspicious of his failure to enroll in a recognized academy. There were frequent letters from Ornans to Paris, mostly to berate the errant son for his supposed dissolute life in the wicked city. The family was unconvinced of the fact that Gustave was spending considerable time at the Louvre studying the old masters.

His first five years in Paris, 1840–1845, were a period of transition in Courbet's painting. Conforming to the ideals of his day, he usually chose literary or romantic subjects for his canvases. For instance, the erotic *Lot and His Daughters* dates from this period. But as Courbet was no intellectual, literary and romantic subjects meant little to him, and he was increasingly drawn to landscapes and portraits. On a visit home in 1842, he did a portrait of his father, actually a favor because he preferred to paint the face he saw in the mirror. In fact, his first success was "Self-Portrait with the Black Dog" (1842), which won him admission to the government's Salon of 1844. The following year, the Salon accepted four of the five canvases he submitted, and he made his first sale. A Dutch dealer gave him 420 francs for two pictures and commissioned a portrait.

The Salon of 1847 rejected all of Courbet's entries, and he accused the jury of excessive conservatism and conventionality. Perhaps he was right, for in that year many prominent artists were rejected—Delacroix, Daumier, and Théodore Rousseau among them—so that one could almost congratulate oneself on being excluded. A number of these men discussed establishing an independent annual exhibition, but the project was rendered unnecessary by the Revolution of 1848.

Government and art are a risky compound, and the mixture can be safely achieved only with the most enlightened direction. Otherwise, the amalgam tends to make common that which is least common in essence. Artists rarely know much of politics, and politicians can be counted on to know nothing of art. The artists and politicians of 1848 engaged in an affair which was more than a *mariage de convenance;* it got intensely emotional. That was the year to lay down the hoe and take up the paintbrush. The Salon jury, in a mood which conservatively might be labeled liberal, gave the nod to quantity by accepting 5,500 pictures, seven of which were by Courbet. The lesson was not lost on a good many of the artists. It was obvious that the democratic Republic loved art with a passion, and the artists forgot what they, more than other men, ought to know: that art has nothing to do with forms of government, because it transcends politics.

Courbet had been indifferent to the February revolt, which brought down the July Monarchy, but the bloody June Days, when Republicans engaged in mutual slaughter, horrified him. His sympathies were with the mob, that is, the more radical or socialistic faction, though he refused as a matter of principle to bear arms for his principles. Hoping to give the enemy a fatal blow with his paintbrush, he drew up a vignette for the paper *Salut public* which was edited by a triumvirate: Baudelaire, Champfleury, and Toubin. If the point needed to be made, Courbet demonstrated that the paintbrush is less deadly than the sword.

Courbet had known Baudelaire only a short time and was uninterested in his poetry, in fact in all poetry. Baudelaire, who often slept at Courbet's, usually in a drunken or drugged state, reflected in his living and in his poetry the spiritual frustration of his time. Courbet did a portrait of the poet (1848), but the subject did not appreciate the canvas. This friendship did not compromise Courbet politically as much as did his continued friendship with Maximilian Buchon, the Realist from Ornans. Through him, Courbet was recognized to be a democrat and a republican, though for the moment such a designation was politically safe.

One of the reforms justified the support which many artists had given the Second Republic. The jury for the Salon of 1849 was selected by the exhibiting artists rather than by the Académie des beaux-arts. Seven of Courbet's pictures were accepted, and his "After Dinner at Ornans" won a second-prize gold medal. The director of *Beaux-Arts* bought this painting for the government, and it was then presented to the Lille Museum. This was the beginning of fame and financial success.

In 1850 Courbet painted the "Stone Breakers." He had seen these men and believed them the personification of poverty. Somewhat later, Proudhon called this large canvas (it was seven feet by ten) the first socialist picture and Courbet the first socialist painter:

The *Stone Breakers* is a satire on our industrial civilization, which constantly invents wonderful machines to . . . perform . . . all kinds of labor . . . and yet is unable to liberate man from the most backbreaking toil.

Certainly Courbet saw the social significance of his work after it had been pointed out to him by Proudhon, an example of how much the viewer brings to a work of art.

Courbet painted several eminent musicians in this era. Chopin's portrait was done in 1848, only a short time before the pianist's death, and Berlioz was persuaded by a friend to sit for his portrait in 1850. He did so grudgingly and had his sentiments verified when Courbet loudly sang during his sittings. His musical genius was so unmistakably absent that Berlioz could only suppose he was being purposely insulted. Naturally he found the portrait bad and even refused it as a gift. It is now regarded as one of Courbet's best.

During the winter of 1849–1850, Courbet was at work on a gigantic canvas, eleven feet by twenty-three. The death of his maternal grandfather in the previous year probably gave him the idea for the picture, which was called "Burial at Ornans." It was accepted for the Salon of 1850–1851, along with eight other canvases. The picture contained forty life-sized figures, all of them inhabitants of Courbet's home town. He sought out the models one at a time and soon discovered that his problem was not whom to include but whom to leave out. The citizenry regarded a place on Courbet's canvas as a civic right, and the clamor to be among the favored forty was intense and disagreeable. The social triumph of these forty immortals was temporary. Parisian art critics advised Courbet that his subjects were too mean and ugly to be worthy of art, and the "Burial" attracted more hostility than his other canvases in the Salon. The townspeople of Ornans then attacked Courbet for making them appear grotesque, but, as a Realist, Courbet had no mollifying answer.

II

The Realists were a later nineteenth century group in revolt against Classicism and Romanticism. Both of the latter schools often took subjects far removed from contemporary life, but the Realists commanded that the everyday, the apparent, the material subject be the artist's concern. They were particularly opposed to elegance and sentimentality, often preferring commonplace and seamy themes.

It has been suggested that certain aspects of the nineteenth century promoted the development of the Realist school both in painting and in literature. Following the French and Industrial revolutions, political and economic power shifted to those whose creed was practicality, and who, out of self-interest, championed a more liberal climate. This faith in the practical and existential involved a loss of faith in the immaterial, in idealism, in imagination, and in the metaphysical. Naturally, some painters and writers reflected this *Zeitgeist*, though it did not necessarily follow that their works won immediate popularity by conforming to the spirit of the time: a group new to social and political leadership is likely to adopt the artistic standards of its predecessor. Here we have Courbet himself, writing, no doubt, with the aid of literary friends:

The basis of realism is negation of the ideal, a negation towards which my studies have led me for fifteen years and which no artist has dared to affirm categorically until now. . . . Romantic art, like that of the classical school, was art for art's sake. Today, in accordance with the most recent developments in philosophy, one is obliged to reason even in art, and never to permit sentiment to overthrow logic. Reason should be man's ruling principle in everything. My form of art is the final one because it is the only one which, so far, has combined all of these elements. Through my affirmation of the negation of the ideal and all that springs from the ideal I have arrived at the emancipation of the individual and finally at democracy. Realism is essentially the democratic art.

And here is a passage which Courbet wrote in 1861 for the benefit of a group of art students:

I hold also that painting is an essentially *concrete* art, and can consist only of the representation of things both *real* and *existing*. It is an altogether physical language, which, for its words, makes use of all visible objects. An *abstract* object, invisible or nonexistent, does not belong to the domain of painting. . . . Beauty as given by nature is superior to all the conventions of the artist. Beauty, like truth, is relative to the time when one lives and to the individual who can grasp it.

The Realists were generally captivated by the promises of nineteenth century science. By 1850 the marriage of science and technology had begun to transform science from philosophy to utility, and as science began to wade in the pond of practicality its advantages were more clearly perceived by the public. Visitors at the Exposition universelle of 1855, while interested in new building construction materials and in farm machinery, were particularly attracted to a section called Home Economy. Here they saw a collection of inexpensive household items designed to raise the living standard of the poor. Science, of course, did not divorce itself from speculation, but, in entering this bigamic state, scored a triumph over pure philosophy and theology, neither of which could produce plows or domestic comforts. The Realists' belief that the cure for the evident evils in the world lay in science is well put by Gustave Flaubert in these words written in 1869 to George Sand:

Experience shows (it seems to me) that no form is intrinsically good; Orleanism, republic, empire, no longer mean anything, since the most contradictory ideas can be filed in each of those pigeon-holes. All the flags have been so defiled with blood and shit that it is time we had none at all. Down with words! No more symbols! No more fetishes! The great moral of the present régime will be to prove that universal suffrage is as stupid as divine right, though a little less odious.

The problem shifts, therefore. It is no longer a question of striving for the best form of government, since one form is as good as another, but of making Science prevail. That is the most urgent. The rest will follow inevitably. Pure intellectuals have been of greater use to the human race than all the Saint Vincent de Pauls in the world! And politics will continue to be absurd until it becomes a province of Science. A country's government ought to be merely a section of the Institute—and the least important one of all.

The division of cultural history into periods or art schools may be convenient for historians, but the results can be misleading. Elements of all philosophical and artistic schools and truths co-exist. A momentary vogue will emphasize a particular verity, but the pendulum of popularity will inevitably shift, and yesterday's truth will seem tomorrow's blindness. Rival creeds, if temporarily eclipsed, are not obliterated for the reason that human nature is relatively constant. A movement like Realism was not first conceived in the nineteenth century (if one remembers that matter as opposed to spirit has always been an issue), but was merely a recent manifestation of an ancient facet of our civilization. We have already noted the apparent triumph of the secular, the practical, and the utilitarian by 1850, but it would be childish to regard such a victory as anything more than transitory. Yet, we find Courbet confident in the finality of his art form.

If man's qualities and sensibilities do not appreciably change in a given era, we may conclude, then, that apparent changes are owing to changing ideals. In Courbet's Realism, the absence of an ideal is elementary to the system, though it can be argued that other Realists idealized applied science as the panacea for humanity. In any case, all Realists were contemptuous of metaphysical ideals. Classicism and Romanticism are by no means synonymous, but each possesses an ideal which lies beyond the realm of the material. The two schools are generally regarded as antithetical; another view is that they are really complementary. Classicism satisfies us with a glimpse of perfection, while Romanticism warms us with its personal touch with humanity. Man, who is neither exclusively bestial nor exclusively divine, requires both ideals for a balanced view.

The greatness of art depends upon the artist's depth and not upon extreme specialization. Courbet, in his own definition of art, recognized only one aspect of life, the mundane. The most serious charge to be brought against Courbet and Realism is materialism, and the usual argument over Realism, which worries the question of whether the common is beautiful, should be a secondary consideration. In its disdain for the immaterial ideal, Realism is vulnerable to the charge of being amoral and, in this way, is antisocial and the sign of a decadent society. Realism is not merely attendant upon a utilitarian age; it is a sign that the superficial and the obvious give satisfaction. Whatever is photographic does not omit details for the mind to fill in. "The truth—yes," said Maupassant; "the whole truth—no."

In a less philosophical vein, Realism was attacked by Ingres, a grandfather in art by the time of the Second Empire. He thought that any anticlassic art was merely the art of the lazy. "It is the doctrine of those who want to produce without having worked, who want to know without having learned." Ingres had been director of the French Academy in Rome, 1834–1841, and his words were heavy with prestige. Certainly his influence was a factor in restraining French artists from following Courbet.

III

We pick up Courbet's story in 1853, the year he presented his "Wrestlers," the "Sleeping Spinner," and the "Bathers" at the Salon. The critics were again harsh. One suggested that the "Spinner" needed a bath. As for the "Wrestlers," the *Journal pour rire* remarked:

These two men are fighting to see which is the dirtiest. The victor will receive a four-cent bath ticket. None of the muscles of these wrestlers will be found in its usual place. The disorder is easily explained by the strain of the struggle. Often a beautiful disorder gives an artistic effect.

The central figure in the "Bathers" was a solid nude, modeled by Courbet's mistress of the moment, and the critics found her disgustingly fat. At a private showing of the Salon for the imperial family, Napoleon III, who had better taste in women than Courbet, struck the picture with his riding crop. This attracted the Empress's attention and, having just seen Rosa Bonheur's "Horse Fair," she inquired, "Is she a Percheron too?"

The "Bathers" was purchased by Alfred Bruyas, whom Courbet met in 1853. Bruyas was a wealthy patron, who became Courbet's best friend and bought a number of his canvases, including the "Sleeping Spinner" and "Man with the Pipe." The chief delight in this art lover's life was to collect portraits of himself, of which he commissioned a total of sixteen.

Also in 1853, Courbet met Count Nieuwerkerke, the Director of Museums. Nieuwerkerke invited the artist to lunch, as he put it, on behalf of the government. It was a friendly gesture, and Nieuwerkerke explained that the government would be pleased to have him paint a picture for the Exposition of 1855. The terms: that he submit a sketch in advance, and that the finished picture be passed by a group of artists selected by Courbet and by a committee chosen by Nieuwerkerke. If the Director sought to placate Courbet, he used the wrong approach, as Courbet did not admit the competence of anyone, beside himself, to judge his art. Nieuwerkerke, who was a traditionalist, could not agree. Courbet then announced that he planned an exhibition of his own to rival the government's, and the interview ended in bitterness.

In the meantime Courbet had a small show in Frankfurt, which was notably more successful than his previous shows in Paris. Prince Gorchakov offered to buy "Man with the Pipe," but Courbet had already promised it to Bruyas. Refusing the flattering offer from the great aristocrat gave Courbet the opportunity to suggest his own selflessness, though the truth was that he had a great financial stake in Bruyas, whom he hoped to develop into what we today call an angel. Courbet told Gorchakov that the same commitment had prevented his selling the picture to Louis-Napoleon in 1850. This was a double falsehood; Courbet did not know Bruyas in 1850, and Napoleon had had to withdraw an offer of two thousand francs for the picture owing to a reduction in his income. The artist had been only too willing to sell to a Bonaparte despite many statements he made to the contrary.

Courbet spent four months of 1854 living sumptuously at Bruyas's in Montpellier. He did two portraits of his host, one of himself, and a large canvas called "The Meeting," which depicted his arrival and reception by Bruyas. The picture is ample evidence of Courbet's egotism. Bruyas and his attendant are shown in obsequious attitudes, and even their dog stands in awe-stricken quiet at the approach of the great master. Of all the figures, Courbet alone casts a shadow. When "The Meeting" was exhibited in 1855, the critics referred to it by one of two titles: "Bonjour, M. Courbet!" and "Fortune Bowing Before Genius."

In the midst of luxury at the Bruyas's, Courbet had a few troubles. He survived an attack of cholera, the same plague which the French troops were at that moment transporting to the war zone on the Black Sea. He attributed his recovery to a medication of his own invention: twelve drops of laudanum in a linseed enema. (Any reader attracted by this home remedy ought to be advised that Courbet suffered from hemorrhoids for the following twenty years.) His illness was capped with some inconvenience in love:

My love affairs here have grown complicated. Jealousy on the part of Camelia, a young girl from Nancy; disclosure of our relations, Rose in prison. Blanche succeeds her. The commissioner annoyed by Blanche. Blanche exiled to Cette. Tears, visit to the prison, vows of love, I go to Cette. Camelia in prison; *mère* Cadet in a frenzy. *Mère* Cadet and I make love. Mina, in anguish, takes a new lover.

His affairs were physical, his mistresses were often his models, and he never married:

I still have Rose. Rose wants to go to Switzerland with me, saying that I may abandon her wherever I please. My love will not stretch far enough to include a journey with a woman. Knowing there are women all over the world, I see no reason to carry one with me.

Courbet contemplated having a private showing in 1855, which would dim into insignificance the Exposition universelle. Bruyas *père*, however, did not relish the idea of a competition with the government and refused the 40,000 francs deemed necessary by his son and Courbet. The artist then swallowed his pride and prepared to submit fourteen canvases to the jury. In particular, he worked on a new gigantic picture, the "Atelier," which would contain thirty figures:

The scene is laid in my studio in Paris. The picture is divided into two parts. I am in the center, painting; on the right all the active participants, that is my friends, the workers, the art collectors. On the left the others, those whose lives are without significance: the common people, the destitute, the poor, the wealthy, the exploited, the exploiters, those who thrive on death.

A jury of thirty examined the more than seven thousand works submitted for the Exposition universelle and ultimately chose over eighteen hundred of them. They accepted eleven of Courbet's fourteen, which would have been a triumph for anyone less self-assured. The "Burial at Ornans" and the "Atelier" were, in all probability, rejected because of their enormous size.

Count Nieuwerkerke was not responsible for their omission, because, though he presided over the jury, he cast no vote.

Courbet was now determined to proceed with his original plan, and, for a six-month period, rented a small area on the Exposition site. His second move was a frantic plea for financial support, written to Alfred Bruyas, so that he might build a gallery. The message to Bruyas: "Paris is furious at my rejection," plus a modest estimate that his show would make 100,000 francs. Everyone cooperated with Courbet, including the government he hated as despotic. The Minister of *Beaux-Arts*, Achille Fould, gave Courbet permission to charge an entrance fee, and most private collectors lent him whatever he requested. The Lille Museum was an exception, finding itself unable to part with "After Dinner at Ornans" for even a moment.

The show opened on June 28, 1855, with forty paintings, and Théophile Gautier, who was hostile to Courbet, was the first to enter. It was a bad omen. Proudhon gave what encouragement he could, but the critics generally felt Courbet's performance to be in bad taste. The public showed little interest, even after Courbet cut the entrance fee, and a financial failure was only too apparent. Even the Realist Champfleury, who had prepared the catalogue for the show, became convinced that Courbet was insincere and only bent on causing a sensation. Here is the gist of Courbet's catalogue, presumably his own ideas but written by Champfleury:

The appellation of realist has been imposed upon me just as the appellation of romanticists was imposed upon the men of 1830. At no time have labels given a correct idea of things; if they did so, the works would be superfluous.

Without discussing the applicability, more or less justified, of a designation which nobody, it is to be hoped, is required to understand very well, I shall confine myself to a few words of explanation to dispel misunderstandings.

Unhampered by any systematized approach or preconception, I have studied the art of the ancients and the art of the moderns. I had no more desire to imitate the one than to copy the other; nor was I any more anxious to attain the empty objective of *art for art's sake*.

No! I simply wanted to extract from the entire body of tradition the rational and independent concepts appropriate to my own personality.

To know in order to create, that was my idea. To be able to represent the customs, the ideas, the appearance of my own era according to my own valuation; to be not only a painter but a man as well; in short to create a living art; that is my aim.

One can only applaud Courbet for wishing to create, for it is the highest function of man. Moreover, the creative life is the happy life, because creation involves the individual in the stream of universality—or truth. It is our touch with perfection. One might define creation two ways, though avowedly they are clearly related: the discovery of unity out of the chaos of natural phenomena; the discovery of the perfect analogy which achieves universal response. Is it not true, by this reckoning, that the creation of art becomes considerably more difficult if the artist rejects tradition and ideals and insists upon "my own personality" and "my own valuation"? No one insists upon a rigid adherence to a standardized form, which can become as sterile as extreme individualism; but, in order to partake of concepts and passions, men must stand together on the same plane.

If this seems a narrow definition of creative art, it is well to note that our language may be at fault. The failure to distinguish clearly between art and skill, owing to the meaning of the word *artisan*, has left us semantically obliged to call every man who draws pleasantly an artist. The world contains many talented craftsmen, or artisans if you will, whose products are skillfully made and delightful to behold. Artists, however, are not merely skillful, nor can they always tell you what they are about, for the true artist has entered the metaphysical realm. Accordingly, Courbet's philosophical views might well be contrasted with some of his canvases. His principles are disavowed by his best paintings, which clearly transcend the narrow confines of Realism. Like all great artists, Courbet was moved by an inner vision which he neither understood nor needed to understand in order to create, and his principles might well be ignored were they not the cooperative effort of his critic-friends and in harmony with an artistic current of the time.

Courbet seemed to change his subjects in 1856, a year in which he submitted nothing to the Salon. His attention veered to landscapes and hunting scenes, hunting being the only exercise he enjoyed. In 1857 Courbet sent six canvases to the Salon, the most notable being "The Quarry," "Doe Lying Exhausted in the Snow," and "Young Women on the Banks of the Seine." Except for the latter, which featured prostitutes, the work was better received than Courbet had previously experienced, and he won a medal as in 1849. A new critic, Jules-Antoine Castagnary, began taking an interest in Courbet. They had as a basis for their friendship anticlericalism and republicanism, but Castagnary was cautious at first:

His brush is vigorous, his color is solid, his depth often surprising. He grasps the external appearance of things. . . . But he does not see beyond that because he does not believe in painting.

Meanwhile, Courbet had begun to travel extensively: Montpellier, Bordeaux, Dijon, Le Havre, Besançon, Brussels, and Frankfurt. Abroad, he made it clear how much he enjoyed the freedom from "that government" in Paris. Courbet could sense great liberty in those areas where his pictures sold well, and by this criterion the peoples of the German states were the freest in Europe. Frankfurt was the center of Courbet's popularity, and there he sold his "Doe Lying Exhausted in the Snow" in 1858.

We do find Courbet in Paris the following year, however, giving a party in his studio. Whatever he may have otherwise written about his displeasure over the Realist classification, he called his party a *fête du réalisme*. Only artists and writers were invited. A number of realistic entertainments were arranged by the host, including a cancan by Titine, a rejected play by Fernand Desnoyers, and a Haydn symphony played by Champfleury on the double bass.

It was clear that Courbet had considerable prestige by 1861. The government, of course, and the official art world still regarded him as a pest, but he won his third second-class medal that year in the Salon. He had submitted five canvases, the most notable being "Oraguay Rock" and "Fighting Stags." Of greater significance was a request he received from a group of students who were discontented at the Ecole des beaux-arts. They wanted him to open a school, and the great rebel agreed to do so.

The school opened at 83 rue Notre-Dame-des-Champs, and the enrollment, thirty-one at first, quickly increased to forty-two. The students' tuition went for rent and equipment, not to Courbet. At first the students were presented with a letter, probably written by the critic Castagnary, and dated December 25, 1861; the students were told that they were not students and that the school was not a school:

There can be no schools; there are only painters. Schools are useful only for the study of the analytical processes of art. No school can lead by itself to synthesis.

Courbet was willing to demonstrate his methods, and he did provide models. A stuffed buck was not too unorthodox a model, but when Courbet introduced and housed a live horse and ox in the studio the landlord was furious. Unhappily for him, Courbet had a four-month lease, which ran its course. The school then closed, foundering on a philosophical point. After all, the refusal to housebreak the animals was an act of faith in Realism.

Shortly afterward Courbet became the guest of a wealthy dilettante, Etienne Baudry, who lived at Rochemont in the Saintonge. Courbet stayed ten months, joining a group of artists and writers. He produced more than sixty canvases during this period and began work on a large picture which he called "subversive." The painting, which he named "Return from the Conference," was eleven by seven feet, eight inches. Not wishing to embarrass Baudry by doing an anticlerical canvas at his home, Courbet made arrangements to work at a nearby imperial stud farm. Here he fashioned the likenesses of seven drunken priests returning home from a religious conclave. To make the staggering procession completely absurd, the fattest of the seven rode a struggling donkey.

The secret of the painting was not long kept, and the outraged

local citizenry forced the director of the stud farm to oust Courbet. He then got the unfinished canvas into the home of a ferry-
man by the name of Faure, who was somewhat reluctant to
receive the donkey. Finally finished, Courbet submitted the painting, with three others, to the Salon of 1863. It was rejected by the
jury and not even allowed in the Salon des réfusés, which was
inaugurated that year by Napoleon III. The work caused a scandal
and was regarded as downright bad painting, aside from its
atrocious taste. An ardent Catholic ultimately bought it in order
to destroy it, but a photograph and a preliminary sketch remain.
Strangely enough, Courbet withheld his best works from this
Salon; he had reached the egotistical point where he ascribed all
adverse criticism to people having "sold out to the government."

IV

The year 1863 saw several crises in French art, which weakened
the position of Courbet's enemies, the academicians. The first
concerned the reform of the "art machine," that is, the governmental apparatus, which dominated French painting. The old
académies had been revived by the Constitution of the Year III
(1795) under the title Institut de France. Actually, the Institut
was composed of five academies. The Académie des beaux-arts,
which concerns us, had a membership of forty "immortals":
fourteen painters, eight sculptors, eight architects, six composers,
and four engravers. Royal patronage of the arts had been a feature
of European society since the days when national governments
took precedence over ecclesiastical authority. The tradition of
government assistance for art was thus so strong that even the
overthrow of legitimate monarchy did not long disturb it. The
forty immortals of the Académie des beaux-arts controlled the
Ecole des beaux-arts, the French Academy in Rome, the official
Salons, and the Hôtel Drouot—the center for sales. The whole
apparatus was financed by the state.

The decision to reform this system does not appear to have been
initiated by the Emperor or any of his ministers, but by Count
Nieuwerkerke and the architect Viollet-le-Duc. The former, of

Dutch origin, was a sculptor who had done little work. He owed
his position as Director General of Museums and Superintendent
of *Beaux-Arts* to Princess Mathilde Bonaparte. Though he as-
siduously courted the artistic world with weekly soirées at the
Louvre, he remained suspect and was never accepted as a confrere.
On his side, Nieuwerkerke was resentful that the Académie
failed to appreciate his talents as a sculptor, and in revenge he
saw to it that official plums fell to students not affiliated with the
Ecole des beaux-arts. As president of the jury, he controlled the
Salons and announced policies and awards. He was, in short, a
dangerous enemy for the academicians, as his authority was second
only to the Minister of *Beaux-Arts*, an office generally filled by
a politician.

Eugène-Emmanuel Viollet-le-Duc was another opponent of the
academicians. He had refused instruction at the Ecole des beaux-
arts and had resisted the vogue of classicism. His taste ran to the
medieval, which he studied outside any organized school. The
French government employed him to work on public monuments, and in the meantime, he began compiling two works
which are still regarded as authoritative: *Dictionnaire raisonné de
l'architecture française du XIᵉ au XVIᵉ siècle*, and *Dictionnaire
du mobilier français, de l'époque carlovingienne à la Renaissance*.
It is obvious that Viollet-le-Duc knew the Gothic period thoroughly, and, while there is disagreement about the taste of some
of his restorations, he was a skillful draughtsman and architect.

Yet Viollet-le-Duc was virtually isolated in his medieval camp,
as the battle lines in French art were occupied by the classical
and contemporary factions. His independence led him to publish
in 1846 an attack upon the Academy's monopoly of teaching, and
he persisted in the assault. The academicians ignored him, and it
is remarkable that his honors were bestowed by foreigners. The
Royal Institute of British Architects, for example, awarded him a
gold medal in 1863. Perhaps it was his countrymen's indifference
that whetted Viollet-le-Duc's ambition to be the master of fine
arts in France. Such a role would allow him to blast the classi-
cists from the Ecole des beaux-arts and inaugurate a renaissance
based on the Middle Ages.

The problem was to win the Emperor's confidence. His Majesty knew virtually nothing of art, but his well known generosity and his solicitude for the improvement of French institutions offered Viollet-le-Duc the opportunity to gain the imperial support in a matter of reform without requiring a discussion of philosophies of art. He was introduced to court at Compiègne by the novelist Prosper Mérimée, who was close to the Empress, having been her French tutor, and here he ingratiated himself by advising on furnishings and helping to produce the moronic skits of which Her Majesty was so fond. Meanwhile, he interested the Emperor in the restoration of the nearby fortress of Pierrefonds, which was accomplished in 1862.

Soon afterward Nieuwerkerke received instructions to reorganize the Ecole des beaux-arts, and the plans which he drew up unmistakably showed the influence of Viollet-le-Duc. New courses were outlined which placed greater emphasis on the history of art and upon aesthetics, and which made the study of French monuments equal to those of the Greeks and Romans. The importance of the Prix de Rome was reduced by shortening the sojourn from five to two years. In a clause calculated to infuriate the academicians, it was proposed that winners of the Prix de Rome spend their two years in countries of their choice, not necessarily Rome or even Italy. To balance the fury of the academicians, another clause was inserted lowering the maximum eligible age for the prize from thirty to twenty-five, which thoroughly annoyed the students. Another blow was the removal of the Ecole des beaux-arts from the control of the Académie des beaux-arts. Henceforth, the school would be governed by a board presided over by the Minister of *Beaux-Arts*. Napoleon signed the decree on November 13, 1863.

The pillars of French art were seemingly struck at their foundations. There were cries of tyranny and indignation from the Academy, Ingres refused to accept the decree, and his pupil, Hippolyte Flandrin, collapsed in tears. But the crowning insult was yet to come. Five days later a ministerial decree named Viollet-le-Duc professor of art history and aesthetics. It was a question of rival philosophies of art, of unexpected governmental interference, and of vested interests—those of the academicians and the students. The classical ideal was to be challenged in the classroom by a man who was not merely a medievalist, but who insisted that the nature of materials and the uses of a building must determine its conception. Viollet-le-Duc believed he had liberated French art.

Hippolyte Flandrin revived to answer back:

You talk of liberty, of liberty of teaching. I say to you that there is an age to learn and an age to judge and choose. It is only at this latter age that there can be any question of liberty, this liberty which so concerns you. I hold that in a school of fine arts, as in any other, it is the government's duty to teach only uncontested truths, or at least those that rest upon the finest examples accepted for centuries. You can be sure that once out of school the pupils will create the truth of their own time from this noble tradition: truth that will have good title to its name, because it will be the product of a true liberty, while the teaching of the pros and cons in the same place and, so to speak, from the same mouths can only produce doubt and discouragement.

Count Nieuwerkerke arrived at the Ecole des beaux-arts on January 29, 1864, to install the new professor, accompanied by Prosper Mérimée and Théophile Gautier. The latter was prepared to write an account of the first lesson for the *Moniteur*. Viollet-le-Duc took the speaker's chair and began his address, "Messieurs" —and the riot began. Each student had been assigned a noise. The packed hall was loud with the clucking of chickens, the trumpeting of elephants, the roar of lions, the braying of donkeys, the mewing of cats, and the yapping of dogs. A select few merely shouted insults. Nieuwerkerke got up to make indignant gestures, inaugurating the second phase of the assault: potatoes, eggs, paper bullets, and pennies.

Having nobly resisted the siege for nearly thirty minutes, the dignitaries began a retreat. This was the signal for loud applause. Quickly, then, the students formed ranks and followed the group out. Nieuwerkerke turned to glare at the students and was treated to a mass *salut dérisoire*. The dignitaries then set out on foot for the Louvre and were trailed by anything but a solemn procession. One group of students would begin the air from *William Tell*:

"O Ciel! tu sais si Mathilde m'est chère!" And the second group would respond, "A sa Mathilde, O Ciel qu'il coûte cher!" Then the aria would be interrupted by shouts of, "Oh, Beaver!"

Nieuwerkerke could understand the Rossini reference to Mathilde Bonaparte, his mistress and benefactress, but he expressed his confusion to Gautier when it came to "Oh! Beaver!" The embarrassed Gautier pretended not to know, though the shout was unmistakably a reference to a new house near the Park Monceau, which Nieuwerkerke had just built. For those not conversant with zoology, it is necessary to add that in building his house the beaver makes important use of his tail.

The procession followed Nieuwerkerke right into the Louvre, where the police interfered. Mathilde was wild with anger, but Napoleon III, who had been much annoyed by the open liaison between Mathilde and Nieuwerkerke, was vastly amused. Nieuwerkerke was soon appointed Senator by way of compensation, but the Emperor took no action against the students. As for Viollet-le-Duc, who had spoken but one word, his professorship was transferred to Hippolyte Taine, who received an ovation from the students.

V

We find Courbet in 1865 grieved by the death of Proudhon. The two had met in 1848 when Proudhon was first elected deputy, and the latter had lauded Courbet as being a socialist painter. Indeed, they were kindred spirits. Proudhon was a humanitarian and hated the exploitation of the poor, as did many other thinkers of the nineteenth century. The social conditions of early industrialism in the West were unquestionably bad, but it has not always been realized that the poverty and squalor of the industrializing society is flagrant because it is concentrated. Poverty, lack of sanitation, and exploitation were known before the nineteenth century, but they were less observed in rural communities where one was deceived by fresh air and rustic charm. That inhuman practices were merely more apparent in the nineteenth century in no way, of course, excuses them.

Two results can be noted which will, in part, explain the radicalism of the Realists and underscore what has previously been written here about their faith in materialism. Sensitive altruists were increasingly inclined to search out economic solutions for the evils they perceived, just at a time when industrialization, by raising the possibility of a high standard of living for all, spurred the peoples of the West to think of material welfare. Secondly, it is more than probable that economic welfare had become an ideal, for, if one recalls men like Saint-Simon, Proudhon, and Marx, one sees their lack of faith in the ideals of liberal government or in religion. As critical as misery itself was the fact that so many thinkers could see no farther than the realm of the exploited.

Proudhon was a man of contradictions. He disbelieved in Western liberalism, but he hated and feared the proletariat. Ultimately he opposed political power and the state as a principle of evil. This was in direct contradiction to traditional Christian teaching, which has held that the state is necessary because of man's sinful nature. Proudhon was anti-Marxist in that he believed that sovereignty rested in the commune. The state would not be political, but "economic"; that is, it would be an agency to control production and distribution. How many of these ideas Courbet shared we do not know. He flattered himself on his knowledge of politics—an unjustifiable pride—and claimed to understand Proudhon.

The association with Courbet was the stimulus for Proudhon's writing a book on art. He originally intended a pamphlet, but concluded with a book: *Du Principe de l'art et de sa destination sociale (The Basis of Art and Its Social Objective)*. Courbet was asked to collaborate and did contribute ideas, but the work is obviously Proudhon's. He knew nothing of aesthetics, thought that art for art's sake was degrading, and judged art by its social significance. For him, the artist was a social leader who should not divorce art from politics:

I define . . . art as an ideal representation of nature and of ourselves directed towards the physical and moral improvement of our species. . . . The aim of art is to guide us to a knowledge of ourselves

through the revelation of all our thoughts . . . all our tendencies,
our virtues, our vices, our absurdities, and thus to contribute to the
development of our dignity, to the improvement of our personalities.

Courbet's association with Proudhon made the former believe
his forte was political and social symbolism, whereas in truth
his portraits and landscapes were his best work. Proudhon's death
grieved Courbet, and, planning to do a bust and portrait, he requested a photograph and a death mask. The bust was never
completed, but "Proudhon and His Family" appeared in the Salon
of 1865. It was thought bad at the time and is still regarded as
one of his poorest works.

For three months after Proudhon's death, Courbet painted at
the seaside resort of Trouville. He produced more than thirty-
five canvases, mostly seascapes and portraits of fashionable
women. This flood of canvases suggests at once the artist's vigor
and shallowness. One of his subjects was Joanna Heffernan, the
mistress of James McNeill Whistler: "The Beautiful Irishwoman."
Whistler had earlier been influenced by Courbet, but by 1865 he
had rejected Realism, holding that the defiance of tradition merely
satisfied the artist's vanity.

The Salon of 1866 was relatively successful for Courbet. The
critics were more favorable, but Maxime Du Camp touched him
in his vulnerable spot: "If a knowledge of how to paint were
enough to make an artist, M. Courbet would be a great one."
Courbet had this to say of himself: "I am unquestionably the
great success of the exhibition. There is talk of a medal of honor,
of the legion of honor. . . ." Nieuwerkerke approached Courbet
about the purchase of the two most successful pictures from the
Salon: "Woman with the Parrot" for the government and "Covert
of the Roedeer" for the Empress Eugénie. There developed an
honest misunderstanding about details, but before it could be
ironed out Courbet had fired an irate letter at Nieuwerkerke accusing him of bad faith. One wonders to what extent Courbet's
politics would have changed had he been able to consummate any
of these abortive sales to members of the imperial family.

The government planned another Exhibition universelle for

1867 like the one held in 1855. Courbet, again planning to compete with the rest of the universe, began the construction of a gallery. His fecundity in canvases had, by this time, made him a wealthy man, and he was able to finance the gallery himself. He planned to collect three hundred of his own paintings for the show, and, as a pleasant gesture, donated three minor pictures to the official Salon. As his enthusiasm waxed, he developed the lunatic idea that Napoleon III would demand the privilege of opening his show.

His Majesty, however, failed to arrive at the show's inauguration, and there is no record which states that, deprived of this lofty honor, he sulked at the Tuileries. Indeed, a good many of the hoped-for canvases failed to arrive. Courbet opened with one hundred and fifteen, later adding twenty. The critics again felt the undertaking to be in bad taste, and once again paid admissions were few. One of the ticket collectors seemingly could not distinguish between the money box and his own pocket, which necessitated his incarceration. To cap it all, several canvases were stolen.

In 1868 the government required Courbet to demolish his gallery, ending his competition with the Salon. Yet, he sent only two pictures to the Salon, "Buck on the Alert" and "Beggar's Alms." The latter, crammed with social significance, was another of Courbet's "roadside series," and was ill received. It showed a frightful beggar handing a coin to a gypsy child, while in the background the gypsy mother suckled a second child along the road and a wretched cur, the product of generations of casual breeding, stood glowering.

Quite apart from aesthetics and philosophy of art, many of the pillars of the French Second Empire objected to Courbet's subject matter because it was drawn from a social level they preferred to ignore. Had he idealized his peasants and workers, there would have been fewer complaints. It is true that Napoleon III was genuinely concerned for the amelioration of the masses, but his régime—and its supporters—stood for Order. The Emperor, paradoxically, was often accused of socialist tendencies, but it is undeniable that the era was one of bourgeois predominance.

And the bourgeois bought pictures, often for nonaesthetic reasons. Pictures have, for instance, a financial and social value, and it is notable that Courbet's later financial success was achieved with masses of landscapes, portraits, and still lifes, and not with canvases of social significance. Where is the new millionaire who prefers the sight of the "vile multitude" to a delectable nude?

Courbet received two foreign awards in 1869. He won a first gold medal at the Brussels International Exposition, and at a show in Munich, Ludwig II gave him the Order of Merit of St. Michael. Both Belgium and Bavaria were monarchies. Thus, Courbet felt obliged to assert that there had been no government interference in either case. The artists of Brussels, it seems, had elected the jury; the artists of Munich had required the King to honor him. This made the prizes safely nonmonarchical.

New honors came the following year. Courbet was nominated by the government to serve on the jury for the Salon of 1870. Respecting Emile Ollivier, the new chief minister, he agreed, but ultimately did not receive enough votes to require him to serve. He sent only two seascapes to the Salon: "Stormy Sea" and "Cliffs at Etretat." The reviews were favorable and his sales were mounting. In April of 1870, for example, he sold nearly forty canvases for about 52,000 francs. Then he was offered the Legion of Honor (Chevalier), which he refused, deeming it a monarchical award. Here is a fragment from Courbet's letter to the Minister of *Beaux-Arts*, Maurice Richard:

The state is incompetent in matters of art. When it undertakes to bestow awards it is usurping the function of popular taste. Its intervention is altogether demoralizing, injurious to the artist, whom it deceives as to his true worth, injurious to art which it shackles with official conventions, and which it condemns to the most sterile mediocrity; the wisest course is to keep hands off. By leaving us free it will have fulfilled its duties toward us.

Count Nieuwerkerke resigned the directorship of museums on September 4, 1870, two days after Sedan. Several days later a group of artists met at the Sorbonne, dedicating themselves to protect art in Paris and her environs. They established an Art

Commission and elected Courbet president of it. The Commission
oversaw the sandbagging of monuments, the packing of valuable
books and documents, and the storage of art works from secondary museums in the vaults of the Louvre.

The Provisional government named Jules Simon Minister of
Beaux-Arts and Education. He, in turn, appointed an Archives
Commission on September 24, 1870, with a view to discovering
any frauds or thefts by officials appointed under the Empire. The
bureaucracy was exonerated by this investigation, much to Courbet's annoyance. He resigned his place on the Art Commission on
the grounds that he could not approve the retention of any official who had served the Empire. He forgot that they had been
serving France.

This initial quarrel with the Provisional Government (the
Government of National Defense) festered and grew worse. In
fact, Courbet's attitude mirrored that of a good many Parisians.
He said that the siege was a farce, though the inhabitants wanted
to fight. The government did not want a republic to save France.
"All that crowd of traitors, rogues, and idiots who governed us
have never fought anything but sham battles, killing a great many
men for nothing." He believed General Trochu, Military Governor of Paris, to be a nincompoop. All this from a man who would
do no fighting.

Sentiments such as these account for the flight of the government to Versailles in March of 1871 and the establishment of the
Paris Commune government. Courbet was elected to the governing body of the Commune, representing the Sixth Arrondissement.
He also headed a committee called Commission fédérale des
artistes, whose duty it was to divorce art from government control. The committee abolished the Académie des beaux-arts, the
Ecole des beaux-arts, and the Academies in Rome and Athens.

I am in heaven. Paris is a true paradise; no police, no nonsense, no op-
pression of any kind, no disputes. Paris runs by itself as if on wheels.
It should always be like this. In short it is sheer bliss.

In April, however, bliss gave way to danger. The Versailles troops
increased their pressure, and a majority of the Commune govern-

ment agreed, for the sake of expediency, to give dictatorial powers to a Committee of Public Safety. Courbet, logically, opposed the move, but was outvoted.

Meanwhile, the Vendôme column had become an issue. After Sedan and the collapse of the Empire, many Republicans had called for its destruction on two grounds: they regarded it a Bonaparte monument, and its bronze could be used for artillery. The column had originally been ordered by Napoleon I in 1803, Austrian and Russian cannon providing the bronze, and he intended a statue of Charlemagne on top. Charlemagne never reached the summit, however, but was generously presented to Aix-la-Chapelle, leaving room on the column for Napoleon in imperial Roman garb. A white flag replaced His Majesty in 1814, but Louis-Philippe restored him in an army uniform. Finally, Napoleon III got around to a third statue of his uncle in 1863, once again in Roman dress.

Courbet, as a Republican, was enthusiastic for the column's removal, but, in his capacity as President of the Art Commission, he felt obliged to protect the ornamental bronze sheeting. In a vaguely worded motion he proposed to unbolt the sheeting and remove the column to Les Invalides. The Commission, in September of 1870, apparently agreed, but it must be remembered that this body was self-constituted and completely unofficial. The decree ordering the column to be demolished, April 12, 1871, said nothing about unbolting the sheeting, and was passed one week before Courbet entered the government for his brief tenure. The deed was actually accomplished on May 16th in the presence of a large gathering.

Shortly thereafter, the Versailles troops blasted their way into Paris, and the Commune came to its ghastly end. Courbet, no longer a member of the Commune, did not bother to flee the victorious troops, but his confidence was unwarranted. His arrest came on June 7th, though he asserted his political action had been taken solely in the interest of the national art treasures. He was indicted before the Third Council of War of the first military division in Versailles on July 25, 1871.

The indictment was reasonable. It acknowledged that Courbet

had opposed the establishment of the Committee of Public Safety, that he had acted to preserve art works, and that he had not been a member of the Commune when the destruction of the column had been decreed. On the other hand, he had participated in a movement to overthrow the Government of National Defense, had incited civil war, and was an accomplice in the destruction of a public monument. He took the stand on August 14th and was very decently treated by the military court, but he could not avoid being held responsible for his support of, and participation in, the Commune.

He was not sentenced until September 2nd, and the three-month ordeal had seriously undermined his health. Six additional months in prison were awarded, plus a fine of five hundred francs and a proportionate share of the trial's cost. It was a mild sentence, if one remembers the bitterness of the struggle. Courbet, in addition, shouldered the expenses of thirteen other defendants: 6,850 francs. In prison, he was required to make felt slippers, until in November he was at last allowed to paint. By the end of 1871 his condition demanded hospitalization, and he remained in the custody of a physician until March 2nd, when he was free. It had been a humiliating and shattering experience.

Because of political chaos, there was no Salon in 1871. The following year Meissonier led a group which demanded, on political grounds, that Courbet be permanently excluded from the exhibitions. Poor Courbet had insufficient defenders, for he had made few friends in his life. He returned to Ornans in 1872 to regain his health. Sun and air, painting, and a vigorous sale of canvases combined to restore him, though he suffered from cirrhosis of the liver, which he attributed to having carried water to extinguish a burning house. He even began negotiations for a new mistress, a young peasant girl named Léontine, and he found it "inconceivable" that she should reject "the brilliant position. . . . She will be unquestionably the most envied woman in France." But Léontine preferred the young men of the village. Replied Courbet: "All the village clods possess intellectual qualities almost equal to those of their oxen, without having the same market value."

The instability of the French government after the Empire was actually a threat to Courbet, as the moderates were continually in danger from the reactionary factions. Members of the latter openly favored making Courbet pay for the Vendôme column. In anticipation, Courbet transferred the titles of some of his properties and even shipped canvases to Switzerland to avoid confiscation. His creative power was slipping along with his physical power. Yet the desire to build up a stock of pictures abroad led him to allow others to finish his paintings, though they bore his name. By employing this factory method, his sales were earning him 20,000 francs a month.

Courbet's fears were not unfounded. On May 24, 1873, a Royalist-Bonapartist faction came to power led by Marshal MacMahon, the Duke of Magenta. Six days later a bill was passed obliging Courbet to bear the cost of reconstructing the column. There had been no precedent for saddling a private individual for damage done to public property during civil strife. Yet, he was a tempting victim: rich and possessed of few friends. Courbet instantly gave his sister Zoé instructions about his remaining properties, and had she acted more swiftly the government would have profited little. The confiscation order came on June 19th, and Courbet himself passed into Switzerland on July 23rd. He never saw France again.

La Tour-de-Peliz, near the eastern end of Lake Geneva, became his last home. He hired aides, and the mass-produced art continued. Furthermore, this gigantic production encouraged forgeries which became numerous after 1872. Heavy drinking went with heavy painting. Courbet consumed more than ten quarts of Swiss white wine a day, plus absinthe. Few challenged his claim to be the foremost drinker in Vaud.

Courbet's flight did not end the Vendôme affair; he retained Lachaud, who had defended him in 1871, to battle on in France. Courbet, of course, was increasingly vague about the details, though he had written notes in 1871. These were in the possession of his sister Zoé, but she would not surrender them. Her behavior throughout those troubled years was enigmatic: sometimes loyal, sometimes malicious, sometimes idiotic.

Courbet's case against the confiscation came to trial in June of 1874, but the court not only confirmed the confiscation; it authorized additional seizures. He was still condemned to pay the cost of reconstructing the Vendôme column. The Court of Appeals confirmed this verdict in 1875. The government presented an estimate of 286,549 francs, which was revised in 1877 to 323,091 francs. His lawyers negotiated an agreement which would allow him to pay installments of 10,000 francs a year and would spare him a prison term. No interest would be charged, though he would be assessed 5 per cent on overdue payments. This arrangement, signed on May 4, 1877, lengthened the settlement for more than thirty-two years. It was a crushing burden for a man fifty-eight.

Presumably, Courbet could have safely returned to France, but he was loath to go while the MacMahon group still threatened to prevent a democratic republic. Furthermore, his physical condition was rapidly deteriorating, and he refused to give up wine. He fell into the hands of a quack just when his cirrhosis was producing dropsy. His waist became enormous, sixty inches, and he was tapped several times, each time to the tune of sixteen or seventeen quarts of fluid. The collapse of the MacMahon régime heartened him, but it was too late.

His father and sister Juliette arrived one day before the end, bringing a pound of French tobacco, which evoked his last smile. Death came on the last day of 1877.

X

Emile Ollivier

AND THE LIBERAL EMPIRE

Ici finit le plaisir et commence la peine.
—ALEXANDRE DUMAS

The son of Démosthène Ollivier, Emile was born in Marseille on July 2, 1825. Their home was governed by politics, and Rousseau was the daily fare; Démosthène was an ardent Republican who doubled in Masonry and plotted with the Carbonari. His wife's death in 1834 led him to place his children in a home—he ranked politics before parenthood—and for five years the children saw their father in Marseille only during summer vacations. Démosthène was ever willing, however, to house political refugees from Italy, and in 1839 this generosity led to bankruptcy. He gave up his business, collected the children, and moved to Paris.

Despite his poverty, he placed Emile in the Collège Sainte-Barbe and was rewarded when the boy won the bachelor's degree in 1841 at the age of sixteen. Emile immediately began to teach night school to put himself through law school, and four years later he was licensed to practice before the bar in Paris. Wishing to excel as an orator, he took diction lessons to rid himself of his Provençal accent, and he read widely—history, philosophy, theology, and literature.

After the Revolution of 1848, Démosthène Ollivier was elected Deputy to the Constituent Assembly from Marseille, and he sat with the Mountain. A friend of the Minister of the Interior, Ledru-Rollin, Démosthène secured an office for his son: Commissioner for the departments of Bouches-du-Rhône and Var. The welcoming crowd in Marseille was dismayed by the youth of the new Commissioner (he was twenty-two), but his initial speech won their cheers. In this address and in his subsequent proclamations, he balanced his praise for Republican principles with appeals for moderation and order; by stressing *Fraternity* rather than *Equality* he hoped to unite his people behind the Republic. Many of the provincial people were conservative and feared that the Republic meant the Terror. Ollivier won their confidence by a series of shrewd refusals: he would not allow a local Republican fanatic to become mayor of Marseille; he refused to imprison the Bishop and refused to form a Committee of Public Safety.

He was petitioned from all sides by office seekers, by cranks, and by men who hoped for political immoderation as an opportunity to work out personal vendettas. He met his first crisis on March 11th, when a mob of workmen demonstrated against the presence of foreign laborers who had been brought in during an earlier labor shortage:

You want to be liked; like others. . . . Do you want to show yourselves worthy of liberty? . . . You called them in during prosperous days, because they were indispensable to you. Keep them during difficult days, because they need you. . . . It is not sufficient to write *Fraternity* on our banners; we must become imbued with it, and it must live in our actions.

Concerned for the welfare of the workers, Ollivier established National Workshops, which employed nearly nine thousand men. They worked on a new seawall for Marseille and on developing the Durance Canal. He instituted a labor Committee whose members were elected to represent various trades, and personally presided over discussions of labor problems.

The initial enthusiasm for Ollivier waned in the spring of 1848, as the fear of revolutionary violence vanished, offering the extreme Leftists opportunity to undermine him. They insinuated that his moderation was actually devotion to the July Monarchy and convinced Ledru-Rollin that an investigation was in order. Unfortunately for Ollivier, the inspector shared the extremist views. Consequently, Ollivier's powers were reduced and his title changed: he became prefect of the Bouches-du-Rhône on June 10, 1848.

Several days later he was in serious trouble. A mob of over three hundred men, waving a red flag, entered the courtyard of the prefecture, and Ollivier went out alone to meet them. They accused him of betraying the workers, as he had not championed an eight-hour day, and refused to let him speak. Doubtless they would have killed him except for the timely arrival of a farmer armed with an ax, whose furious intent intimidated the three hundred. Ollivier had previously consented to be the godfather to this farmer's daughter, and was thus repaid.

Refusing to be bullied, Ollivier gave orders next day for the arrest of the mob's leader, who was president of the local *Montagnards*. The workers raised barricades in the streets, and Ollivier found it useless to warn them that the Republic was the friend of Labor and ought not to be compromised by violence. He ordered the local National Guard against the barricades, but the officers were reluctant to take orders from one so young. Thus, he had to order in troops from Aix, Avignon, Arles, and Tarascon, and peace was restored after a day's fighting. Many workers, grateful for Ollivier's obvious sympathy, had refused to join the insurrection, and Ollivier refused to apply repressive measures once the fighting was over. Of course, he was then attacked by the Rightists.

The Provisional President, Cavaignac, then withdrew Ollivier from Marseille and named him prefect of Haute-Marne. Embittered, he went to Chaumont reluctantly, but once there devoted himself to administering efficiently in the hope of popularizing the Republic. He became popular himself and was spoken of as a desirable candidate for Parliament, but the jealous incumbent secured Ollivier's recall as prefect in 1849 to destroy him as a rival. A petition of protest was signed by 32,000 citizens of the department, but Ollivier was not reinstated. Later, he was offered a new post, but refused it in his disgust.

Ollivier now turned to the practice of law, but was inopportunely interrupted by his father's political troubles. Démosthène was not reelected in 1850 as Deputy from the Bouches-du-Rhône and wanted to stand for election in Var. He needed his son's eloquence in the campaign, and Emile heeded the call, though confident his father could not win. The election was lost as foreseen, but their campaign had annoyed Haussmann, then prefect of Var, and Emile Ollivier was charged in Draguignan with attempting to organize clubs for political action. He was acquitted, but the enmity between Haussmann and Ollivier remained.

Back in Paris, Ollivier discovered that being a Republican had become less respectable after the bloody June Days, and he found it hard to obtain clients. In his spare time he began to study Saint-Simon and often went to Holy Father Enfantin's, where he met Michel Chevalier, the Péreire brothers, and Prince Jerome-Napoleon. His unemployment was not quite complete, thanks to the calamities suffered by his relatives. Aristide Ollivier, his brother, publisher of a Republican journal in Montpellier, was killed by a Royalist in a duel following a polemic which Aristide had written. It fell to Emile to defend his brother's paper in court, which he did successfully.

Shortly afterward his father was summoned to appear before the Paris Assize on December 2, 1851, to face a charge of conspiring to overthrow the government. Démosthène Ollivier had been one of the Republicans who, anticipating a coup on the part of the President, advocated the President's arrest. Emile rushed back to Paris from Montpellier to defend his father, arriving during the night of December 1–2. He awoke in the morning to find Louis-Napoleon's *coup d'état* an accomplished fact and Démosthène in flight. Betrayed five days later, the latter was taken by the police. No doubt he would have received a serious sentence—perhaps deportation to Cayenne—had it not been for Prince Jerome-Napoleon, who secured him a passport for Belgium.

For some months Emile Ollivier was idle, utterly dejected by the events of the three preceding years; only in 1852 did he begin to revive. That year he became secretary to a leading lawyer and accepted a few clients of his own, and he renewed acquaintance with a former school friend, Ernest Picard. Not until 1857, however, was he entrusted with cases sufficiently important to win him legal recognition. In particular, the case of the Marquise de Guerry *v.* the Convent of Picpus was significant, as it pitted Ollivier against the Royalist Berryer, prominent in both law and politics. Ollivier's presentation was considered far more brilliant, and the Republicans naturally saw him as a strong candidate for public office.

Meanwhile, Ollivier had become a patron of music. He was often invited to the salon of Comtesse d'Agoult (who used the literary pseudonym Daniel Stern), whose two daughters, Blandine and Cosima, had been fathered by Franz Liszt. Ollivier fell in love with Blandine, and the two were married on October 22, 1857—Liszt's birthday—in Florence. Ollivier was thirty-two, she twenty-one. Cosima married Hans von Bülow in the same year, but this marriage ended in divorce and Richard Wagner became her second husband.

Wagner often visited Liszt in Paris, and at Liszt's suggestion Ollivier undertook to protect Wagner's legal rights in France. Ollivier accepted the task as an obligation to music, for Wagner was neither a paying client nor a good friend. He heard Wagner sing portions of *Tannhäuser* at Listz's and was soon seconding the Princess Metternich's demands for a performance at the Opera. Napoleon III ordered the celebrated Paris premiere to please the Princess, but the Emperor, the Princess, and Ollivier were an ineffective claque at the performance in competition with the Jockey-Club.

Ollivier and Blandine were supremely happy together. True to her father's art, she played the piano beautifully and filled their home with glorious sound. But she did not recover from the birth of their first child, Daniel; lingering several months, she died at Saint-Tropez, only twenty-six.

In the meantime the Republicans prepared to marshal their forces for the election of 1857, but the restrictions upon the liberty of the press and the right to hold public meetings made electioneering by the Opposition difficult. Furthermore, France seemed satisfied with the Empire. The Parisian Republicans drew up a list of candidates, nevertheless, from the "Men of '48"; except for Jules Simon these candidates were relatively aged, which led the Republican command to nominate a younger man— Ollivier—to run in the Tenth District where there was no hope for a Republican anyway. The younger men resented this gerontocracy, and a quarrel—centering at first about a personal antagonism between General Cavaignac and Léonor Havin—split the party into factions immediately before the election.

Consequently, the Republicans presented two slates of candidates, and Ollivier ran in the Fourth District against the government's candidate, Varin, and the older Republican Garnier-Pagès. The latter was eliminated in the first balloting, giving Ollivier the combined Republican vote and victory in the runoff. Four other Parisian Republicans were elected: Carnot, Cavaignac, Goudchaux, and Darimon, giving the Republicans victory in half the city's electoral districts. Only one Republican Deputy was elected in the provinces: Hénon from Lyon.

The victorious Republicans were not of one mind about taking the oath to support the Empire, which was required upon assuming one's seat in the Corps législatif. The older members favored striking a pose of high-principled refusal and, thus, abdicating their seats, while the young preferred to become a loyal opposition. Only Ollivier, Darimon, and Hénon took the oath; they were seated on the left rear benches in the Corps législatif and studiously avoided by the other members. In 1858 elections were held to fill the vacant seats, and returned two more young Republicans, Picard and Favre. The Three had become The Five, and Ollivier was recognized as their leader.

The first hint of Ollivier's policy came in the same year, following Orsini's attempt upon the life of Napoleon III. The government asked for additional security powers, which were not only repressive but unnecessary, for the assassination attempt had been made by an Italian who commanded no following in France. Ollivier spoke against granting the emergency powers and recalled the example of William III of England, who, after thirteen years of rule, was regarded as the restorer of the public liberties. This speech foreshadowed the alliance between the Empire and liberalism, to which, in 1858, most Bonapartists and Republicans were hostile.

The Liberal Empire was never promulgated as such. Instead, the dictatorship dating from 1851 was abandoned in piecemeal fashion, beginning in 1859, giving the impression of grudging concession to popular demand. Victor Duruy, the Emperor's most durable and successful Liberal Minister, believed that Napoleon III was more liberal than the Bonapartists. In the face of his own party's opposition, His Majesty could at best move slowly toward parliamentary monarchy, while his natural inertia and his painful illness contributed to his apparent hesitation.

Historians have generally not been kind to Napoleon III, feeling that the drift toward Liberal Empire was opportunistic and not dictated by any sincere desire to be liberal. The Emperor understood, however, that he owed his throne to the strength of the Napoleonic Legend, a legend whose myths he had accepted as reality from childhood. Consequently, he was as imbued with the totalitarian aspects of Bonapartism as with its Jacobin aspects, two seemingly irreconcilable elements made compatible by the notion that Liberty could only derive from Order.

The War of 1859 against Austria on behalf of Italian nationalism was the first of the Emperor's liberal measures; he provoked the war despite the opposition of his party and his wife. The Cobden-Chevalier Treaty of 1860, negotiated by free traders, produced a reduction in tariffs, which Napoleon forced upon the French manufacturers. Later that year, the Decree of November 24, 1860, reestablished Parliament's right to reply to the speech from the throne, commanded the ministers without portfolios to defend the government's projects in parliamentary debate, and opened parliamentary debates to publicity for the first time. "The Empire," said Proudhon, "has made a half-turn to the Left."

In the spring of 1861, a bill to liberalize control of the press came before the Corps législatif, and Ollivier, in speaking for a free press, thanked the Emperor for the decree of the previous November and recognized his "courage and generosity":

When you are head of a nation of thirty-six million people; when you have been acclaimed by that nation; . . . when you are the most powerful of sovereigns; when destiny has drained herself of favors for you; when everything has been given to you; when, by a celebrated good fortune, you have emerged from prison to mount the throne of France after suffering exile; when you have known all the sadnesses and all the joys, there remains to taste only one pleasure which surpasses all the others: to be the one who courageously and voluntarily initiates a great people into liberty, who rejects his faint-hearted and faithless counselors to put himself directly in the presence of the nation.

The Republicans were stunned and disconcerted by Ollivier's speech, for only Darimon had known in advance that Ollivier approved the Decree of November 24th. It was bad enough to have the Emperor stealing their liberal thunder without having the Republican leader in the Corps législatif applaud the theft. An angry Carnot publicly questioned how a man whose father had been proscribed by Napoleon III could now speak of the Emperor as the initiator of French liberties; but a minority of the Republicans, including Jules Ferry and Léon Gambetta, suspected that Ollivier's decision to support liberal reforms within the framework of the Empire was the only alternative to Republican impotence. A majority of the older Republicans referred to this minority as the "Little Olliviers."

Morny, President of the Chamber and one of the few Liberal Bonapartists, naturally welcomed Ollivier's speech. The two men had had a much publicized encounter in the Chamber after the news of the Decree of November 24th:

Morny: Well, I suppose you are happy?
Ollivier: Yes, only you are founded or lost.
Morny: How's that?
Ollivier: You are founded if this is only the beginning; you are lost if this is the end.

Hopeful that the Empire was making an important conquest, Morny carefully edited Ollivier's speech of thanks before its official publication, but his editing did not pass unnoticed. A Deputy inquired from the floor why the phrase *chance légendaire* (celebrated good fortune) had been changed to *héros légendaire* (legendary hero), and why the clause "as for me who am a Republican" had been expunged from the text.

Morny explained only his second revision. He had ordered the revision to avoid calling Ollivier to order, since the remark was unconstitutional in character. He added that Ollivier was free to reestablish the original clause and the Chamber free to insist upon it. The incident was embarrassing for Ollivier, who was grateful for Morny's attention but not yet ready to cast free from the Republicans. Consequently, he wrote Morny a note to clarify his original words, and Morny duly had the note published in the *Moniteur*. The older Republicans, however, were rightly fearful that Morny had made a major breach in their ranks. Ollivier's *Journal* reveals that on that day he recognized that continuing to put his principles above party discipline would likely lead to expulsion from the party; he did not intend to leave of his own accord, but neither did he intend to oppose liberal reforms proposed by the government.

To avoid being compromised by Morny, Ollivier avoided his company whenever possible. A chance encounter outside the Chamber late in 1861 was the occasion for Morny to assure Ollivier that the Empire would continue to go in a liberal direction. The next year, Ollivier agreed to meet Morny in private for the first time. The latter was confident that a parliamentary régime would, in time, be established, and he hoped to be the first responsible Prime Minister. Such assurances, coming from the Emperor's half-brother, could only have encouraged Ollivier in the path he had already chosen, and when—upon the death of his wife—Ollivier received an especially sensitive letter of condolence from Morny, his reserve began to disappear.

As the election of 1863 approached, some of the Republicans favored ejecting Ollivier from the party ranks, but Gambetta argued successfully that the party had an obligation to support every one of The Five. Consequently, Ollivier ran as a Republican, and this time in both Paris and Var. He was beaten in Var, as his father had been before him, but won in Paris. Morny congratulated Ollivier on his election and hotly castigated the Minister of the Interior, Persigny, for having opposed Ollivier with an official candidate.

Fearing a clean break with the Republicans, Ollivier refused an invitation to call on the Emperor, but he did not balk when Morny suggested that they work together in Parliament for legislation beneficial to laborers. In February of 1864, then, when a bill came before the Corps législatif to liberalize the laws restricting combinations, Morny appointed Ollivier the reporter for the parliamentary commission named to examine the bill. Rouher, Minister of State, was furious at the Emperor for allowing the bill in the first place—he remarked that the Emperor had just joined the International—and at Morny for daring to show such confidence in a member of the Left. The Republicans were equally annoyed, and accused Ollivier of selling out to the Empire.

The provisions of the old Chapelier Law of 1791, which prohibited workers from combining and striking, had been incorporated into the Code Napoléon. The proposed Law of 1864 allowed workers the right to form coalitions, but not to associate. Association meant a permanent organization; coalitions existed only for temporary periods, giving workers the right to defend themselves by organizing. The law, furthermore, would give workers in coalition the right to strike, providing they avoided violence and were striking for "justifiable grievances"—meaning for genuine economic reasons and not for revolutionary or obstructive reasons. In this way the government hoped to improve the rights of workers without admitting the principle of unions, which were regarded as dens of conspiracy by the employers of the day.

In their eagerness to attack Ollivier, the Republicans bitterly denounced the bill, despite the fact that the law was intended to improve the workers' lot, and allied themselves with those on the extreme Right who regarded the measure as dangerously radical. Of course, the Republicans argued that the measure was inadequate, but Ollivier answered that it was better to take what could be had than to dwell upon the impossible. "I do not limit myself to criticizing what it lacks; I am thankful for what it gives me." The Coalitions Law passed 222 to 36, and marked the public break between Ollivier and the Left.

The Morny-Ollivier alliance was now an accepted fact. Upon his return to Paris from a winter vacation, January, 1865, Ollivier went first to see Morny. The latter suggested that their next project be a liberal press law, that once again Ollivier should be its reporter, and that Ollivier should now be willing to go to the Tuileries to meet His Majesty. Morny refused Ollivier's suggestion, however, that Morny should become reconciled with Prince Jerome-Napoleon, and he assured Ollivier that the Liberal Empire would develop slowly under the Emperor's direction without the aid of the erratic cousin.

The sudden death of Morny in March of 1865 must have been a serious shock to Ollivier, but it came as a boon to the conservative Bonapartists and the Republicans. The "Little Olliviers" drifted back into the Republican camp; and, except for a handful of loyal men, Ollivier seemed isolated and without political future. Naturally, the Deputies were curious about Ollivier's next move and were attentive when he rose to speak on March 27th. He began by thanking the government for its liberal reforms, but criticized its failure to do more:

You say to me, "If the government follows the advice you give, it will be committed to a fatal path; to resist is the principal art of governing." I believe the exact opposite. I am convinced that governing is the art of yielding, the art of yielding without seeming to be forced, the art of yielding at the proper moment to the legitimate expressions of a people. . . .

If Charles X had not attempted a *coup d'état* against his own constitution; if, in 1829, he had returned to the fine policy of 1819; if, instead of following Polignac, he had listened to Chateaubriand, Royer-Collard, or Guizot, he would not have learned a second time how bitter is the bread of exile.

If Louis-Philippe had not marred so many noble qualities with a senile stubbornness; if he had not shut himself off from association with able men, from electoral reform, and from lowering the property qualifications; . . . if he had been more solicitous for French glory and for the people's suffering and for their rights, he would not have rediscovered—in his later years—the trials of his youth, and all the agitation of 1847 and 1848 would have been terminated by a Barrot and Thiers ministry and not by a Revolution. . . .

But let us not misconstrue: to yield is not sufficient. It is necessary to yield at the proper moment—neither too soon nor too late. . . . As for the Empire, it is not too soon; it is not too late: the time is now.

He concluded by turning to the Republicans and harkened back to the days when he, as a Republican, believed that form of government was fundamental to all other questions: "I was in error. The best government is that which exists from the moment the nation accepts it." If one subordinates progress to form of government, he told them, one is simply surrendering to the necessity of revolution.

Napoleon III, it is true, was pleased by Ollivier's speech, but after Morny's death His Majesty was almost as isolated at court as Ollivier was in Parliament. The Empress, Rouher, and most of the courtiers were conservative, and Rouher feared Ollivier as a possible rival for power. Against Rouher, Ollivier could count on the support of Walewski, Morny's successor as President of the Corps législatif, though Walewski was weak and without Morny's authority. In the cabinet, Duruy would support Ollivier, but what was one minister against a conservative majority? Prince Jerome-Napoleon also favored Ollivier, but the imperial cousin was regarded as a pest by the Emperor and heartily disliked by the Empress.

Napoleon III declined to meet this opposition head-on, but, while postponing new liberal reforms, he worked to retain Ollivier's support in the hope of future reforms. Morny, before his death, had arranged for Ollivier to be invited to the Tuileries. His first visit, on May 6, 1865, happened to coincide with the Emperor's tour of Algeria, but he was received by Eugénie. He found her friendly and kind, eager to hear him discuss the principles of liberalism, which she admitted made no sense to her; but during the audience he agreed to serve on an investigating committee which Her Majesty was sponsoring to look into cases of juveniles held in La Roquette prison.

The Empress summoned him again on June 27th, ostensibly to discuss the committee's work, but the Emperor quickly interrupted the meeting and turned the talk to politics. The meeting had obviously been staged, a minor illustration of Napoleon III's love for the devious method. Asked what reforms should be forthcoming, Ollivier spoke for freedom of the press and for unhampered elections. The interview was a personal success for both men. Napoleon III was convinced that Morny had been right—and Rouher wrong—in judging Ollivier as an honest man and not merely an ambitious politician. And Ollivier had been charmed by the Emperor: "What great things we will do together if Napoleon III really wishes to establish liberty!"

In 1866, however, Napoleon's speech from the throne gave no hint of further reforms; apparently, the conservative Bonapartists had prevailed at court. As a response to this speech, the fourteen Independent Deputies, led by Thiers, proposed suggesting that the stability of France could no longer be threatened by the "wise progress" of political institutions. Rouher attacked the suggestion as implying parliamentary government, and the government beat down the proposal; but in losing, the Independents rallied 63 votes (without Republican support) against the government's 206, a notable protest against Rouher's policy.

Nevertheless, Ollivier had begun to despair for the future of liberalism. The Emperor's natural inertia and his painful illness robbed him of the vitality necessary to combat the conservatives, and a do-nothing policy seemed to be the result. Yet, by the year's end, the régime had suffered embarrassing defeats in foreign affairs—the unexpected Prussian victory at Sadowa and the necessity of evacuating Mexico—and Napoleon III was forced to continue the consolidation of the régime: the establishment of a Liberal Empire according to the dictates of the Napoleonic Legend. The conservatives regarded the régime's setbacks as the product of the liberal reforms already instituted, but His Majesty's actions were generally conceived in the spirit of the Legend's holy writ. He had given France order; he must now give her liberty. In those healthier, happier years beginning in 1859, he had drifted toward liberalism because he could; in the years of sickness and shadows he drifted toward liberalism because he must.

Toward the end of 1866, the Emperor conferred with Walewski at Compiègne about new reforms. They agreed to propose a more liberal press law and to require cabinet ministers to go before the Chamber to explain and defend government policies. The latter proposal would have the incidental effect of reducing the authority of the Minister of State (Rouher) by making him merely a liaison between the executive and legislative branches, as had been originally intended, instead of the sole spokesman for the government. Ollivier had hoped for the institution of true parliamentary government, but agreed to support these projected reforms.

Walewski then approached Ollivier with an offer of a cabinet post, stating that the Emperor needed Ollivier's support; but Ollivier was reluctant to join the government before parliamentary government had been established, and finally consented only if three conditions should be met: freedom of the press; acceptance of the principle of German unity; a constitutional amendment making it possible for a minister to retain his parliamentary seat. These terms were given to the Emperor on January 2, 1867, who asked for several days to consider them.

Meanwhile, Ollivier regretted his decision and, on the tenth, called on Napoleon to insist on the advisability of remaining outside the cabinet for the moment. The talk was friendly, and the Emperor said: "We are in agreement. A resolute and liberal step is necessary: I merely hesitate over the proper moment." Clearly, too, the Emperor wished to demote Rouher, but shrank from a direct clash with the Empress. Consequently, he begged Ollivier to interview the Empress immediately in the hope of securing her approval of Rouher's dismissal, and he asked if Ollivier would be willing to interview Rouher in the Emperor's study. Ollivier agreed to both interviews.

His meeting with the Empress produced nothing. Revealing herself intransigent, Eugénie sanctioned neither Rouher's removal nor new liberal reforms which would be of consequence. Ollivier was then confirmed in his decision not to join the cabinet until such time as parliamentary government would be guaranteed. In later life, he admitted that his own intransigence at this point was a mistake, for he left the field open to Rouher and the conservatives.

Abetted by the Empress, Rouher ignored his scheduled meeting with Ollivier. This defiant stand, however, failed to bluff Napoleon III, who, on January 19, 1867, decreed that all ministers

would participate in the debates of the Corps législatif and that
new laws relative to the freedom of the press and of assembly
would be presented. Rouher, then, changed his tactics and pretended to champion the reforms he actually did not favor and
intended to sabotage. Accordingly, he agreed to honor the Emperor's suggestion that he discuss the projected reforms with
Ollivier.

Believing that Rouher's new orientation was sincere, Ollivier
cooperated with Rouher in good faith; his disillusionment came
shortly. He found that Rouher was organizing a secret ring of
Deputies devoted to defeating all of the Emperor's reform
projects, and he found himself the victim of slander. Rouher
whispered that Ollivier had been so ambitious for office that he
had been eager to traffic with his opponent, and when Rouher
began again to show his true conservative hand few doubted
that Ollivier was anything but a vile intriguer. Prince Jerome-
Napoleon was among those who recognized Rouher's trick and
refused to join the general outcry against Ollivier, but Rouher
—using his new prestige gained in discrediting Ollivier—then
turned on Walewski and forced his resignation as President of
the Corps législatif.

Thus, as in 1866, the conservative Bonapartists had triumphed
over the Emperor and Ollivier. In July of 1867, Ollivier furiously
attacked Rouher in the Chamber, using the phrases "grand vizir,"
"mayor of the palace," and even "vice-emperor without responsibility." He was called to order by the new President, Eugène
Schneider, but not before Rouher had been severely stung. To
placate Rouher, Napoleon presented him with the Grand Cross
of the Legion of Honor, whereupon Ollivier refused further invitations to the palace.

The Republicans, who had been among the first to participate
in Rouher's campaign to vilify Ollivier, found it opportune in
1868 to open a subscription for a monument to honor Baudin,
one of their number who had fallen during the *coup d'état*
of 1851. To test his party loyalty, they asked Ollivier to sign the
subscription list. He rejected their proposal on the grounds that
such a monument was an encouragement to revolution, and that

too much had been accomplished in the direction of Liberal
Empire for him to sanction revolution. The Republicans chose to
interpret this as Ollivier's approval of the *coup d'état*, and they
were agreed that he should not be accepted as a Republican
candidate for the elections of 1869, forcing him to run as an
Independent.

He knew that his campaign would be futile unless the charge
of opportunism, made by Rouher in 1867, could be proved false.
Thus, he decided to publish a book which would reveal the
constancy of his political position. Originally entitled *The Nineteenth of January*, referring to Napoleon III's liberal decree of
that date, Ollivier ultimately published his book on March 3,
1869, under the title *A Report to the Electors of the Third
District of the Seine*. The key document reproduced in the book
was a letter from the Emperor dated January 12, 1867, and he
had felt obliged to ask His Majesty's permission to publish it.
Permission was readily granted on the grounds that "I repent
neither the sentiments nor the ideas which I manifested to you
at that time."

In less than a month's time, the book sold 20,000 copies.
Sensational because it was the first revelation of the private
talks between Napoleon, Walewski, Ollivier, and Rouher in
1867, the book also revealed that Ollivier had been instructed
to talk to Rouher, and that there had been no "selling out" to
Rouher—indeed, that Rouher had been the scoundrel in the
affair. Ollivier had been helpful in bringing about the reform
decree, true to his principle of loyal opposition in the interest of
liberalism, while Rouher had maneuvered to defeat the Emperor's will.

The zealotry with which Rouher set out to defeat Ollivier's
attempt at reelection in 1869 suggests that he felt his own career
at stake. He used his influence to have the Third District in
Paris gerrymandered; likely a Republican stronghold in any
event, the removal of more moderate voting sections to neighboring districts ensured a Republican victory. And in Var, where
Ollivier had stood unsuccessfully before, the prefect received
word from Rouher to spare no effort to beat Ollivier again.

Rouher's strategy succeeded in Paris. The balloting began on May 24th, and Ollivier was overwhelmed two to one. But His Majesty interfered in Var, refusing to allow an official candidate, and while Ollivier did not have the official designation he was soon known to be the Emperor's man. In the provinces the chore of beating a Republican was not too difficult, and Ollivier won 16,000 to 8,000. That there were 12,000 abstentions reveals that many of the conservatives refused to vote for Ollivier despite the Emperor's will, and had an official Bonapartist candidate been entered it is doubtful that Ollivier could have been elected. Even under the favorable circumstances of the election, no one was more astonished at his victory than he himself.

The election of 1869 produced forty Opposition Deputies, of whom thirty were Republican, giving the Opposition only eight more parliamentary votes than in 1863. These figures mislead, however, for two reasons: the Opposition was less scattered than before and could become more effective through Republican discipline. Secondly, the popular vote for Opposition candidates increased markedly: 3,355,000 votes against 4,438,000 for official candidates. Therefore, in the face of a solid victory for its candidates, the government still had reason to be nervous.

The conservative Bonapartists demanded that Napoleon III crown their victory by reconstituting the cabinet along more conservative lines; but Ollivier, utilizing his new prestige as the "Emperor's man," rallied 116 Deputies, who signed a petition favoring responsible government. (The 116 Deputies did not include the Republicans.) Napoleon III made a typical response to this double pressure; he gave the appearance of favoring both sides. Actually, of course, he favored Ollivier's liberal program, and he announced on July 12th that he was ready to take his "third step"—the Decrees of November 24, 1860, and January 19, 1867, being the first two. He granted the Corps législatif the right to choose its own officers, increased its power to initiate and amend legislation, and gave it the right to vote the budget by sections. Deputies could, henceforth, become ministers without losing their parliamentary seats, but he stopped short of decreeing ministerial responsibility.

To placate the conservatives at least momentarily, the Emperor reconstituted his cabinet in their favor on the same date, appointing men who were, in general, opposed to the Emperor's new decree and who could not long have commanded the confidence of the Chamber under a situation of ministerial responsibility. As true parliamentary government seemed near at hand, it is small wonder that the new ministers suspected their tenure would be short. Even the chief conservative was missing from their ranks: Napoleon III had rid himself of Rouher by abolishing the Ministry of State and retiring its incumbent to the Presidency of the Senate.

Among Ollivier's followers there was some disappointment that true parliamentary government had not been fully instituted, but Ollivier had learned that Napoleon III moved slowly and carefully in the face of serious opposition. Consequently, he congratulated the Emperor on the reforms and accepted an appointment as President of the Var Departmental Council. The Republicans expressed their disappointment, too, the violence of their opposition increasing after July 12th; but did their violence really represent their disappointment or their fear? If the Empire was on the verge of becoming parliamentary, what would be left for them? In the meantime, the reforms announced on July 12th were sanctioned by a decree of the Senate (*sénatus-consulte*) on September 8th.

In October, Ollivier and Napoleon III began discussions relative to supplanting the conservative cabinet of July 12th. When inviting Ollivier to Compiègne on October 31st, the Emperor suggested that he come at night and in disguise to avoid interference by the press and the court circle. Thus, Ollivier boarded the train in the Gare du Nord without his glasses and wearing a false nose. He conferred with the Emperor in secret for two hours, setting down his terms for entering the government: responsible ministry; peaceful settlement of all questions dividing Prussia and France; and occupation of Rome at least until the Vatican Council had finished its sitting. These terms were acceptable to the Emperor.

Ollivier also wanted the conservative Minister of the Interior, Forcade de La Roquette, removed upon his own entry into the cabinet, but the Emperor said that he would require at least a month to prepare this direct challenge to the conservatives. Consequently, Ollivier agreed to wait while the Emperor prepared the ground. In the interim, the Emperor was suddenly aware that he had not discussed with Ollivier the fact that the constitution did not provide for a Prime Minister, and he wrote to Ollivier accordingly.

Ollivier answered that he had never mentioned the office of Prime Minister because he thought the Emperor ought to continue to preside over cabinet meetings. Responsible government did not necessarily imply a Prime Minister, but merely homogeneity within the cabinet with the ministers devoted to the majority in Parliament. Under such circumstances, Ollivier would accept a cabinet appointment.

A second letter from Napoleon requested that Ollivier draw up a list of possible ministers, adding that he was on the verge of sending Forcade de La Roquette to the Council of State. Then, on November 29th, His Majesty went before the Corps législatif to open a special session: "France wishes liberty, but with order," he said. "As for order, I am responsible; but help me, Gentlemen, to preserve liberty." In response, a new parliamentary group drew up a petition for responsible government, which attracted 136 signatures and which the Republicans promised to support. This gave the Emperor a clear mandate to disimiss the conservative ministers.

On December 27th Ollivier received the following letter from the Emperor, which was published the next day in the *Moniteur:*

Monsieur le Député, The ministers having given their resignations to me, it is with confidence in your patriotism that I ask you to designate the men who can form a homogenous cabinet with you, which will faithfully represent the majority in the Corps législatif, which will be resolved to apply—both in letter and in spirit—the *sénatusconsulte* of September 8.

I am counting on the devotion of the Corps législatif to the major interests of the country, as on yours, to aid me in the task which I am undertaking to make the constitutional régime function correctly. . . .

Actually, Napoleon III gave Ollivier free reign to select only ten of the twelve ministers; as the Emperor was responsible for the national defense, he thought the ministers of War and the Navy should have his confidence. General Le Boeuf and Admiral Rigault de Genouilly, in consequence, were retained from the previous cabinet at Napoleon's request. Ollivier's only difficulty came in filling the post of Foreign Affairs, which Count Daru finally accepted. Ollivier himself took the Ministry of Justice, to which he added the Ministry of Cults. The cabinet was finally assembled on January 2, 1870. On that day the ministers agreed that French foreign policy should proceed on the assumption that the hegemony of Prussia in Central Europe was a *fait accompli*, and that the Emperor should be asked to terminate his private correspondence with French ambassadors abroad. Thus was the Ministry of January 2nd launched.

The machinery of responsible government was as yet imperfect, and years of experience would be required to make the new form efficient and practical. In particular, the adjustment of the monarch's role was difficult, for the transition from dictatorship to limited monarchy in the course of one reign compelled Napoleon III to effect an evolution accomplished in England during the reigns of the four later Stuarts. Though the analogy is not perfect, the Government of January 2nd resembled cabinet government in the time of William III and Anne more than in the time of the first two Georges.

As Napoleon III continued to preside at cabinet meetings, the post of Prime Minister did not exist. The leading minister, in this case Ollivier, was actually a vice premier and was given the title Keeper of the Seals *(Garde des Sceaux)*. As for ministerial responsibility, the Senate's decree of September 8th stated that the ministers would be "dependent" on the Emperor, deliberating in council under his presidency, but "responsible" to the Lower House and impeachable by the Senate. The apparent ambiguity in the Ministry's responsibility probably derived from an attempt to express the Ministry's simultaneous responsibility to Parliament and loyalty to the crown. The Emperor continued to be responsible to the people directly.

The new ministers were men of integrity, and though seven of the twelve had had no ministerial experience, their appointment unleashed a wave of optimism which was immediately

registered on the Bourse. This confidence was reflected by the
Duc de Broglie, Doudan, Montalembert, and Girardin, whose
writings avowed that the government had been reconstituted on
a firm basis. Even some Republicans, like Picard, admitted that it
might soon be necessary to rally to the Empire.

While all the ministers favored responsible government, the
cabinet was actually divided. One faction, led by Ollivier, wished
to keep the Emperor's influence strong; the other group, led
by Daru and Buffet, hoped to continue the development of responsible government along the British model. Ollivier's position
was partly conditioned by his personal attachment to the monarch, whom he had begun to address as *"Cher Sire."* Naturally, the
Emperor favored Ollivier: "You are the first of my ministers to
understand me."

On January 3rd the ministers paid their respects to the Empress, whose conservative and clerical views were well known.
Her reply to the ministers was significant: as long as the ministers had the Emperor's confidence, they could count on her
"good will." By omitting the word, she made it known that the
ministers did not have her confidence. In the days that followed,
her hostility to Ollivier was so evident that the second Mme.
Ollivier went to the Empress's "Mondays" only rarely. (He
married Marie-Thérèse Gravier in 1869.)

Baron Haussmann was the first of the conservative Bonapartists
to have challenged Ollivier (after the election of 1850 in Var)
and was the first to feel the ire of the new liberal cabinet. Having threatened to resign as prefect of the Seine should Ollivier
become a minister, Haussmann had failed to do so—counting
on the Emperor's personal support—and the cabinet unanimously
voted his removal from office. Haussmann was hated, despite the
wonders he had worked in the transformation of Paris, for supposed irregularities in the management of funds and for his arbitrary manner. Parliamentary investigations had been unable to
touch him, thanks to imperial protection, and it was a bitter
moment for Napoleon III when he had to sign the cabinet's order
for Haussmann's dismissal. He did so, but with tears.

During the Ministry's first week, the Republicans made known their intention to remain in opposition, though privately many of them despaired for the party's future. Then, on January 10th, the government suffered a cruel shock, which restored Republican hopes; Pierre Bonaparte shot a Leftist editorial writer.

Fifty-four at the time, Prince Pierre was the third son of Lucien. He was reared in Italy, where he spent much effort as an agitator in the Papal States; living a violent life, he had once before been involved in murder. In 1848 he followed his father's republicanism rather than the Bonapartism of the family name, so that under the Empire he was tolerated but not made part of the family circle. His services were refused by Napoleon III, and though entitled to be called "Highness," Pierre was rarely seen at court.

Preceding the murder, Prince Pierre had engaged in a journalistic duel with Paschal Grousset, a writer on *La Marseillaise*, who had attacked Napoleon I in an article. Grousset finally sent two seconds to arrange for a duel with arms, one of whom was Victor Noir (Yvan Salmon). Instead of meeting Pierre's seconds, they called on him personally—bearing arms, and he received them armed as was his habit. A short argument followed, ending with the death of Victor Noir and the flight of his companion.

Ollivier acted swiftly. The murderer was arrested the same evening, and preparations were made for his trial. The victim's newspaper moved equally swiftly, publishing a call to revolution penned by Henri Rochefort:

I have had the weakness to believe that a Bonaparte could be something other than an assassin! I dared to suppose that a straightforward duel was possible with this family where murder and snares are tradition and custom. . . . For eighteen years now France has been held in the bloodied hands of these cutthroats, who, not content to shoot down Republicans in the streets, draw them into filthy traps in order to slit their throats in private.

The government could not have been more embarrassed. The journal had to be seized for inciting revolution, which would only give the appearance of official partisanship. Who would remember that Prince Pierre had been *non grata* at the Tuileries—in fact, a Republican? Worse, a Senate decree of June 4, 1858, provided for special criminal jurisdiction in cases involving members of the imperial family. As the law applied in this case, a special jury would have to be picked from among the members of the departmental councils, and the possibility of a whitewash could not be denied.

Ollivier did his best to remind the public that the government represented justice and liberty, adding that the government represented force only when threatened. But the Republicans intended to squeeze every possible advantage from the unfortunate incident and rallied nearly 100,000 people for Noir's funeral. The Republican leadership was divided on how far it could push the mob in the face of vigorous government defense measures, and the uprising sputtered and died for lack of direction. Rochefort was condemned to six months in prison for provoking civil strife and for offense to the Emperor's person.

In the meantime the High Court was convened in Tours to try Prince Pierre. The evidence was inconclusive, and the Court ultimately decided to accept the defendant's plea that he had fired in self-defense. He claimed that he thought the two seconds had come to kill him, and their unorthodox procedure in arranging the duel gave some credence to the Prince's version of the affair. Consequently, he was acquitted, a decision hardly comforting to a government newly instituted in the name of liberty and justice.

The Government of January 2nd was reform-minded. An ancient grievance that justices of the peace meddled in politics was now answered with an order that judicial and political powers should be clearly separate. Similarly, teachers—as employees of the state—were warned to avoid political activity. Freedom of the press was decreed, though it was still illegal to publish material insulting to the Emperor, designed to promote disobedience in the Army, or to provoke revolution. The General Security Law of 1858, voted after the Orsini attempt, was unanimously revoked by the Chamber upon the cabinet's initiative. Other reforms were outlined and their study begun: a civil régime for Algeria, industrial legislation, and electoral reform in particular.

The reform of the Senate's powers meant constitutional amendment and, hence, a plebiscite. Originally, the Senate had been given the sole power to pass on the constitutionality of legislation and to amend the constitution. The liberals now favored dividing the legislative powers between the two houses, and on March 28th they proposed to give the two houses equal authority and make the Ministry responsible to both houses. Ollivier went before the Senate to speak in favor of the amendment; he argued with effect that the Senate had the opportunity to give France a free government and that this liberty, available for the first time without a revolution, would therefore not be subject to the reaction ruinous to revolutionary régimes.

Impressed, the Senate unanimously voted the constitutional changes requested on April 20th, but failed to clarify the ambiguity in the Ministry's responsibility. The Emperor still nominated and dismissed ministers, who deliberated in council under his presidency, and who were dependent upon him; they were also responsible to Parliament. Ollivier knew that this ambiguity could cause trouble.

Ollivier's election to the Académie française at this time was a measure of the intelligentsia's confidence in the sincerity of Napoleon III; had they suspected him of bad faith the embargo upon his ministers would not have been lifted so promptly. The election was obviously political, as Ollivier had published little and as Montalembert—practically on his deathbed—took the initiative in the nomination.

The cabinet split over the necessity to hold a plebiscite. Those favoring the plebiscite were those who also favored the Emperor retaining considerable authority; Daru and Buffet, who championed the creation of a prime ministership, resigned when the cabinet voted for the plebiscite. The Republicans were anxious when the plebiscite was announced, fearing a substantial imperial victory, but the government was far from confident—anticipating public indifference rather than opposition. The day was May 8, 1870:

The people approve the liberal reforms of the Constitution by the Emperor in effect since 1860, done in conjunction with the principal governmental bodies, and, thus, ratify the Senate Decree of April 20, 1870,

After the disappointing returns in the election of 1869, the government was overwhelmed by the results of the plebiscite: 7,358,786 voted Yes, 1,571,939 voted No, and 1,894,681 abstained. These figures were comparable to the plebiscite which ratified the *coup d'état* of 1851, when 7,439,216 voted Yes, 640,737 voted No, and 2,171,440 abstained. The Republican Gambetta gave the verdict: "It is a landslide; the Emperor is stronger than ever."

Ollivier thought of taking the Ministry of Foreign Affairs himself after Daru's resignation, but decided instead to devote his attention to consolidating the Liberal Empire. Prince Jerome-Napoleon recommended the Duc de Gramont to Ollivier as an experienced diplomat. Gramont, Ambassador to Austria for eight years, cut a fine figure, but he mistook his own grand manners and beauty for diplomatic skill and thought himself at least the equal of Bismarck. This reckoning was not shared by Bismarck, who had styled Gramont "an ox" and "the most stupid man in Europe," remarks which were swiftly carried to Gramont.

Despite the public's interest in the constitutional reform of 1870, no one could entirely forget the lengthening shadow of Prussia. The liberal-national movement, which Napoleon III represented, was suddenly checked in 1866 by Prussia's victory over Austria, a victory which was national but not liberal. Both sides had bargained for French neutrality: Prussia had promised to restrict her territorial expansion to areas north of the Main River in compliance with Napoleon III's desire to strengthen the secondary states of the Germanic Confederation, and both Austria and Prussia promised Napoleon that Venetia would go to Italy. Military opinion held that Austria and Prussia were evenly matched and that a war between them would be a lengthy affair; Napoleon, hence, anticipated that the war would leave him arbiter of Europe. From that lofty perch he would allow the formation of a stronger Prussia, which would be federated with the smaller states of the Germanic Confederation. He did not mean to unify the German nation (as he had not meant earlier to unify the Italians), but to create a federation of independent German states.

The difficulty with this design, as Thiers pointed out in the Chamber, was the possibility that the Germans would proceed from federation to unification and upset the balance of power. But Bonapartist principles dictated that Napoleon III be as solicitous for German nationalism as he had been for Romanian and Italian nationalism; the notion was that the Bonapartist frontiers, drawn to make nationalities free and self-governing, would produce general peace and stability in Europe. Incidentally, of course, bits of territory lost by France when the Bonapartist world collapsed in 1815 would be returned as the price of Napoleon III's arbitration.

These calculations were outmoded by the brilliant Prussian success at Sadowa. As a long war of attrition was avoided, Prussia was left in a powerful position to dictate terms to Austria; the services of the utopian arbiter were not required, which meant, in addition, that the frontiers of 1814 could not be claimed. The suddenness of the Prussian victory, in short, put Napoleon III on the sidelines, and the government in Paris understood that a serious loss of prestige was inevitable unless the French were capable of a bold stroke. Drouyn de Lhuys, Marshal Randon, and Persigny advocated immediate French intervention to dictate peace to both sides, and perhaps had Napoleon not been suffering an especially acute attack of the stone during the week of Sadowa a show of military strength would have been made. Inaction must have encouraged Bismarck to believe that he was dealing with weakness and division in Paris.

Benedetti, French Ambassador to Prussia, was ordered to Nikolsburg, where Bismarck was to receive the Austrian emissaries, in the hope of salvaging something which would be beneficial to French prestige. During the armistice negotiations, the French maintained the fiction that they were mediating between the two Germanic powers, and Benedetti hinted that France would require compensation for her services. Austria ceded Venetia to France for transfer to Italy, but Bismarck avoided committing himself about "a little tip" for France. Instead, he proceeded to arrange his own terms with Austria, which the French supinely supported in the hope of Bismarck's good will.

The Nikolsburg terms became the Treaty of Prague. Prussia excluded Austria from Germany by bringing the Germanic

Confederation to an end, but—except for Venetia—Austria was allowed to maintain her territorial integrity. Leaving the German states south of the Main independent, Prussia annexed Hanover, Schleswig-Holstein, electoral Hesse, Nassau, and Frankfurt; the remainder of the North German states were to be organized into a confederation with Prussia. The Austrian indemnity was so modest, finally, that in assessing the defeat the Austrians saw that their major loss had been to Italy by way of Napoleon III.

Only when the terms had been agreed upon did Benedetti advance the French claims for compensation: the frontiers of 1814 (Saarbrücken and Landau) with an added dash of Rhineland territory or perhaps Luxembourg. But a government which seems to be hanging around for tips creates the same impression as its human counterpart—servility and weakness—and Bismarck sensed he had become the master. He rejected the demands as offensive to German national sentiment, but implied that he would support compensation at the expense of Luxembourg and Belgium. Benedetti, invited by Bismarck, penned the draft of a treaty suggesting the French claims to this non-German territory. The draft did not sanction the forceful annexation of Belgian or Luxembourgeois territory, but merely France's right to negotiate the purchase of the territory—purchases which would be ratified by plebiscites. No matter how legal the transaction, Bismarck knew the British would balk at French annexation of Belgian territory, and he filed Benedetti's draft away as a useful reference.

Meanwhile, Napoleon III determined to press for Luxembourg alone. Negotiations were opened for its purchase with the King of the Netherlands, who was also Grand Duke of Luxembourg, and arrangements were begun for a plebiscite. It happened, however, that Luxembourg, which had been a member of the former Germanic Confederation, was garrisoned by Prussian troops, and, in 1867, Bismarck inspired a rumor in Parliament that "German" soil was about to be surrendered to France. Both the Dutch and the French were intimidated by the resultant outcry, and the negotiations for the sale collapsed. With them went Napoleon III's hope that he would crown the sale with a Franco-Prussian alliance. This diplomatic defeat was all the more stinging as the French government had prematurely hinted that its Luxembourg policy had been successful.

In exasperation, the French turned toward Austria in 1867, proposing an alliance. These overtures failed because the Austrian internal situation was serious after two failures in war; furthermore, Hungarian influence had become the dominant factor in the Monarchy's foreign policy, and the Magyars wished to avoid a return to the arena of German affairs. Though hopeless, negotiations continued by fits and starts into 1869. French attempts to encourage the Austrians by bringing Italy into an alliance also failed, because the Italians would treat only on the basis of a French guarantee to evacuate Rome.

The failure of France to gain her 1814 frontiers and to regulate the Rhine question to her satisfaction was later taken as proof that war with Prussia was inevitable. In 1870, however, the country as a whole anticipated no trouble, and Daru, when Foreign Minister, had proposed a reduction of 10,000 men in the contingent called up from the class of 1870. The measure passed the Corps législatif with a sizable majority, though the reduction was criticized by the Republicans as insufficient. On June 30th Ollivier announced to the Chamber that peace seemed assured. His confidence derived in part from one of the conditions he had set as a basis for assuming office: that the Prussian gains of 1866 be regarded as legitimate and a *fait accompli*.

The Emperor, as nominal chief of the military establishment, was far from happy with the Army system both for military and for political reasons. The Army was basically professional, and its organization was founded upon principles derived in the period of reaction against the Revolutionary era. The Charter of 1814 abolished conscription as a wicked Republican principle, but when recruitment produced a royal Army something larger than a police force, the government had had to compromise. In 1818 a new military law revived the draft, but to maintain the purity of royalist institutions the law described conscripts as "auxiliaries" and recommended renewed efforts to recruit volunteers.

The size of the Army was fixed at 240,000, and the annual draft was never to exceed 40,000 men. The annual class eligible for conscription numbered roughly 300,000, meaning that 260,000 men could not be called up, even in time of war. Members of the Université were automatically exempt, as were those who had physical disabilities or family obligations; but if their names were drawn they were counted as part of the annual quota and could not be replaced. Thus, the Army never received the full 40,000 men and, in general, trained only a fraction of what was received. The remainder were put on reserve with the obligation to keep their mayors informed of changes in residence. This system remained in principle, though the size of the Army and of the annual contingents was occasionally modified.

This professionalism was enhanced by the "blood tax." Upper- and middle-class conscripts could purchase substitutes, and generally avoided service; and because many urban workingmen could not pass the physical examinations for Army service a large part of the conscripts came from the peasantry. The Army offered them a career and favored long-term service in the hope of accustoming the conscripts to military life. Reenlistments were then more likely and the annual conscription lists could be reduced, but the system did not make France a nation of trained reservists.

The Prussian system, in contrast, was based on the innovations of the French Revolutionary and Napoleonic era, and as an heir to those traditions Napoleon III grew up to admire the Prussian system on the grounds that a small professional army, augmented by trained reserves, represented equality and democracy. In 1843 he wrote of the Prussian system: "It is based on justice, equality, and economy, and has for its object, not conquest, but independence." Becoming Emperor, he was not able to impress the French Army with his views until after Sadowa, and at that late date the nation had become so confident in the invincibility of its professional Army that reforms, which were both expensive and inconvenient, seemed like madness. In consequence, it proved impolitic to push the necessary reforms, and by 1870 only minor improvements had been realized.

On the other hand, historians have been inclined to forget that the constitutional reforms of 1870 produced a wave of optimism in France. Only a few suspected the true nature of the Prussian peril, and the government had taken office on January 2nd with a friendly statement on German nationalism. France was on the verge of a new and happier era, and the Emperor, addressing the Corps législatif relative to the results of the plebiscite, concluded, "More than ever before, we may envision the future without fear."

This sanguine atmosphere was rent on July 2nd with the news of General Prim's offer of the Spanish throne to Leopold von Hohenzollern-Sigmaringen, brother of Carol I of Romania. While he had no proof, the French Foreign Minister, Gramont, did not doubt for a moment that Bismarck had inspired the Spaniards in their choice—an assumption which later proved to be correct. On the other hand, the evidence available at the moment implied that the Spaniards were free agents in their enthusiasm for the Romanian prince, and granting that the avoidance of a Hohenzollern prince in Spain was a genuine French interest, one would have supposed the circumstances dictated that Gramont approach Madrid on the matter. Furthermore, as a member of a cabinet pledged to peaceful relations with Prussia, he should have avoided any action contrary to cabinet policy.

His zeal to turn on Berlin instead of Madrid suggests that he had been waiting for an opportunity to square off against Bismarck, and in doing so he focused public attention upon Prussia and awoke memories of the diplomatic humiliation of France engineered by Bismarck in 1867. It is noteworthy that he did not bother to ask for cabinet consideration of the crisis, but, after consulting with the Emperor alone, sent a telegram to Berlin on July 3rd demanding an explanation. Bismarck's response, of course, was an expression of complete ignorance about Madrid's policy.

The cabinet deliberated for three hours with the Emperor at Saint-Cloud on the morning of July 6th to frame the official attitude toward the Hohenzollern candidacy. A ministerial declaration was prepared, which Gramont read to the Corps législatif that afternoon. It opened with a profession of friendship for Spain

and respect for her sovereignty, and noted that, dating from
1868 when the Spanish throne had been vacated, France had kept
a strict neutrality in the selection of a new monarch:

[But respect for the rights of a neighboring people] does not oblige
us to stand aside while a foreign power, by placing one of its princes
on the throne of Charles V, threatens to upset the present balance
of power in Europe to our detriment and to imperil the interests and
the honor of France.

This eventuality, we ardently hope, will not come to pass. To prevent it, we count on both the wisdom of the German people and on
the friendship of the Spanish people.

If it be otherwise, fortified by your support, Gentlemen, and by
that of the nation, we shall know how to fulfill our duty without hesitation and without weakness.

The cabinet, in other words, upheld Gramont's earlier implication
of Prussia in the Hohenzollern candidacy, and Ollivier later
defended this *démarche* on the grounds that Prussia, whether
conspiring to bring a Hohenzollern cousin to the Spanish throne
or not, was involved by the nature of the circumstances; secondly, that international sympathy for the French cause might be
mustered by showing how deliberately Bismarck was provoking
trouble.

These explanations, however honest, cannot avoid the fact that
Gramont's hasty action on July 3rd committed the cabinet to
dealing with both Prussia and Spain; and, considering the failure
of France after 1867 to win friends among the influential powers,
any expectation of allies in 1870 was unrealistic. Approaching
Spain alone was the only safe course. Furthermore, the final paragraph of the cabinet's declaration of policy carried a hint of
war for which the entire cabinet was responsible; but Gramont
probably emphasized this portion of the declaration, by the
power of his delivery, beyond the intentions of the majority of
the ministers, and Ollivier left the Chamber alarmed by the warlike demonstrations with which the Deputies received the speech.
Who would have known, as a result, that the French government
was actually pledged to peace and to friendship with Prussia?

Meanwhile, as Bismarck had been playing the innocent in

Berlin, Gramont ordered Benedetti, the French Ambassador, to join the Prussian King at Ems. He was instructed to ask the king to issue a statement disapproving Leopold's acceptance of the Spanish throne and suggesting the withdrawal of that acceptance. King William refused to issue the statement, but he did advise Leopold's father, Prince Anthony, of the advisability of withdrawing, and on July 12th Anthony renounced the Spanish throne in his son's name.

The affair seemed at an end, and Bismarck greeted the news badly. He had calculated from the start that unification of Germany required the prior defeat of France, for he was not content with a federal union of Germany which Napoleon III favored, but wanted Prussia to swallow up the rest of Germany. The preponderance of Prussia in the German world after 1866 had alarmed the South German states, especially Baden, Bavaria, and Württemberg, and in order to keep them out of the French camp and loyal to the military alliances he had forced upon them, Bismarck understood the necessity of making France appear the aggressor. The Hohenzollern candidacy had been tailored to enrage the French; but, thanks to "Papa Anthony's" renunciation, the cause seemed lost.

Gramont was as disappointed as Bismarck, for nothing had been said about Prussia's part in the withdrawal; and, since Gramont's initial attack had been made to force Prussia's hand, he felt it desirable to negotiate further to extract a satisfactory response from Berlin. Thus, his first mistake led to his second. Egged on by the conservative Bonapartists, including the Empress, Gramont sent off a second telegram to Benedetti demanding that he ask for King William's pledge that the Hohenzollern candidacy for the Spanish throne would never again be authorized from Berlin. Ollivier was not informed of this message until the following morning—July 13th—when he immediately considered resigning from the cabinet.

His annoyance was justified: the cabinet had been ignored by Gramont. Furthermore, the Emperor had permitted Gramont's action despite his promise to consult the cabinet, seemingly giving way in the face of the conservatives at court and impressed

by the warlike spirit of the crowds in the streets. Doubtless, the
Bonapartists hoped that, by forcing the Emperor to take a strong
line, authoritarian government could be restored. A military
victory—and they had no doubt that the Prussians could be easily
swept aside—would serve to consolidate the dictatorship. Understanding what was at stake, Ollivier decided to remain in the
cabinet to save the Liberal Empire. In addition, he knew that
his resignation would be interpreted abroad as his branding
France the aggressor, and he wished to avoid that possibility;
finally, he was personally attached to Napoleon, and shrank from
deserting him in a time of trouble.

Instead, Ollivier asked the cabinet to declare that the incident
of the Hohenzollern candidacy was closed (still the thirteenth)
no matter what William's answer should be. The cabinet upheld
Ollivier's proposal eight to four and vetoed the War Minister's
proposal to begin mobilization. Thus, Ollivier triumphed over
Gramont in the cabinet, but elsewhere—at court, in the streets,
and in Parliament—Gramont's demand that France receive a
satisfactory guarantee from Prussia won increasing support.
Foreign observers in Paris were of the opinion that the majority
in the cabinet, including the Emperor, was being dragged toward
war against its will.

The cabinet lunched with the Empress Eugénie on the thirteenth, and she was hardly polite. Marshal Le Boeuf, who backed
her against the majority of the cabinet, insulted Ollivier at lunch
by calling him the "Emperor's betrayer"; but, despite all, Ollivier
was convinced by the day's end that the Emperor and the majority in the cabinet would stand firm for peace.

Meanwhile, Benedetti had received Gramont's second instructions and once again sought out the King at Ems. William refused
to commit himself about a future Hohenzollern candidacy, but
he did admit his previous consent to Leopold's candidacy and
authorized Benedetti to report that he had also approved the
withdrawal of Leopold's candidacy. The King ended the interview by reiterating his refusal to make any guarantees about any
future Hohenzollern candidacies, but the information he had
given Benedetti clearly indicated that Prussia had backed down

on Leopold's candidacy and ought to have satisfied even Gramont.

In reporting the interview to Bismarck, the King telegraphed the nature of Benedetti's request, indicating that the interviews had terminated with the King's refusal to make any guarantees about the future. He neglected to mention the concession he had made to Benedetti, perhaps because he may have made it later in the day after the telegram had been transmitted, and he left the publication of the report to Bismarck's discretion. Bismarck saw at once that by condensing the King's telegram—especially as there was no mention of the concession to Benedetti—he could publish an account of the interviews which would make it seem as if the French Ambassador had made an impudent demand, which the King had impudently refused: "a red rag for the Gallic bull."

The edited dispatch was published in the *Gazette of North Germany* on July 14th, the news of it reaching Paris the same day. Ollivier realized that the Prussians were bent on provoking war, and he discussed with the Emperor the possibility of calling for a European congress as the only device left to prevent its outbreak. Bismarck's red rag, however, had done its work: the court, the people, and both Chambers were aroused, and Napoleon and Ollivier were swept along against their will. Ollivier was forced to ask Parliament for military credits, which were granted enthusiastically. Just as enthusiastically, the Deputies shouted down those few who thought it advisable to examine all documents relative to the crisis, an examination which would have revealed that Benedetti had secured the Prussian King's consent to have the Hohenzollern candidacy canceled. Probably no other parliamentary body, given the circumstances, would have behaved more rationally.

Napoleon III was a piteous object during the last days of the crisis: a sick man caught between the conservative Bonapartists at court and the liberal Bonapartists in the cabinet. Only he knew the weaknesses of the Army and had taken seriously the reports on the excellence of the Prussian Army sent by Stoffel, military attaché in Berlin; he knew that neither Austria nor Italy had

made any commitment to come to the aid of France. Did he fail
to discuss these points with the cabinet on the fourteenth because
he felt the war to be inevitable? Or because he saw no way to
back out of the Prussian trap without a fatal loss of prestige for
his dynasty? Or because—in the face of Marshal Le Boeuf's
reassurances about the readiness of the Army—he felt it hopeless
to convince anyone that the Army was not ready? Or because he
was ill and had been recently told of the necessity to have an
operation? Stymied and confused, he had greeted the suggestion
of a European congress with grateful tears, but the conservatives
would have none of it.

Thus did Gramont, supported by the Empress and Le Boeuf,
lead the government into Bismarck's trap, and Ollivier—the
peace-loving Ollivier—had to ask a roaring Lower House to
support the proposal for war. In the process he dropped a most
unfortunate remark; as Prussia's action left no alternative to
war, Ollivier said that he accepted the war "with a light heart."
He meant, of course, with a clear conscience, but in the later
light of death, defeat, and a harsh peace, his gaucherie was seized
upon by the Republicans as evidence of the Empire's callousness.

Bad news from the front was not long forthcoming. Napoleon
III, who had gone off with the troops, telegraphed to Paris of the
defeats suffered during the first week of August, indicating that
it would be wise to prepare the capital for possible siege. It was
shocking news after only a week's campaign. The cabinet decided
to convoke the Chamber on the eleventh; then advanced the date
to the ninth; it also forced the dismissal of Marshal Le Boeuf,
the conservative Minister of War, but the extreme Left and Right
preferred to use the defeats to rid themselves of Ollivier and the
Liberal Empire.

The Empress worked during the night of August 8–9 to select
a new slate of ministers, so confident was she that the cabinet
would be turned out on a vote of no-confidence. Ollivier, meanwhile, got wind of a Leftist uprising in the bud and proposed
that the cabinet ask His Majesty to return to Paris to rally loyal
opinion around his person, but the Empress countered that he
must not return without a victory. Ollivier then frankly told her

that the monarch was an obstacle at the front, because he could not command in his physical condition and no one else could command because of his presence. In the face of cabinet unanimity, Eugénie gave in to the necessity of recalling the Emperor on the morning of the ninth, but when Ollivier left her presence for the Chamber she reversed her decision upon discovering support in the Privy Council. Persigny, Rouher, and Baroche—all conservatives—prevailed over the cabinet, and the Emperor was not advised to return.

In the meantime Ollivier had invited General de Montauban, the Comte de Palikao, to become Minister of War replacing Le Boeuf, and Palikao agreed to serve if promoted to be Marshal of France. Thus he was in Paris on the morning that Ollivier asked the Chamber for a vote of confidence. The vote was never in doubt: the Right, which had opposed military reforms, combined with the Left, which had urged military reductions, and swept up a Chamber stunned by news of disaster. The ministers present voted for themselves, accounting for the only votes the cabinet received. The Empress then notified Ollivier to inform the Chamber that she was inviting Palikao to form a cabinet.

Out of office, Ollivier suffered increasing abuse as the military disasters compounded. Had he not left Paris before the siege began, he most likely would have been assassinated. Henri Rochefort openly advocated his murder, saying, "The jury will acquit the assassins." Those who refrained from accusing Ollivier of treason castigated him for incapacity; he was widely caricatured as a turkey, a symbol for stupidity. Both conservative Bonapartists and Republicans made him a scapegoat for the defeat, and thus helped to identify the Liberal Empire with national disgrace. A few saw more dispassionately, Maxime Du Camp, for example, who wrote the following lines to Flaubert on September 19, 1870:

The nation weeps and laments, is in despair, proclaims its innocence, and casts the blame upon the Empire. The nation is in the wrong; she has her fate in her own hands, and this is what she has made of it. . . . The moral reforms which might have saved her have been utterly neglected. . . . Morality molds character, and character is the

basis of national life. You may rest assured that nothing of that kind
will be done. The French nation will be informed that she is the first
nation of the world, that she has been betrayed and handed over to
the enemy—in a word, that she is exempt from all blame.

Napoleon III had been shocked at the suddenness of Ollivier's
fall and had written him a comforting letter—in exile; the Emperor never permitted Ollivier to be criticized in his presence—
but the imperial words had lost their meaning in Paris. Ollivier,
having gone to Turin on August 12th on a fruitless mission to
secure Italian help for France, was warned by Prince Jerome-
Napoleon not to return to Paris. The Republicans overthrew the
Empire on September 4th, and Ollivier learned that his house in
Passy had been sacked and that an order for his arrest had been
issued in the Department of Var.

During his three years of exile, Ollivier's chief support came
from the Egyptian government. In 1865 Ismaïl Pasha had employed him to represent Egypt in cases pertaining to the Suez
Canal Company for an annual salary of 30,000 francs. The money
continued to come to Ollivier in exile, but he lived in constant
dread of unemployment. Confident that the day of his justification would come, he prepared to write the history of the Liberal
Empire; and, hoping to hasten his justification, he sought the
exiled Emperor's blessing as a Bonapartist candidate for the
National Assembly from Corsica. Napoleon, however, had already lent his support to Conti, who had been the Emperor's
chef de cabinet after Mocquard.

After Conti's death in 1872, both Rouher and Ollivier aspired
to his seat. Napoleon asked Ollivier to stand aside: Rouher was
the elder and had not accrued the odium of the defeat. As
Ollivier wrote, "Failure is never pardoned: you can be stupid
and dishonest with impunity, providing you succeed. If you fail,
your good intentions will not amnesty you." Another blow to
Ollivier was the death of Napoleon III on January 9, 1873, which
left the Empress Eugénie the titular head of the Bonapartists.
She never surrendered the notion that liberalism caused the Empire's downfall, and refused to permit Ollivier to be invited into
her circle.

Late in 1873, he decided to risk ending his exile and went to La Moutte, his estate in Var. Some unfinished business was pending: his reception by the Académie française. Having been elected in 1870, he had been forced by political events to request that his reception be postponed, a postponement which the Académie readily granted, as many academicians shared the national hostility to Ollivier. But now he finished his reception address and sent it to Emile Augier, who had been named to receive him, and the reception was scheduled for March 5, 1874.

In the meantime the Académie appointed a special commission to review Ollivier's speech before it could be given publicly. The commission, which included men like Guizot and Favre who had been knights in the battle for liberty during the Second Empire, denied Ollivier the right to make any friendly reference to Napoleon III. They succeeded, in fact, in arranging an indefinite postponement of Ollivier's reception; he took his seat, however, without the reception ceremony, but remained an unwelcome outsider. Not until 1892 did he make a formal speech in the Académie, and only after the turn of the century did he participate in discussions. Through all the hostility and isolation, he never wavered in his faith that the Liberal Empire would have survived except for the war.

During these years Ollivier twice presented himself for public office. In 1876 he stood for Parliament in Var and was whipped three to one. Ten years later, he ran for the Departmental Council of Var, again unsuccessfully. His opponent introduced a false letter into the campaign, allegedly written by Bismarck to Ollivier:

If I had had the misfortune to bring upon my country all the woes which you have brought upon yours, I would spend the rest of my life on my knees asking God's pardon for what I had done.

The legend of Ollivier's guilt remained so strong in France that such a letter was absolutely believable, and even after 1892, when Bismarck began to reveal his own role, the legend did not fade. Its persistence can be accounted for, in part, by recalling that fatal phrase "light heart"; misunderstood at the time and forever after rendered out of context, accepting the war with a "light heart" suggested that Ollivier had gleefully led the nation to ruin. For forty-three years he lived to bear the onus of his countrymen's hatred.

He spent many years preparing a gigantic apologia. Its actual writing encompassed the last twenty years of his life, and as his sight began to fail he ended by dictating to his wife and daughters. His case ran to seventeen volumes under the heading *L'Empire libéral, études, récits, souvenirs*. The loyalty of his wife sustained him through this work, and on his deathbed, in 1913, he took her hand, saying, "I thank you for all that you have been in my life."

Henri Bergson, who was elected to fill Ollivier's chair at the Académie in 1914, had four years to study Ollivier's career before making his reception speech. He became convinced that an injustice had been done to Ollivier and designed his reception speech to rectify the wrong. Consequently, Bergson's reception by the Académie after the war proved sensational. Others had seen the truth relative to the outbreak of the War of 1870, but no one had made an effective presentation in favor of Ollivier.

The French, however, have never found it in their hearts to pardon Napoleon III and his Second Empire. To use Ollivier's phrase, "Failure is never pardoned." The gentlemen of the Third Republic had more unpleasant words for Napoleon III than for either Charles X or Louis-Philippe, both of whom preferred "traveling" to reforming, neither of whom lost wars or provinces. An obvious conclusion is that failure in war is a greater sin than political intransigence; but, recalling the despair of the Republicans after the plebiscite in 1870, is it not possible that the reforms of 1869–1870 were sufficiently promising for the reconciliation of liberty and order that the Republicans after 1870 never dared admit it?

EPILOGUE

A familiar remark, perhaps apocryphal, is attributed to Napoleon III: "How could you expect the Empire to function smoothly? The Empress is a Legitimist; my half-brother, Morny, is an Orléanist; my cousin, Jerome, is a Republican, and I am said to be a Socialist. Among us, only Persigny is a Bonapartist, and he is crazy." For those of us in whose minds and hearts this kindly, humorous Emperor has lived, the quip rings true.

Bibliographies

The Duc de Persigny

AND THE RENASCENCE OF BONAPARTISM

The biographical materials on Persigny are eulogistic and unreliable: H. Castillo, *Le Comte de Persigny*, Paris, 1857, and J. Delaroa, *Le Duc de Persigny*, Paris, 1865, come under this heading. Persigny's secretary, Count d'Espagny, published the *Mémoirs du Duc de Persigny*, Paris, 1896, and included an introduction which faithfully reflects the thesis in the memoirs: that Persigny had an infallibility in matters imperial. Though this volume does exaggerate Persigny's importance, the exaggerations are a key to the man's character.

As for the renascence of Bonapartism, note my article "Louis-Napoleon: A Tragedy of Good Intentions," *History Today*, IV, 219–226 (April, 1954), which includes a summary of the *Works* of Napoleon III. F. A. Simpson, *The Rise of Louis Napoleon*, London, 1909, is excellent for the period 1808–1848, and the standard official biography, Blanchard Jerrold, *Life of Napoleon III*, 4 vols., Paris, 1874–82, is valuable for the same period but increasingly unreliable after 1848. Persigny's adherence to Bonapartism is related in all the above-mentioned works as well as in André Bellessort, *La Société française sous Napoléon III*, Paris, 1932. From this period, too, one ought to mention Persigny's own work, *De la destination et de l'utilité permanente des pyramides*, Paris, 1845.

Pierre de la Gorce, *Histoire du Second Empire*, 7 vols., Paris, 1894–1905, is a superb work and without peer as a survey of the period. Volume I contains a discussion of Persigny's role in the Orléans confiscation, while Volume IV takes up the Roman Question and the elections of 1863. Additional material on the religious problems facing Persigny as Minister of the Interior will be found in Jean Maurain, *La Politique ecclésiastique du Second Empire de 1852 à 1869*, Paris, 1930. Also note J. J. F. Poujoulat, *Lettre à M. de Persigny à l'occasion de sa circulaire contre la Société de St. Vincent de Paul*, Paris, 1861.

In the realm of foreign affairs, it is well to cite first A. Debidour, *Histoire diplomatique de l'Europe, 1814–1878*, 2 vols., Paris, 1891, which is a fine work; then two articles by A. Pingaud, "La Politique extérieure du Second Empire," *Revue historique*, CLVI, 41–68 (1927); and "Un Project d'alliance franco-russe en 1858," *Séances et travaux de l'Académie des Sciences Morales et Politiques* (Compte rendu, 1928), LXXXVIII, 145–164. I have used several other articles which suggest that Franco-Russian relations weighed heavily on Napoleon's Italian policy: Ernest d'Hauterive, "Mission du Prince Napoléon à Varsovie (1858)," *Revue de deux mondes*, 7th Period, LXV, 823–854 (June 15, 1928); G. Pagès, "Les Relations de la France et de la Russie en 1860," *Revue historique du Sud-Est européen*, V, 277–287 (October-December, 1928); and Pierre Rain, "Les Relations franco-russes sous le Second Empire," *Revue des études historiques*, LXXIX, 629–658 (1913).

Lord Cowley was Persigny's counterpart in Paris; see the first Earl Cowley, *Secrets of the Second Empire* (F. A. Wellesley, editor), New York and London, 1929. Several English memoirs pertain: third Earl of Malmesbury, *Memoirs of an Ex-Minister*, 2 vols., London, 1884; and Sir Herbert E. Maxwell, *Life of the Fourth Earl of Clarendon*, 2 vols., London, 1913.

A recent book is worthy of note: Lynn M. Case, *French Opinion on War and Diplomacy During the Second Empire*, University of Pennsylvania Press, Philadelphia, 1953. This study contains masses of valuable information and presents the thesis that public opinion exercised control over decisions of diplomacy and war. Finally, two important books which suggest the background of the Treaty of 1860: Arthur Louis Dunham, *The Anglo-French Treaty of Commerce of 1860 and the Progress of the Industrial Revolution in France*, University of Michigan Press, Ann Arbor, 1930; and H. N. Boon, *Rêve et réalité dans l'œuvre économique et sociale de Napoléon III*, The Hague, 1936.

In Horace de Viel-Castel, *Mémoire sur la règne de Napoléon III, 1851–64*, 6 vols., Paris, 1883–84, there are many caustic observations on Persigny. If Viel-Castel must always be taken with reservation, it is also clear that Persigny was a tempting target for those who had an eye for the ridiculous. Marcel Boulenger, *Le Duc de Morny, Prince français*, Paris, 1925, relates the Morny-Persigny antagonism, while Frédéric Loliée, *The Gilded Beauties of the Second Empire*, New York and London, 1910, includes the flighty Mme. de Persigny.

The Duc de Morny

AND THE GENESIS OF PARLIAMENTARIANISM

The best biography of Morny is Marcel Boulenger, *Le Duc de Morny, Prince français*, Paris, 1925. An earlier work usually regarded as standard is Frédéric Loliée, *Le Duc de Morny: The Brother of an Emperor and the Maker of an Empire*, London, 1910. Loliée has the advantage of translation, but his work contains many inaccuracies. A recent biography which is popularized—but not bad—is Robert Christophe, *Le Duc de Morny, "Emperor" des Français sous Napoléon III*, Paris, 1951. Christophe either omits the larger issues or deals superficially with them. A bad example of popularization is Maristan Chapman (pseu.), *Imperial Brother*, New York, Viking Press, 1931; it is unreliable.

Morny's biographers have drawn on certain memoirs, which should be acknowledged here. The last volume of L. D. Véron, *Nouveaux mémoires d'un bourgeois de Paris*, 6 vols., Paris, 1853–55, contains some pro-Morny information on the *coup d'état*. Cartier de Villemessant, *Mémoires d'un journaliste*, 6 vols., Paris, 1872–78, is another pro-Morny source. Villemessant was editor of *Figaro* and a friend of Morny. Another friend of Morny was the Comte d'Alton-Shée, whose *Mémoires*, Paris, 1868, are useful. I have also used Edmond and Jules de Goncourt, *Journal, Mémoires de la vie littéraire*, 9 vols. (Edition définitive), Paris, 1935. André de Maricourt, *Mme. de Souza et sa famille*, Paris, 1907, is also good.

In the first volume of Maxime Du Camp, *Souvenirs d'un demi-siècle*, 2 vols., Paris, 1949, there is material on Morny and the *coup d'état*. Also note an article by a descendant, Le Duc de Morny, "La Genèse d'un coup d'état," *Revue des deux mondes*, 7th period, XXX, 512–534 (1925). There is a recent book on this subject, Pierre Dominique, *Louis-Napoléon et le coup d'état du deux décembre*, Paris, 1951.

For Morny's embassy to Russia, see *Un ambassade en Russie*, 1856, ed. by Paul Ollendorff, Paris, 1892. There is an excellent article by Victor Boutenko, "Un projet d'alliance franco-russe en 1856," *Revue historique*, CLVI, 277–325, while the history of Franco-Russian relations in this period is covered in François Charles-Roux, *Alexandre II, Gortshakoff, et Napoléon III*, Paris, 1913. For Morny's difficulty with Rouher, see Robert Schnerb, *Rouher et le Second Empire*, Paris, 1949.

Albert Guérard, *Napoleon III*, Cambridge, Mass., Harvard University Press, 1943, contains a good survey of the Mexican affair, while the Jecker letter of 1869 can be found in *Papiers secrets et correspondance du Second Empire*, ed. by Poulet-Malassis, Paris, 1873. The Mexican situation is admirably presented by Ralph Roeder, *Juárez and His Mexico*, 2 vols., New York, Viking Press, 1947.

Perhaps the most interesting book about Morny is Alphonse Daudet, *Le Nabab*. There is an English translation, *The Nabob*, by W. Blaydes, New York, 1902. Daudet was appointed *attaché de cabinet* by Morny in 1861 and served until 1865.

Montalembert

AND LIBERAL CATHOLICISM

The standard biography of Montalembert is R. P. Lecanuet, *Montalembert d'après son journal et sa correspondance*, 3 vols., Paris, 1895. Emmanuel Mounier has edited an anthology of extracts drawn from Montalembert's writing entitled *Montalembert*, Paris, 1945, which can serve as a guide to his voluminous political and religious works.

For a good general survey of French religious history covering this period, see Adrien Dansette, *Histoire religieuse de la France contemporaine de la Révolution à la Troisième République*, Paris, 1948. (A second volume brings this study up to date.) More intensive and valuable is Jean Maurain, *La Politique ecclésiastique du Second Empire de 1852 à 1869*, Paris, 1930, which contains an excellent bibliography. Also note an earlier work by A. Debidour, which is anticlerical but good: *Histoire des rapports de l'Eglise et de l'Etat en France de 1789 à 1870*, Paris, 1898. Another excellent survey is E. E. Y. Hales, *Pio Nono: A Study of European Politics and Religion in the Nineteenth Century*, Eyre and Spottiswoode, Ltd., London, 1954.

The best critical survey of Liberal Catholicism is Georges Weill, *Histoire du Catholicisme libéral en France (1828–1908)*, Paris, 1909. Leroy Beaulieu, *Les Catholiques libéraux: L'Eglise et le libéralisme de 1830 à nos jours*, Paris, 1885, is a proliberal work, while Justin Fèvre, *Histoire critique du Catholicisme libéral en France jusqu'au Pontificat de Léon XIII*, Paris, 1897, is antiliberal. Volume II of La Gorce, *Histoire du Second Empire*, 7 vols., Paris, 1894–1905, contains good material on the religious factionalism and the opposition of the Académie to the régime.

Jacques Offenbach

AND PARISIAN GAIETY

Biographies of Offenbach range from thinly veiled political polemics to straightforward eulogies. One of the most recent books is Jacques Brindejont-Offenbach, *Offenbach, mon grand-père*, Paris, 1940, which protests against discussing the public life of France in order to interpret the private life of Offenbach. Presumably the author had in mind a work by Siegfried Kracauer, *Jacques Offenbach ou le secret du Second Empire*, Paris, 1937. An English edition of the latter book was published in London in the same year. Two other biographies have been regarded as standard: André Martinet, *Offenbach, sa vie et son œuvre*, Paris, 1887; and Louis Schneider, *Offenbach*, Paris, 1923.

Shorter sketches of Offenbach are found in Volume III of Comte Maurice Fleury et Louis Sonolet, *La Société du Second Empire*, 4 vols., Paris, 1911; and in Louis Sonolet, *La Vie parisienne sous le Second Empire*, Paris, 1929. These works also suggest something of Offenbach's milieu, as does Maxime Du Camp, *Paris: Ses organes, ses fonctions, et sa vie*, 6 vols., Paris, 1875. Another writer who worked on the society of the Second Empire was Frédéric Loliée; see in particular *The Gilded Beauties of the Second Empire*, New York and London, 1910.

I found three works helpful for the artistic background of this period: Jacques Barzun, *Berlioz and the Romantic Century*, 2 vols., Boston, Atlantic Monthly Press, 1950; Maxime Du Camp, *Literary*

Recollections, 2 vols., London and Sydney, 1893; and Ivor Guest, *The Ballet of the Second Empire, 1858–1870*, London, A. & C. Black, 1953.

Sainte-Beuve:

SULTAN OF LITERATURE

The latest biography of Sainte-Beuve is André Bellessort's excellent *Sainte-Beuve et le XIXᵉ Siècle*, Paris, 1954. André Billy, *Sainte-Beuve*, 2 vols., Paris, 1952, is also excellent and recent. Matthew Arnold's article on Sainte-Beuve in the *Encyclopædia Britannica* is the work of an admirer; for a contrary view, see the late edition of Marcel Proust, *Contre Sainte-Beuve*, Paris, 1954. Robert G. Mahieu, *Sainte-Beuve aux Etats-Unis*, Princeton, 1945, is a study of Sainte-Beuve's influence upon American literature. Interesting biographic material can be found in *Le Livre d'Or de Sainte-Beuve, publié à l'occasion du centenaire de sa naissance, 1804–1904*, Paris, 1904.

A psychologist who was interested in Sainte-Beuve's method was C. K. Trueblood, "Sainte-Beuve and the Psychology of Personality," *Character and Personality*, VIII, 120–43 (1939). Sholom J. Kahn, *Science and Aesthetic Judgment*, New York, Columbia University Press, 1953, is not specifically a study of the Second Empire, but the questions studied are relevant. Marie-Louise Pailleron's survey, *Les Ecrivains du Second Empire*, 2nd ed., Paris, 1924, is valuable, as is Philip Spencer, "Censorship of Literature under the Second Empire," *Cambridge Journal*, III, 47–55 (1949). Michel Mohrt, *Les Intellectuels devant la défaite, 1870*, Paris, 1942, is interesting, but obviously written with 1940 in mind.

Le Journal d'Edmond et Jules de Goncourt, 7 vols., Paris, 1887–1895, is a well known source for the literary life of the Second Empire, and Ximenès Doudan, *Lettres*, 4 vols., 2nd. ed., Paris, 1879, is also important. Doudan was secretary to the Duc de Broglie. Francis Steegmuller's recent *The Selected Letters of Gustave Flaubert*, London, Hamish Hamilton, Ltd., 1954, and Philip Spencer, *Flaubert: A Biography*, London, Faber & Faber, Ltd., 1952, shed much light on the period.

Both Martin Turnell, *Baudelaire, A Study of His Poetry*, London, Hamish Hamilton, Ltd., 1953, and Peter Quennell in his edition of Charles Baudelaire, *My Heart Laid Bare*, New York, Vanguard Press, Inc., 1951, suggest disapproval of Sainte-Beuve's treatment of Baudelaire; but André Maurois's *Lélia, The Life of George Sand*, New York, Harper & Brothers, 1953, puts Sainte-Beuve in a more favorable light. The two most recent biographies of Sainte-Beuve's benefactress are A. Augustin-Thierry, *La Princesse Mathilde*, Paris, 1950, and Marguerite Castillon du Perron, *La Princesse Mathilde*, Paris, 1953.

The Countess

OF CASTIGLIONE

The work of Frédéric Loliée ought to be cited first, because so many subsequent books have heavily relied on him. English translations are available for most of his works. In order of appearance, note *Les Femmes du Second Empire*, Paris, 1906 (English edition, New York and London, 1907); *The Gilded Beauties of the Second Empire*, New York and London, 1910 (first published in 1909); *The Romance of a Favourite*, London, 1913. Loliée is so highly regarded by many historians that it is essential to note that he makes many errors. He is not even consistent in his own work, as anyone who compares two of his books will discover.

Abel Hermant has used a great deal of Loliée in his *La Castiglione*, Paris, 1938, but he has done additional research and discovered new material, most of it important and revealing. In contrast, there exists a book by Hector Fleischmann, *Napoleon III and the Women He Loved*, n.d., which should be used with extreme care. It seems highly unreliable, based primarily on gossip. Another unreliable work, and one usually cited as such, is Horace de Viel-Castel, *Mémoire sur la règne de Napoléon III, 1851–64*, 6 vols., Paris, 1883–84. Viel-Castel was a friend of Mathilde and an assistant to Nieuwerkerke in the Louvre. His material is fascinating, but must be used with care. An English abridgment and translation appeared in two volumes in London, 1888.

On June 11, 1951, the remaining papers of the Countess of Castiglione were put up for sale at the Hôtel Drouot. An extensive catalogue of the pieces, including many direct quotations from the letters, was made by Etienne Ader, *Correspondances inédites et archives privées de Virginia Castiglione*, Paris, 1951; with an introduction by André Maurois, this catalogue constitutes a major source.

Henry d'Ideville devoted Chapter X of his *Journal d'un diplomate en Italie, Turin, 1859–62*, 2nd ed., Paris, 1892, to the Countess. Here he gives the account of his visits to her, which are invariably quoted by other sources. Robert de Montesquiou, *La Divine Comtesse*, Paris, 1913, is primarily drawn from information furnished by Léon Clery, who was one of the Countess's three lawyers.

One work, though it is not specifically devoted to the Countess, merits notice, because it states that a son was born to Napoleon III and the Countess: Robert Sencourt, *Life of the Empress Eugénie*, London, 1931. The supposed offspring was Dr. Hugenschmidt, who was in attendance at the Countess's death. Sencourt says that Hugenschmidt was raised by Thomas W. Evans, the American dentist employed at court. In a subsequent book, Sencourt, whose real name is Robert Esmonde Gordon George, makes no mention of Hugenschmidt at all (*Napoleon III, the Modern Emperor*, New York, D. Appleton-Century, Co., 1933).

It is fitting to append several general works on the society of the Second Empire. Count Maurice Fleury and Louis Sonolet, *La Société du Second Empire*, 4 vols., Paris, 1911, has noteworthy illustrations, and André Bellessort, *La Société française sous Napoléon III*, Paris, 1932, is an excellent survey.

Louis Pasteur

AND THE BACTERIAL REVOLUTION

The standard biography of Pasteur was written by his son-in-law, René Vallery-Radot, *La Vie de Pasteur*, Paris, 1900. English translations of this work are available. Vallery-Radot married Marie-Louis Pasteur in 1879; she was the only daughter of Pasteur to survive childhood. A child of this marriage, Pasteur Vallery-Radot, recently published an interesting volume of Pasteur's life: *Pasteur: Images de sa vie suivies de quelques episodes dramatiques de sa carrière scientifique*, Paris, 1947.

Other biographers of Pasteur draw heavily on René Vallery-Radot's work, but perhaps see the subject more objectively. L. Descour, *Pasteur and His Work*, New York, n.d.; Louis Lumet, *Pasteur*, Paris, 1923; Henri Mondor, *Pasteur*, Paris, 1945; and R. Dubos, *Pasteur, Free Lance of Science*, Boston, Little, Brown & Co., 1950, are reputable and interesting books. One other biography is particularly useful for this period: J. M. D. Olmsted, *Claude Bernard, Physiologist*, New York, Harper & Brothers, 1938.

One of the chief sources on Pasteur are his own works: Louis Pasteur, *Oeuvres*, 7 vols., Paris, 1922–29. Of special interest, too, is his article, "Le Budget de la science," *Revue des cours scientifiques de la France et de l'étranger*, 5th year, No. 9 (Feb. 1, 1868).

Several books which indicate the paucity of scientific facilities in the nineteenth century are Maxime Du Camp, *Paris, ses organes, ses fonctions et sa vie*, 6 vols., Paris, 1875 (see Vol. V in particular); and and article by Henry E. Guerlac, "Science and French National Strength," which is found in E. M. Earle, *Modern France*, Princeton, Princeton University Press, 1951. Finally, a brilliant book which contains a discussion of Pasteur's role is E. C. Large, *The Advance of the Fungi*, New York, Henry Holt & Co., 1940.

Victor Duruy

AND LIBERAL EDUCATION

Basic to any study of Duruy are his own memoirs, *Notes et souvenirs*, 2 vols., Paris, 1901. The first volume is valuable in particular, as it reveals the development of his philosophy of education. Also see Charles Dejob, "Le Réveil de l'opinion dans l'université sous le second Empire. La Revue de l'instruction publique et Victor Duruy," *Enseignement secondaire*, March-May, 1914. Volume IV of La Gorce, *Histoire du Second Empire*, 7 vols., Paris, 1894–1905, discusses the state of French teaching, as does Volume V of Maxime Du Camp, *Paris, ses organes, ses fonctions, et sa vie*, 6 vols., Paris, 1875.

In his fifth volume, La Gorce, *op. cit.*, discusses the battle between the religious and educational camps; he believed that Duruy represented materialism. An excellent source on these issues is Jean Maurain, *La Politique ecclésiastique du Second Empire de 1852 à 1869*, Paris, 1930, which includes a fine bibliography. We still need a good biography of the leading anticlerical of the period; meanwhile see Flammarion, *Un Neveu de Napoléon I, le Prince Napoléon* (1822–91), Paris, 1939. George Duveau, *La Vie ouvrière en France sous le Second Empire*, Paris, 1946, suggests the attitude of the working class toward the expanding educational system, while D. W. Brogan, *France Under the Republic, 1870–1939*, New York, Harper & Brothers, 1941, portrays the ultimate triumph of Duruy's educational principles.

I have also used Napoleon III, *Histoire de Jules César*, 2 vols., Paris, 1865, as well as references to this work which appear in Maxime Du Camp, *Literary Recollections*, 2 vols., London and Sydney, 1893, and in Marcel Emerit, *Madame Cornu et Napoléon III*, Paris, 1937.

Gustave Courbet,

REALISM, AND THE ART WARS
OF THE SECOND EMPIRE

I am much indebted to a recent biography of Courbet for the details of the artist's life. It is an excellent book: Gerstle Mack, *Gustave Courbet*, New York, Alfred H. Knopf, Inc., 1951. A second work which contains good materials has been edited by George Boas, *Courbet and the Naturalistic Movement*, Baltimore, Johns Hopkins Press, 1938. Notice in particular the Introduction by Boas and the following three chapters: Eleanor Patterson Spencer, "The Academic Point of View in the Second Empire"; Albert Schinz, "Realism in Literature"; and Ruth Cherniss, "The Anti-Naturalists."

For further ideas on Realism, see Jacques Barzun, *Berlioz and the Romantic Century*, 2 vols., Boston, Atlantic Monthly Press, 1950.

The chapter entitled "Interchapter: The Century of Romanticism," is the appropriate section. Then there is the fine volume by Robert C. Binkley, *Realism and Nationalism, 1852–1871*, New York, Harper & Brothers, 1935. The opening chapter on science and technology is ably done. And every student of Realism must see the new book by Francis Steegmuller, *The Selected Letters of Gustave Flaubert*, London, Hamish Hamilton, Ltd., 1954.

Maxime Du Camp is always a noteworthy source on the Second Empire. Two works in particular apply here: *Literary Recollections*, 2 vols., London and Sydney, 1893; and *Souvenirs d'un demi-siècle*, 2 vols., Paris, 1949. Another book, which contains brief sketches and significant remarks by artists, has been edited by Robert Goldwater and Marco Treves, *Artists on Art from the XIV to the XX Century*, New York, Pantheon Books, Inc., 1945.

Further reading on Proudhon can be found in Edward H. Carr, *Studies in Revolution*, London, Macmillan & Co., Ltd., 1950, while for Viollet-le-Duc, see Paul Gout, *Viollet-le-Duc (1814–1879)*, Paris, 1914. The latter work is actually Supplement III of the *Revue de l'art chrétien*.

Emile Ollivier

AND THE LIBERAL EMPIRE

The best recent biography of Ollivier is Pierre Saint Marc, *Emile Ollivier (1825–1913)*, Paris, 1950. He has drawn heavily on several good sources: Emile Ollivier, *L'Empire libéral, études, récits, souvenirs*, 17 vols., Paris, 1895–1915; Marie Thérèse Ollivier, *Emile Ollivier: Sa jeunesse, d'après son journal et sa correspondance*, Paris, 1918; and Pierre de la Gorce, *Histoire du Second Empire*, 7 vols., Paris, 1894–1905.

Volume VI of La Gorce is excellent for the Government of January 2 and for the coming of the War of 1870. Two other general works provide good background: Robert C. Binkley, *Realism and Nationalism, 1852–1871*, New York, Harper & Brothers, 1935; and Hauser,

Maurain, Benaerts, and L'Huillier, *Du libéralisme à l'impérialisme, 1860–1878* (Vol. XVII of *Peuples et civilisations*), Paris, 1952.

More specialized works which contain important material on the origins of the War of 1870 are Lynn M. Case, *French Opinion on War and Diplomacy During the Second Empire*, Philadelphia, University of Pennsylvania Press, 1953; Albert Sorel, *Histoire diplomatique de la Guerre franco-allemande de 1870*, Paris, 1875; Robert H. Lord, *The Origins of the War of 1870*, Cambridge, Mass., Harvard University Press, 1924—an excellent book which suggests that King William was more conscious of Bismarck's intrigues than is generally held; and Laing G. Cowan, *France and the Saar, 1680–1948*, New York, Columbia University Press, 1950, which maintains the doubtful thesis that the War of 1870 was caused more by the Rhenish problem than by the Hohenzollern candidacy.

J. Monteilhet, *Les Institutions militaires de la France, 1814–1932*, Paris, 1932, is a good survey, and Victor Duruy, *Notes et souvenirs*, 2 vols., Paris, 1901, contains a number of observations about the failure to reform the military establishment as well as about the Empress's influence on the declaration of war. Du Camp's remarks about the defeat are taken from *Literary Recollections*, 2 vols., London and Sydney, 1893.

INDEX